Organizational
Learning
Capability

ORGANIZATIONAL
LEARNING
CAPABILITY

Arthur K. Yeung
David O. Ulrich
Stephen W. Nason
Mary Ann Von Glinow

New York   Oxford
OXFORD UNIVERSITY PRESS
1999

Oxford University Press

Oxford   New York
Athens   Auckland   Bangkok   Bogotá   Buenos Aires   Calcutta
Cape Town   Chennai   Dar es Salaam   Delhi   Florence   Hong Kong   Istanbul
Karachi   Kuala Lumpur   Madrid   Melbourne   Mexico City   Mumbai
Nairobi   Paris   São Paulo   Singapore   Taipei   Tokyo   Toronto   Warsaw

and associated companies in
Berlin   Ibadan

Copyright © 1999 by Oxford University Press, Inc.

Published by Oxford University Press, Inc.
198 Madison Avenue, New York, New York 10016

Oxford is a registered trademark of Oxford University Press

Library of Congress Cataloging-in-Publication Data
Organizational learning capability / Arthur K. Yeung . . . [et al.].
p.   cm.
Includes bibliographical references and index.
ISBN 0-19-510204-5
1. Organizational learning.   I. Yeung, Arthur K.
HD58.82.0744   1998
658—dc21   98–3797

1 3 5 7 9 8 6 4 2

Printed in the United States of America
on acid-free paper.

PREFACE

The four of us began our learning journey in 1992, when we received funding from the International Consortium of Executive Development and Research (ICEDR) and the University of Michigan Business School to answer a simple question: How do organizations learn?

Organizational learning, knowledge, and intellectual capital have been frequently discussed in the literature and among managers, but relatively little broad-based, rigorous empirical research had been done to examine how organizations approached the learning process. After reviewing this literature, and with support from our sponsors, we decided to create and administer a survey on how organizations learn. This survey was based on frameworks and ideas in the literature, taken from case studies and theories of learning, and it drew heavily on the work of Chris Argyris and Jim March.

We believed that an empirical assessment of how organizations learn would complement the case studies, personal experiences, and frameworks that had been published in other learning work; and we were lucky enough to have the kind of sponsorship that enabled us to send surveys to companies throughout the world, so that key informants could answer questions about how their businesses dealt with the learning process. Ultimately, we collected data from about 400 companies in 40 countries. Our study of these data, we believe, is one of the largest empirical studies to date on how organizations learn.

As we pursued this research, we also decided to complement our empirical work with in-depth case studies. Todd Jick, a member of our research team, prepared a case on Alcatel Bell's learning process as it entered the global telecommunications market; Steve Nason took the lead on the Samsung Electronics case as this company learned about the microelectronics market; Arthur Yeung examined how Hewlett Packard's Video Communication Division changed from an analytical instrument manufacturer to a key player in emerging video technologies. Collectively, these cases and the empirical research gave us rich insights into the processes whereby organizations learn.

After we collected our data and did preliminary analyses, we had to struggle to articulate our findings in a way that would be readily accessible to managers yet rigorous enough for academic research. After much angst and difficulty in trying not to oversimplify, we derived our simple "g × g" expression: Organizational learning capability = Generating ideas × Generalizing ideas with impact. This definition helped us focus and synthesize our efforts. We also began exploring the different learning styles inherent in how organizations generate knowledge and the processes by which ideas are generalized across boundaries. Our empirical data were particularly helpful in understanding learning styles; our case studies and consulting experiences helped us with idea generalization. At the same time, we focused on the learning disabilities, or blockages, that hindered many of the companies in our survey sample from learning. We found that executives may articulate a learning strategy and even invest considerable resources in it, but unless certain disabilities are overcome, a company's learning capability can be seriously impaired.

As we began to present our work at conferences of both managers and academics, two things happened. To our delight, managers who had been intellectually convinced that learning was important, but were confused by the morass of terms, concepts, conjectures, and assertions in the academic literature, started to use our ideas for assessing learning capability and made investments to improve learning. Academics also helped us to explore the theories underlying our findings. Now, we believe our research and thinking about learning will serve many audiences. For executives who understand that their organization's ability to learn is important, we offer both empirical evidence that learning matters and specific tools for generating and generalizing ideas with impact. For managers who want to improve their units' capacity to learn, we provide diagnostic tools and action templates that can be quickly adapted to most situations. For chief learning officers, or those responsible for creating learning organizations, we offer blueprints and examples that might be followed to improve learning practice. For academics interested in how learning theory can be tested and applied to practice, we offer empirical results on learning styles, disabilities, and processes.

We decided to take this project beyond the scope of the journal articles that we have already published on this topic and turn our results into a book, in the hope of reaching a wider audience—that is, all those humble HR managers and unit leaders who are beginning to go from the belief stage to action on learning within their organizations. Our goals, as both academics and consultants committed to helping managers with the practical issues of running a company, have been to shift ideas on learning from theory to reality; to move beyond broad, grandiose statements about learning to specific management tools that can make learning happen; and to replace the mystique of learning with sound research.

Of course, our learning journey requires many acknowledgments and thanks. We appreciate the time and effort put in by all the survey respondents who completed our questionnaires and by the managers in companies in which we collected case-study data. We acknowledge the intellectual heritage of the many researchers and theorists who have helped us craft our own work, including most notably Chris Argyris, Jim March, Ikujiro Nonaka, David Garvin, and Jerry Porras. We are deeply grateful for the funding from the University of Michigan, which was sponsored by Ron Bendersky (who is also a colleague and friend) and Doug Ready at ICEDR, whose financial support and agenda triggered our research. We are also grateful to Todd Jick, whose work on the cases, instruments, and research design was crucial to the effort. We also wish to acknowledge William Snyder, who helped identify the initial list of learning disabilities, and Fred Luthans, who encouraged us to publish our early work in *Organizational Dynamics*.

And in writing this work, we especially want to thank Martha Nichols. We drafted this in many stages, and turning it into a readable and coherent book was no minor task. Martha has a wonderful sense of style and touch, and she helped us clarify our ideas and select our words so that the work will be accessible to many. Finally, we thank the Internet and various e-mail servers that allowed authors in the four corners of the world to share information and edit chapters more quickly than if we had had offices next door.

We hope our learning journey generates new insights, challenges, and ideas that can be generalized to each reader, going beyond what is presented in this book. In fact, that's the whole point of learning:

never resting on one's laurels or ceasing to question what comes next. No matter how much of a believer in learning you already are, you need to translate such beliefs into real management practices that ensure organizational learning capability.

Hong Kong, China   A. Y.
Ann Arbor, Michigan   D. U.
Hong Kong, China   S. N.
Miami Beach, Florida   M. A. V. G.
March 1998

CONTENTS

Organizational
Learning
Capability

CHAPTER ONE

Organizational Learning

From Theory to Reality

As the 1990s draw to a frenetic close, management theorists aren't the only ones holding forth about the need for organizational learning. Executives at some of today's top companies now discuss "knowledge" and "the fifth discipline" with the seriousness normally reserved for capital expenditures, unit costs, and market share.

Consider Harley-Davidson. CEO Rich Teerlink has invested in a "Harley University," in which customers can attend extensive training workshops on the safety and maintenance of motorcycles; dealers learn about service and business success in other sessions; and employees participate in classes on leadership, values, and change. Even more important, this CEO mentions the need for learning in almost every speech he makes—to employees in one-day leadership conferences, to shareholders at annual meetings, to distributors in workshops, and to customers at motorcycle rallies. Underlying these various efforts is a strong belief that learning leads to competitiveness. Here's Teerlink in a mid-1990s presentation to managers:

> The "old ways" will not lead to success in the future. New knowledge, skills, and capabilities are essential to success. Continual improvement and learning are fundamental for success in leaders—and in all employees for that matter. Continuous and constant questioning of the status quo is a fundamental requisite for continuous improvement. All employees must be willing to question why things are being done the way they are. Open-minded review of *every* aspect of an organization is essential for success.[1]

3

Harley-Davidson has woven this commitment to learning throughout its strategic-thinking process. One of the company's five core values is "intellectual curiosity," another reference to "questioning the status quo," which is not the stuff of standard management practice. Its mission statement cites the importance of learning new ways to meet and exceed customer expectations. And in Harley-Davidson's case, this commitment has paid off. In the late 1970s, Harley was acquired by AMF, and for the next few years, the company struggled to meet quality and service standards. By the time Harley executives took the company public again and out from under AMF's umbrella, it was in crisis. Market share had fallen, and consumer confidence in the quality of its motorcycles had plummeted even more.

During the 1980s, Harley-Davidson rebuilt its image and its market share. Its product quality improved, and Harleys began to appeal to new market segments, such as yuppie buyers, symbolizing a "free" American lifestyle. Still, the company's spectacular comeback left CEO Teerlink worried that complacency would arise among his employees. After all, they could read almost weekly in the business press about the "Harley miracle," in which workers successfully turned the company around. He felt he needed a rallying cry, and his emphasis on learning became an effective slogan around which employees could focus attention and energy. It helped them feel good about what they had done, yet gave them a reason to keep improving.

Although academics have been studying organizational learning for more than 40 years,[2] Harley-Davidson's experience indicates that the renewed interest in learning comes at a time when corporations face unprecedented challenges in the marketplace, the larger society, and indeed the whole international arena. Pressures to reduce costs, customers' high expectations for speed and customization, the constant drive to meet global competitive demands, the changing nature of work, the shrinking pool of educated workers, perceived changes in the traditional social contract, and exponential development in information technology have all shifted the rules of the business game. Ikujiro Nonaka, the well-known Japanese business expert, puts it this way:

> In an economy where the only certainty is uncertainty, the one sure source of lasting competitive advantage is knowledge. When markets shift, technologies proliferate, competitors multiply, and products become obsolete almost overnight, successful companies are those that consistently create new knowledge, disseminate it widely throughout the organization, and embody it quickly in new technologies and products.[3]

Since the 1980s, many books and articles have been written about "organizational learning," a concept first elaborated by Chris Argyris and Donald Schon in their 1978 book of this title. There Argyris and Schon distinguished between double-loop and single-loop learning. Peter Senge further popularized organizational learning theory in his 1990 book *The Fifth Discipline*. Venerable Peter Drucker, along with Nonaka and other management theorists, has trumpeted the needs of knowledge workers and "knowledge societies." And "chief learning officers" (CLOs) are popping up across the Fortune 500 with lightning speed.

So what's wrong with this picture? If everyone is on board, from the halls of academe to the corner office, why is it so tough to put these ideas into practice? What is learning, anyway, and how does it manifest in both individuals and organizations? Do all organizations—or individuals, for that matter—learn the same way, or are there different learning styles? Most important, how can companies build what we call *organizational learning capability*—the capacity to generate and generalize ideas with impact, across multiple boundaries, through specific management initiatives?

These questions are at the core of this book. While learning theory is quite popular, the field has generated little in-depth research or practical management advice up to now. By weaving together detailed case studies, a review of the past literature, and the rich data gleaned from a worldwide survey of companies and our consulting practices, this book takes learning theory into the real world. It covers four specific learning styles, as well as the three building blocks of organizational learning capability: generation of ideas, generalization of those ideas, and identification of organizational learning disabilities.

Even if most managers know that learning matters, it's extremely difficult to create a true learning organization. *Organizational Learning Capability* explains why it's so hard, presents a new model for thinking about learning in organizations, and tells managers—the people on the front lines of the learning "war"—how to make it work.

Why Learning Matters: The "White-water" Business World

Learning is a topic so rich and diverse that no book, not even this one, can capture all nuances of it. But in the organizational context of the new millennium, it's quite clear that companies *need* to learn in order to survive. They must acquire competence, in individual employees and across boundaries; they must be able to change continuously, both internally and externally; they must be fast and agile in responding to competitive and customer changes. The need for this kind of learning matters to all public and private organizations, because managers are now grappling with new and constantly changing business challenges.

To begin with, the work force has recently shifted in a number of ways. Demographics—aging workers and a smaller number of new entrants—are against companies committed to increasing the competence and learning skills of their employees. With the aging workforce, companies find it more difficult to re-train employees to keep up with rapidly changing technology and job design. This is true not only in Japan and the United States but also in most of the industrialized countries of the world. In addition, data from numerous sources indicate that the quality of public education, most notably in North America, has declined. According to a study in the late 1980s, only 70 percent of U.S. students complete high school, compared with 98 percent in Japan. Only one-third of U.S. high school students take a science class in any given year. A whopping 25 percent of all Navy recruits cannot read at the ninth-grade level.[4] As a result of this educational decline, real workplace competence has become an increasingly scarce resource. Firms now have to compete as never before to attract, motivate, and retain well-educated, highly talented individuals. The shortfall has huge implications for industries, like high technology, which depend on skilled workers for their lifeblood.

The nature and pace of work are also rapidly changing. A decade ago, Ray Stata, Chairman of Analog Devices, argued "that the rate at which individuals and organizations learn may become the only sustainable competitive advantage, especially in knowledge-intensive industries."[5] His words now ring more true than ever. Organizations that cannot adapt and react to business changes will fall behind in technology and service; those that are bound by tradition and not committed to change will risk failure. IBM, General Motors, Sears, and American Express are all examples of successful firms that did not adapt fast enough to business trends in the 1980s and suffered the consequences. They needed to make deep changes to be more competitive. While IBM made dramatic changes and improvement under Lou Gertsner in the 1990s, Apple—one of IBM's most serious rivals in the past—is now struggling for its life.

Jack Welch, CEO of General Electric, recently noted that even a business that's taken 30 years to build can be lost in two years if it doesn't adapt and change.[6] Welch is consumed with the notion of *speed* in all domains of GE business and wants to ensure that employees are empowered to make faster decisions, that market intelligence is quickly integrated into changing business plans, and that cycle times are reduced on all GE initiatives.

To ensure speed, or the capacity for rapid change, the ability to learn becomes critical in all aspects of a business—from product design to manufacturing technology to distribution to meeting customer expectations. Learning is the ability to assimilate new ideas from others and from past experience and to translate those ideas into action faster than a competitor can. Not learning may lead a firm to stick with an existing product line beyond reason or not to respond to a competitor's initiative in time to make a difference.

In fact, managers are increasingly turning to internal organizational processes and capability as a means to win in the marketplace. Emphasizing customer service has become a truism of current management thought, and the ability to serve customers, respond quickly, ensure stable relationships, and offer continuity of service comes from an organization's internal processes. Competitiveness therefore moves from the inside out. That which is done inside the firm (creating a shared and adaptable culture, as well as the capacity to learn) becomes essential for success in the external business arena.

Of course, many changes are unpredictable; whether they happen within a company, the industry, or the global economy, they happen in ways that cannot possibly be anticipated. But here again, learning from one's mistakes or even public relations nightmares becomes a critical factor for quick response. In a "white-water" work world, as Peter Vaill, a professor at George Washington University, has phrased it, change is measured in increasingly smaller increments, and the ability to learn is central to business performance.[7]

When Johnson & Johnson's Tylenol crisis occurred in 1982, for example, executives discovered they had to respond fast. Customers had long trusted the company to produce high-quality products, yet just a few contaminated bottles were threatening to sink the entire brand and one of the company's most lucrative businesses. J&J learned that its credo—a commitment to patients and quality—should be applied across all businesses. By immediately disclosing the incident to the public and taking the products off the shelf, the company assured customers of its commitment to quality and made that credo real. Though these actions were risky and costly in the short run, J&J learned that the ability to act quickly and decisively built brand equity and helped maintain market share for all products.

By the time General Motors sued NBC for false reporting on *Dateline* in 1993, NBC and GE executives had already learned to act fast. In part, they may have paid attention to the experiences, both good and bad, of companies like Johnson & Johnson, Union Carbide, and Exxon. But NBC and its corporate parent averted negative publicity not only because they'd read horror stories in *Business Week* or the *Wall Street Journal* but also because they absorbed the lessons into their own operations. When the General Motors lawsuit was announced, General Electric, the owner of NBC and a parent with very deep pockets, was named with NBC in the suit. A crisis team quickly formed, including representatives from finance (to assess the cost), legal, public relations (to assess the image problem of the suit), and senior executives. For three or four days, GE and GM fought their differences out in the media headlines. GE lawyers argued that the Dateline news crew was a subcontractor acting as an independent producer. General Motors argued that GE and NBC were still liable for what this subcontractor had done: they had planted a small explosive device on a GM truck to ensure that the gas tank exploded on impact so that it could be filmed.

The night before *Dateline* was to air, Jack Welch of GE, with his passion for speed and closure, talked with Jack Smith of GM and said he wanted to settle, regardless of the legal nuances. The GM settlement included a lump sum payment of $2 million and a public apology by Jane Pauley on *Dateline* the next night (although rumor has it that the Jane Pauley apology may have been more difficult to extract that the $2 million). GE executives have learned that to settle and move on was better than to fight and win, with the risk of long-term bad publicity. And they were right. The GM versus GE headlines only lasted a week, and most people have already forgotten the incident.

As consultant Cal Wick sums it up:

> In companies across the country, the ability to learn is becoming a condition for employment, one that requires every successful manager's deliberate attention and commitment. Work and learning are interlocking components that drive managers and companies to success. Companies must learn better than their best competitor or their business is doomed to fall behind. Learning has become the key to organizational survival. Becoming a learning organization isn't a panacea for all business frailties. It doesn't mean a company can avoid every pitfall, but it does guarantee that the company will make a quicker comeback.[8]

Learning matters for the overall corporation's ability to assess and adapt to changing conditions. Learning matters for product divisions as they attempt to create innovative products and services. Learning matters for managers as they effectively and promptly cope with crises. Learning matters for executives who are charged with articulating and implementing ever-evolving strategies. And learning matters for employees, the ones who must obtain new skills and build workplace competence. In brief, learning matters for everyone, but managers—especially HR managers and senior executives—are the people who must establish a sustainable organizational commitment to it.

What Is Organizational Learning, Anyway?

The idea of learning from one's mistakes is fairly easy to grasp; yet it may be hard to live up to this idea from day to day and even harder to apply it to tasks like adapting to new customer needs or new competitors. For one thing, individual learning within an organization is not the same as organizational learning. Organizational learning is more than the sum of what each individual learns. According to Fiol and Lyles, two of the scholars in the field, it represents systems, histories, and norms within the organization that are transmitted to new organizational members.[9] Hedberg, another learning theorist, puts it this way:

> Although organizational learning occurs through individuals, it would be a mistake to conclude that organizational learning is nothing but the cumulative result of their members' learning. Organizations do not have brains, but they have cognitive systems and memories. As individuals develop their personalities, personal habits, and beliefs over time, organizations develop world views and ideologies. Members come and go, and leadership changes, but organizations' memories preserve certain behaviors, mental maps, norms, and values over time.[10]

This view of organizational learning bears some similarity to the "good" aspects of a bureaucracy: the creation of systems and procedures robust enough to endure the turnover of individuals. Therefore, managers who want to build learning organizations must focus on both individual and organizational learning. Individual learning occurs as members within the organization acquire knowledge through education, experience, or experimentation. Organizational learning occurs as its systems and culture retain this knowledge and transfer it from individuals.

Sound simple? Of course not. Another glance at what various business writers have said about organizational learning shows why it's so tough to get a management handle on it. For Slocum and Dilloway, "Learning organizations have leaders who design cultures and systems in such a way that employees are continually challenged to help shape their organization's future."[11] Shaw and Perkins claim that organizational learning "is the capacity of an organization to gain insight from its own experience, the experience of others, and to modify the way it functions according to such insight."[12] Fiol and Lyles say, "Organizational learning means the process of improving actions through better knowledge and understanding."[13] Senge argues that a learning organization is one "that is continually expanding its capacity to create its future."[14] For Wick it is "an organization that continually improves by readily creating and refining the capabilities needed for success."[15]

Managers aren't much better at defining how to do this. The call for a "cultural revolution," for instance, has been made by many U.S. senior executives. Task forces have been assigned, speeches made, workshops held, consultants retained, and numerous discussions held about letting go of the old and building the new. The rationale for changing one's culture has been heard time after time, and we see phrases like the following:

- Our old ways of doing things are too slow, too cumbersome.
- With global competition, we must become more competitive. To be more competitive, we must change fundamentally how we do our work.
- The 1990s will be a decade dominated by change. Successful companies must fundamentally change how they work and build in new ways of working with employees.
- Managers must focus on the "soft" values that determine "hard" outcomes. The values influence why we do what we do. In a decade of change and competition, we must redefine old values.

Fine words all, but all abstract. Harley-Davidson and General Electric aside, it's hard to imagine how an organization's "capacity to create its future" or its "redefining old values" can become an operational reality or what these words mean in terms of day-to-day management. In a *Fortune* article, Walter Kiechel once quoted Robert Quinn, who wisely pointed out that the notion of a learning organization could become a very big conceptual catchall to help us make sense of a set of values and ideas we've been wrestling with, everything from customer service to corporate responsiveness and speed. While Kiechel views such an expandable definition as positive, Quinn's comment also highlights what is not clear about current organizational learning theory.

In essence, the learning organization has become a management Rorschach test: whatever one wants to see in the learning organization is seen. Personal biases filter the concept of learning and enable it to become all things to all people. Disciples of quality see the learning organization as the next venue of quality efforts. Change agents see in the learning metaphor the essence of their work. Organizational anthropologists who study culture see the learning organization as their natural extension. Yet if the metaphor of the learning organization becomes all things to all people, it will add little value to any individual worker or to the company at large.

To avoid this trap, our book focuses on *organizational learning capability* and differentiates three concepts: learning, change initiatives, and culture change. Let's clarify our basic definition: an organization's fundamental learning capability represents its capacity to generate and generalize ideas with impact (*change*) across multiple organizational boundaries (*learning*) through specific management initiatives and practices (*capability*). Indeed, we focus on capability, because this word emphasizes what managers actually do. And in an organizational context, "learning" means that knowledge has been transferred beyond individual learners to other people, units, and functions.

When we discuss "change initiatives," we mean a series of specific change programs, not a new mission statement about values or a call to end global warming. Such programs, often construed as fads (reengineering, total quality management), can certainly improve the organization. They may even have a trickle-down or trickle-up effect on various organizational processes, but rarely do they directly affect the entire organization or its overall culture. In general, we believe such change is incremental and evolutionary, not radical or revolutionary.

"Culture change" refers to the extent to which an organization assesses, modifies, and transforms its shared values, beliefs, and mindsets—it is not simply questioning the status quo or implementing "casual dress" Fridays. A number of researchers have shown the importance of the concept of culture change, and even its financial impact,[16] but have failed to operationalize "culture" and "culture change" fully. We see culture as the identity of the firm in the mind of the customer. Harley-Davidson's culture is not what its core values express but the image its strategy, products, values, and services create in the mind of the Harley dealer and rider. This culture, or brand identity, can be changed as companies work to alter both their external customer identity and the internal management practices that create this identity.

Granted, our definitions may still seem abstract. It's true that we emphasize a fundamental organizational capability, one that sustains business innovation and adaptation. But as outlined in the next section, we break this fundamental capability into three practical building blocks. Our model goes beyond an ideal or a set of grand ideas—the "fifth discipline" of Peter Senge, for instance—and hence can be managed and created.

The Three Building Blocks

Organizational learning capability is based on a company's ability to (1) generate ideas, (2) generalize those ideas, and (3) identify learning disabilities. Chapters 4 through 6 of this book will focus on each of these building blocks, reporting the results of our research survey and including case studies of what specific companies have done. In a nutshell, however, *generation* refers to acquiring, discovering, inventing, and sourcing ideas. Centers of excellence, management innovation, creative new products, and the starting up of new plants are all examples of idea generation. And it's here that the four learning styles we've identified in our research come into play: experimentation, competency acquisition, benchmarking, and continuous improvement.

The second building block, *generalization,* involves sharing ideas across boundaries within an organization. Learning cannot occur unless ideas are transferred over time, physical space, and/or the organizational hierarchy. In the case of time boundaries, for instance, ideas should outlive individuals, becoming part of an organization's culture. If ideas are transferred over time, a new manager may not have to "reinvent the wheel." When ideas are shared up and down the management hierarchy, they move across vertical boundaries. They can also cross horizontal boundaries, moving between functional or product units. Ideas shared over the whole supplier–firm–customer value chain cross external boundaries; and those that are transferred between regions or nations—that is, management practices in one location used by others—cross geographic boundaries.

Identification of learning disabilities, the third building block, can turn up problems in a company that lead to failures in generating or generalizing ideas. The reasons for such disabilities are legion; managers may be inhibited from developing innovative ideas because of their own blindness, complacency, risk aversion, simplemindedness, or even the opposition of stakeholders (investors, customers, and employees). As a result, firms become stagnant, wait too long, and fail to change until major crises develop. Many companies, on the other hand, do have pockets of excellence in which managers experiment and innovate. They try new marketing, manufacturing, and organizational arrangements; often these specific initiatives work. But in this case, they are only generating ideas, not generalizing them. Unless the idea is shared across a boundary—be it another organizational level, plant, or unit—it has no lasting impact.

And that's the main point of organizational learning: having an impact. This means that something substantial has changed, and change implies that learning has happened. Routine, piecemeal, and nonstrategic ideas can be shared across boundaries without much effect. One firm we know of spends a large percentage of its training budget ensuring that managers understand internal administrative processes (such as which forms to fill out when), accountabilities (who makes what decisions), and what kinds of approvals are required based on the scope of a decision. You could say this organization has generated and generalized ideas on administrative operations, but these actions don't affect the actual competitiveness of the firm. The managers of this company have not built organizational learning capability.

For real-world business purposes, we define impact as adding value to the firm's stakeholders (investors, customers, and employees) over a long period of time. The following simple equation symbolizes the extent to which an organization has developed its learning capability and may help managers to assess their firm's overall ability to learn:

$$\text{Learning capability} = \frac{\text{ability to}}{(\text{generate} \times \text{generalize ideas with impact})}$$

We will return to the concept of "$g \times g$." What we want to emphasize here is the need for all three building blocks. True learning organizations both generate and generalize ideas; they can also identify and correct any learning disabilities within the organization, because otherwise the ideas will have no impact. Take Matsushita. In their 1995 book *The Knowledge Creating Company,* Nonaka and Takeuchi describe not only how the Cooking Appliance Division at Matsushita generated new concepts in designing a product (its Home Bakery) but also how the concepts and methods were generalized to other Matsushita divisions and then the whole corporation.[17]

In fact, the successful development of Home Bakery—the first fully automatic breadmaking machine that allows users to make quality breads comparable with those of a professional baker—provided an exciting learning experience for Matsushita, a company known up to that point as a price-based competitor for relatively standard products in mature markets. To begin with, the development process for Home Bakery represented a sharp break with the conservative and status quo–oriented culture at Matsushita. It dissolved the usual boundaries within the organization through the formation of interdepartmental project teams. Engineers also stopped spending so much time competing with each other to conjure up new fancy products and concentrated their efforts on creating products with genuine quality that met real customer needs. The development of Home Bakery inspired Akio Tanii, CEO at the time, to adopt "Human Electronics" in 1986, which focused much more of Matsushita's strategic and product-design energy on developing more "human" products that incorporated high technology. The fully automatic coffee maker with an integrated mill and a new generation of rice cookers (such as the Induction Heating Rice Cooker, which cooks rice in a manner similar to that of the traditional Japanese steam oven) are other examples that have hit the market.

Based on our definition, Matsushita has high organizational learning capability. In contrast, companies like General Motors, which are good at developing different pockets of excellence, have not generalized its ideas across the right boundaries.

Making It Work: Learning Organizations in Action

When we consult with business clients about creating a learning organization, we hear them wrestling with questions like

- How can I transform my organization's culture to bring about new values, processes, and behaviors that will help us be more competitive?
- How can I create a learning organization where new ideas are constantly generated and shared throughout the organization?
- How can I build a capacity to change within my organization that will enable us to move more quickly into new markets and implement new technology more quickly?
- How can I leverage my organization's capabilities or competencies to better respond to market conditions?

These are good questions and can form a blueprint for how any company approaches learning. They also indicate the magnitude of the task. Helping managers understand the importance of creating a learning organization is often difficult. The need for learning can be intellectually framed—it is needed to ensure competence, to increase capacity for change, and to remain competitive. But in today's world of 80-hour work weeks and cross-continent meetings, executives need both intellectual and emotional reasons to get fired up about big changes. Clearly, they shouldn't wait for a PR nightmare or a serious dip in revenue to become enthusiastic about learning, although in reality these are often the only things that turn them into learning evangelists.

For those who want to eliminate the need for such last-minute conversions—especially professionals on the HR front lines—building a commitment to learning within a company is the thing to do. It's helpful to start with what people already know. In our workshops on learning organizations, we begin with clients' experiences of individual learning. First, we ask executives to articulate what learning is by describing someone who is a learner and someone who is not (worksheet 1.1). To be more creative, we've asked small groups to identify either TV characters or public figures in each column.

Next, we work on getting clients to see that learning means more than superficial knowledge; it involves a deeper understanding of ideas *and* a commitment to use the ideas. Here, we've found that presentation of a relatively simple case study is useful (worksheet 1.2). In fact, this story about how individuals learn in school is a good analogy to the learning organization. While two organizations may be equally profitable or successful in any given year, they may not both have a commitment to learning. The organization that goes deeper, understanding the essence of the work and why it's been successful, is more likely to replicate that success.

Last but not least, we focus on how managers can translate the benefits of individual learning into organizational learning. By starting with the left-hand column in worksheet 1.3—"What are the benefits to individuals of being learners?"—we generate a predictable list. Learning individuals are typically more creative, fun to be around, focused, current on ideas, and successful. We then draw parallels from each individual benefit to organizations. Learning organizations are generally more innovative and exciting places to work; they are competitive, future-oriented, and profitable.

In addition to working directly with executives, we've also observed many learning organizations in action. Some firms, like Ford, 3M, Motorola, and Harley-Davidson have made learning an explicit part of their business strategy. Others make a commitment to learning by investing in training. Amoco, AT&T, General Electric, GTE, IBM, and Xerox have built physical facilities to house training and education curricula; some have leased or rented space. Other companies like Aetna, Allied Signal, Baxter Healthcare, Boeing, Champion International, Digital, Hershey, PPG, and Westinghouse, invest in designing training and development activities.

Investment beyond financial resources is equally important. In firms where senior managers attend seminars as presenters and participants, and where best practices are constantly shared across functions, divisions, and geographic locations, the commitment to learning increases. Companies in which top executives publicly talk about learning, such as Harley-Davidson, clearly have a leg up. But managers can do more than talk; they can create symbolic events that highlight learning. The human resources function of AT&T, for example, has created awards for outstanding HR individuals, teams, and business partner performance. Nominees are scored by an internal and external panel of judges, and awards are presented at an annual event. The symbolic nature of the event encourages the dissemination of selected ideas throughout the AT&T human resources community.

Steve Kerr, the chief learning officer at General Electric Company, has argued that managers should "honor the past, but get by the past." From his perspective, symbolic events can be used to let go of the past. For instance, in one company, which had recently been reformed through a merger, managers suggested that employees burn all the artifacts of the old company—letterhead stationary, coffee cups, T-shirts. After such a symbolic burning, learning could occur at the new firm.

We believe this book will help line managers understand why they should focus on learning capability; how they can build it; and where to start their efforts—making that first jump into the new, yet honoring what has gone before. More specifically, we aim to inspire HR professionals to design and deliver practices (staffing, organization design, training, education) that encourage learning capability. Burning coffee cups may not be most managers' style, but the efforts of other companies—from the sublime to the ridiculous—can help guide us in creating our own learning organizations.

How This Book Is Organized

Organizational Learning Capability is a handbook devoted to managers and human resource professionals, and to all those responsible for building learning capability within their corporations. In this book, we'll share what we've learned in the last few years through our consulting practices, and we'll give the results of a survey of global companies like AT&T, Eastman Kodak, Ford, GE, Ssangyong Business Group, and NEC.

Our research addresses four basic questions, each of which underpins the rest of this book: What is learning capability? How do organizations learn and/or fail to learn? What are the consequences of learning capability? How can managers assess and enhance organizational learning capability? While we can't provide definitive answers for every company or industry—much more research remains to be done—we will argue six key points:

- There are four styles of organizational learning—experimentation, competency acquisition, benchmarking, and continuous improvement—not just single-loop versus double-loop learning, or adaptive versus generative learning.
- The effectiveness of an organizational learning style depends on its congruence with the broader business context (business strategy, culture, industry characteristics, and so on).
- Different learning styles lead to different performance consequences.
- Organizations learn not only by generating innovative ideas but also by generalizing those ideas across boundaries.
- Organizations are liable to a set of learning disabilities.
- Specific management practices can be used to build learning capability.

This book is organized into eight chapters. After this introduction, chapter 2, "What We Know about Organizational Learning: Different Learning Styles," presents a brief review of the literature, introduces our worldwide survey of companies, and discusses differences in the four learning styles we have identified empirically through our research. Chapter 3, "A Model for Organizational Learning Capability: The Three Building Blocks," specifies idea generation, idea generalization, and identification of learning disabilities, integrating them into a new conceptual model.

Chapter 4, "Generating Ideas with Impact," and chapter 5, "Generalizing Ideas with Impact," detail the first two building blocks, based on our survey research and in-depth case studies of Samsung Electronics, Alcatel Bell, 3M, Hewlett-Packard, and Motorola. Chapter 6, "Identifying Learning Disabilities," describes common failures that prohibit corporations from learning; again, the results of our survey research, as well as case studies of Samsung and several health-care systems, flesh out this discussion.

Chapter 7, "Building Organizational Learning Capability: A Blueprint for Learning Architects," lays out how companies can assess their organizational learning capability and develop action plans to enhance it. We include a number of worksheets with this practicum chapter.

Chapter 8, "Learning Matters, Warts and All: Diary of a True Learning Organization," closes the book by summarizing our research and conclusions, as well as indicating where learning organizations may be heading in the future. The appendices present notes on our research methodology and design, a list of companies that participated, and our survey questions in full.

For us, the most useful aspects of organizational learning theory are based on management concepts that have evolved over the last fifty years, not a series of new fads. Thus, chapter 2 reviews what previous researchers and theorists have discovered about learning. Like any good learning organization, we want to build on the past, not destroy it; in turn, we hope our work provides a foundation for future research.

CHAPTER TWO

What We Know about Organizational Learning

Different Learning Styles

Consider 3M and Samsung Electronics. Both companies are admired for their ability to adapt to changing market conditions; both are successful in addressing their respective business needs. Both are learning organizations—yet their learning styles are very different. Samsung Electronics learns by benchmarking through joint venture partners, trading partners, and suppliers; 3M learns through encouraging employee experimentation.

According to James Collins and Jerry Porras in their popular 1994 book *Built to Last*,[1] 3M has developed a distinct management philosophy. Near its shaky beginning in 1902, this company learned a hard lesson. Early founders bet on the wrong product (corundum mining) and discovered fast that they had to diversify 3M's products to minimize risks. To accomplish this, employees were and still are encouraged to exercise individual initiative in experimenting with new products, as long as these products meet a demonstrable human need. Managerial enthusiasm for experimentation is best captured in phrases like "Encourage; don't nit-pick. Let people run with an idea." "Encourage experimental doodling." "Give it a try—and quick!"

As a result, 3M has been transformed into what Collins and Porras call "a mutation machine"—a company that continually mutates from within, branching out into different product areas. By 1990, they write, "3M had branched into over sixty thousand products and over forty separate product divisions. These spanned such wide-ranging categories as roofing granules, reflective highway signs, video recording tape, overhead projection systems, computer storage diskettes, bioelectronic ears, and 3M Post-it notes."[2] The ability of 3Mers to innovate is based on a unique combination of values, management practices, and learning style. By encouraging employees to experiment with many new products—and by empowering them with the time, resources, and incentives to do so—3M has learned faster and better than its competitors.

Samsung Electronics, a highly successful Korean corporation with $18.8 billion in sales and 84,000 employees in 1996, exemplifies another approach to organizational learning. In the early 1990s, Samsung commanded more than one-fifth of both the U.S. and the world market in microwave ovens and had become the world's third-largest DRAM chipmaker, growing about 60% a year since its founding in 1969. Even so, the company embarked on a major change initiative in 1991, triggered by its inability to fill, in a profitable manner, customer orders that were either too specialized or too small.

After learning that their most successful Japanese competitors were organized around flexible manufacturing systems (FMS), Samsung's top executives decided to restructure its production system along the same lines. Given that the company had no experience in FMS, this was a formidable task. Samsung requested that managers read books, attend seminars, and seek consulting assistance, all fairly standard strategies for learning a new subject area. But more important, it strategically formed business relationships with other companies—through joint ventures, procurement, and trading contracts—and systematically benchmarked the FMS technology deployed by its business partners. Samsung Electronics did indeed restructure its production system, from start to finish, in six months.

If there's one thing we know, from our own research and from an extensive review of the literature, it is that companies learn in different ways. Clearly, both Samsung Electronics and 3M have high organizational learning capability. We will return to these exemplary firms in later chapters, since study of their management initiatives, business strategies, and cultures yields a wealth of practical information about how to approach organizational learning. (An extended case study of Samsung Electronics, in particular, forms the core of chapter 5.) Still, if even two companies differ radically in style and practice, how do we make sense of what learning is and how it applies to specific firms and businesses? How do we get down to basics—and *are* there any learning basics, beyond the fact that organizations learn differently?

The answer to the last question is, of course, yes. Organizational learning is a broad topic, one that has been studied for many years and in which continuing debates occur. Yet it's safe to say that after a good three decades of academic attention, the field has generated a number of useful theses about what learning is and how it happens. These theses integrate a large and diverse literature, are grounded in theory, and have formed the fabric of the learning organization paradigm.

Our own research emphasizes four different learning styles—experimentation, competency acquisition, benchmarking, and continuous improvement—and this differentiation of styles distinguishes what we've done from the work of other researchers. However, our learning typology is based on the important theoretical contributions of March, Argyris, Huber, and Garvin, to name but a few. Given that past writers have covered so much ground, we'll briefly catalog what is known about learning before delving into different learning styles. These basics underpin our own research, and they form the foundation for what we call organizational learning capability.

A Brief History of the Learning Organization

We can trace the concept of organizations as learning systems to the early 1900s. Frederick Taylor, who developed the influential theory of scientific management, believed that when management "truths" were articulated and measured, he could transfer this learning to other employees and thus improve the efficiency of the organization.[3] In the late 1950s, organizational learning was refined and defined by a number of theorists at Carnegie Mellon University, such as Richard Cyert, James March, and Herbert Simon. In 1958, March and Simon wrote, "For as we shall see when we consider organizational standard operating procedures, an organization's choice is heavily conditioned by the rules within which it occurs. These rules, in turn, reflect organizational learning processes by which the firm adapts to its environment."[4]

This work on how organizations make choices led Simon and his colleagues to study models of decision making. For example, they studied how expert chess players were more adept than novices at replacing pieces on the chess board, because experts used cognitive schemas or maps to organize an otherwise random set of chess pieces.[5] These researchers also highlighted the decision-making process of "satisficing," in which the minimally acceptable alternative is chosen rather than the optimal alternative.[6] (For this work, Simon won the Nobel Prize for economics.) The learning research of the Carnegie School was perpetuated by March in his exploration of models for ambiguity and learning. His 1988 review of the organizational learning literature in the *Annual Review of Sociology* remains a classic to this day.[7]

A second stream of research, centered on the work of Chris Argyris and Donald Schon, has led to the current interest in organizational learning. Argyris and Schon introduced the difference between first- and second-order learning. First-order learning, also known as single-loop learning, involves improving the organization's capacity to achieve known objectives and is often associated with routine and behavioral learning.[8] Second-order learning, sometimes called deutero or double-loop learning, reevaluates the nature of the objectives and the values and beliefs underlying them. It addresses contradictions in goals that motivate first-order learning—for example, increasing profits in the short term versus increasing R&D investment to ensure long-term competitiveness. While first-order learning rarely leads to significant change in a firm's basic assumptions, second-order learning involves changing an organization's culture. In other words, it consists of learning how to learn. Individual members who engage in double-loop learning might reflect on and improve their capacity to discover performance gaps, invent solutions, produce actions, and generalize learning outcomes.[9] Chris Argyris has also focused on defenses against learning and how learning is related to actions within organizations. He believes that "smart people" still have to learn how to be successful managers.[10]

In addition, the general study of organizational learning has fallen under a number of different labels. As George Huber points out in his 1991 review of the literature,[11] learning can be characterized by adaptation to changing environmental events, by flexibility and responsiveness, and by change within the organization. In many ways, the "learning organization" has become an umbrella concept that encompasses many topics in the study of organizations. Most recently, Peter Senge and his colleagues at MIT have popularized work on learning. They claim that by applying systems thinking, they can plot the processes of organizational learning. Senge's MIT group has formed a learning center that's become a clearinghouse for research about learning organizations.[12] At least in part because of the popularity of Senge's work and its impact on management—he has been called the guru of organizational learning—the learning organization now receives much more attention in the business world.

Clearly, the study of organizational learning is not new. However, in recent years there's been renewed interest in how learning can help managers build robust organizations. Lately writers sometimes assume that the learning organization will replace "old" concepts like management by objectives or strategic planning, or various Japanese practices like quality circles and intrapreneuring that were widely touted in the 1980s. But just as technology evolves, so does management thought. Table 2.1 outlines management trends, beginning with the 1950s, that cover the work of everyone from George McGregor to Peter Drucker to Warren Bennis to Edward Deming to William Ouchi to Michael Porter to Tom Peters to Gary Hamel and C. K. Prahalad. From our perspective, learning research extends rather than replaces the useful management concepts of the past.

The Learning Basics: Eight Assumptions

The legacy of management thought and theory is certainly rich, but it has also led to a lack of clarity in learning organization research—the "all things to all people" trap mentioned in chapter 1. Dealing with a clutter of concepts is the first challenge in wading through the literature. Unsuspecting readers are faced with a plethora of terms: culture, change, values, strategy implementation, core competence, organizational capability, quality. The field is littered with conceptual and operational imprecisions; some writers refer to learning organizations as those that have changed their culture successfully; others say they are those that have implemented a process improvement program like reengineering. Companies used as examples of learning organizations, such as Motorola, are also cited as cases for quality.

Many models of change, for instance, have focused on how to organize and deliver change initiatives. "But," as John Kotter writes, "in too many situations the improvements have been disappointing and the carnage has been appalling, with wasted resources and burned-out, scared, or frustrated employees."[13] These programs—reengineering, TQM, and so on—were all the rage just a few years ago and the focus of much management attention. But while changing or redesigning processes may well be part of what a learning organization does, such programs are often piecemeal add-ons to an already full plate of change initiatives.

Similarly, notions of organizational culture and culture change are inadequate for describing the learning organization. As Kotter and Heskett note, companies that develop strong cultures that are focused on employees, customers, and shareholders outperform those in similar industries and markets in the long run.[14] Culture change is central to our concept of organizational learning capability, but past literature in this area tends to gloss over how change happens and what specific initiatives might drive it. For concepts like "change initiatives," "cul-

Table 2.1　Evolution of Management Thinking

1990s	Learning organization
	Culture change
	Strategic unity
	Core competence
	Organizational capability
	Empowerment
1980s	Japanese management
	Quality circles
	Excellence
	Leadership
	Mission/vision/values
	Cycle time (competing through time)
	Customer service
	Intrapreneuring
1970s	Strategic planning
	Life cycles
	Value chain
	Zero base budgeting
	Matrix management
	Participative management
1960s	Management by objectives
	Transaction analysis
	Team building
	Job enrichment
1950s	T-groups
	Theory x / theory y
	Managerial grid
	Forecasting

ture change," and "learning" to have any practical value, then, they must be simultaneously differentiated and integrated.

Table 2.2 presents a way to integrate these three concepts. The two dimensions here are learning and change. Organizations demonstrate more or less commitment to either dimension. Those that fall into cell 1 do neither; instead they just maintain the status quo. Cell 2 organizations engage in a series of change initiatives but fail to learn. These are "program-of-the month" companies that start more initiatives than they complete. Organizations in cell 3 work on learning but fail to change. Individuals may generate new ideas, but the ideas aren't generalized into organizational systems. Alternatively, units may experiment with an idea but fail to share what they've learned with

Table 2.2   Integration of Change Initiative, Learning Organization, and Culture Change

Extent to which change initiative is adopted	Extent to which learning organization exists	
	Low	High
High	2 Change initiatives Variation Experimentation	4 Culture change through *learning capability*
Low	1 Status quo	3 Individual learning Learning without diffusion

other units. Finally, cell 4 organizations change *and* learn; in other words, they have organizational learning capability.

Note that differentiating learning, change initiatives, and culture change can help inform management decisions. When beginning any change initiative, for example, it's critical to try new ideas rather than becoming better and better at the wrong thing. Ian Mitroff calls this the "error of the third kind"—solving the wrong problem well—a common organizational failing.[15] When focusing on learning, companies must not only accomplish an initiative but also transfer what has been learned from it across boundaries—and make sure that learning is retained. For managers, this can mean everything from sending e-mail memos to accessing best-practice databases to attending industry conferences in which ideas are shared.

In short, organizational learning comes down to the ability to generate and generalize new ideas with impact. The eight "basics" that follow, derived from the work of many scholars and researchers in the field, further clarify what we mean by organizational learning capability.

1. Learning Organizations not Only Focus on Learning—but Also Meet Their Goals

This may sound overly simplistic, but managers on the line know that business performance from quarter to quarter is not necessarily tied to a company's larger goals or long-term growth. Most definitions of organizational learning emphasize that successful learning entails an organization meeting its goals, and that these goals may not be performance-related per se.[16] For our purposes, the primary goal of the learning organization is improving competitiveness through product and process innovation and continued adaptation to environmental changes.

At times, learning is the end, not the means. Many activities can help create the ability to learn. As we'll discuss in more detail below, Senge has drawn on decades of systems-thinking work to demonstrate that when managers think about whole systems, not just parts, learning is more likely to occur. But while some studies of learning end with increased learning, we want to argue that the capacity to learn has both antecedents and consequences. Companies that learn can adapt more quickly to changing customer needs; they can also better meet their financial goals for growth and profitability.

2. Learning Organizations Follow a Systems Logic

By "systems thinking," Peter Senge means the ability to understand the complex causal relationships among a set of organizational factors and issues. No action in an organization stands alone. All actions are connected in systematic ways to other actions. For instance, the relationships of managers and subordinates are embedded in a larger system of compensation, promotion, and other organizational processes. For Senge, creating a new product from a complete systems perspective means that many discrete elements come together to form a new product or service. He argues that of all the disciplines related to learning (including personal mastery, mental models, shared vision, and team learning), systems theory is the fifth and most important:

> It is the discipline that integrates the disciplines, fusing them into a coherent body of theory and practice. It keeps them from being separate gimmicks or the latest organization change fad. Without a systemic orientation, there is no motivation to look at how the disciplines interrelate. By enhancing each of the other disciplines, it continually reminds us that the whole can exceed the sum of its parts.[17]
>
> Systems thinking is a discipline for seeing wholes. It is a framework for seeing interrelationships rather than things, for seeing patterns of change rather than taking "snapshots." It is a set of general principles—distilled over the course of the twentieth century, spanning fields as diverse as the physical and social sciences, engineering, and management. It is also a set of specific tools and techniques. . . . The essence of the discipline of systems thinking lies in a shift of mind: seeing interrelationships rather than linear cause-effect chains and seeing processes of change rather than snapshots.[18]

Senge proceeds to identify the essential elements of a systems approach to learning. By mapping the circles of causality over time, he believes that organizations can better understand root causes and improve learning. But while systems language is elegant and compelling, it is also sometimes vague and unfocused. It can be hard for managers to act on concepts like "circles of causality," even if the systems notion that activities need to be understood in context is a critical element of learning and has been applied in various ways to improve learning.

In the world of total quality, continuous improvement, and re-engineering, a number of tools draw on systems theory, including process mapping, flow charting, and what Mike Hammer calls "out-of-the-box thinking,"[19] which means breaking set ideas and not thinking about things in the same old way. In the early 1990s, for example, AT&T used process mapping and feasibility analysis to cut steps and costs out of processes, thus improving its order-to-remittance system and supplier management. The company also used this kind of thinking to examine alternative investments for growth, such as becoming more global and creating new business products. In these efforts, AT&T made sure that any change was considered in the context of a broader system of activities.[20] When such tools are applied, organizations learn because they have a better set of data about what people are actually doing and why; this, in turn, can lead to process improvements.

3. Organizational Learning Is Connected to—but Not Limited by—Individual Learning

We've already emphasized that individual learning within an organization is not the same thing as organizational learning. This distinction is important because it points to what companies as a whole must do to create learning organizations. It also reflects managerial attitudes towards learning, organizational learning styles, and possible organizational learning disabilities. If organizational learning simply amounted to the sum of what individuals learned on the job, there would be no need for special consultant workshops, team meetings, cross-training, learning awards, or any of the various change initiatives that theorists and learning specialists have suggested. The fact is, many of these learning initiatives have been successful, and hundreds of researchers and managers can't be misguided.

So why do we need organizational learning, and what is its connection to individual learning? As Snyder and Nason have pointed out, when organizational learning is retained in the norms, routines, technologies, and policies of the organization, it survives the turnover of individuals.[21] Organizational learning is embedded in patterns of behavior not identified or tied to any one individual. Indeed, a firm can only create a "learning identity" for itself when learning is tied to more than one enthusiastic CEO or brave HR manager. Nordstrom's service identity, for instance, is represented by individual employees committed to serving customers, but this identity is not unique to any one individual. Therefore, when the collective identity supersedes individual effort, learning has truly become part of the culture.

We consider learning to be organizational when ideas and knowledge generated by individuals within the organization are shared across organizational boundaries of space, time, and hierarchy. Our definition is very much connected to the second building block of organizational learning capability: generalization of ideas. While individuals within an organization may generate good ideas, they'll have no real impact if they aren't generalized—that is, if they aren't used, expanded on, and revised by other people, units, or functions. For us, the simple expression of $g \times g$ is the essence of organizational learning. It means that ideas generated by individuals have impact and consequence for the larger organization; by the same token, what the organization knows is not limited by what a few individuals or "pockets of excellence" know.

4. Learning Occurs along a Continuum, from Superficial to Substantial

Many theorists have described the difference between what we call superficial and substantial learning. As we've already noted in our brief history, Argyris and Schon laid out the differences between first-order and second-order learning. In a 1985 paper, Fiol and Lyles[22] similarly highlighted the distinction between lower level learning, which occurs within a given organizational structure and set of rules, and higher level learning, which aims at adjusting overall rules and norms rather than specific activities or behaviors.

Table 2.3, which is based on the work of Fiol and Lyles (Ref. 22) and Snyder and Nason (Ref. 21), illustrates how various researchers have distinguished between superficial and substantial learning. Understanding this learning continuum can help clarify what learning really is and why substantial learning is ultimately more valuable. Managers who focus on superficial learning, for instance, may gain a few short-term insights along the way but no long-term learning capability. Their knowledge tends to come from well-established routines, formal rules, and traditional problem-solving skills. Managers and organiza-

Table 2.3   Levels of Learning

	Superficial (lower level)	Substantial (higher level)
Definitions	First-order learning	Second-order learning (Argyris and Schon, 1978)[a]
	Single-loop learning	Double-loop learning (Argyris and Schon, 1978)[a]
	Gaining knowledge	Understanding rationale and processes behind knowledge (Levitt and March, 1988)[b]
	Habit-forming learning	Discovery (Hedberg, 1981)[c]
	Reactive learning	Proactive learning (Miles and Randolph, 1980)[d]
	Evolutionary learning	Designing learning (Shrivastava and Mitroff, 1982)[e]
Characteristics	Occurs through repetition	Occurs through use of heuristics and insights
	Routine	Nonroutine
	Control over immediate task, rules, and structure	Development of differentiated structures, rules, etc. to deal with lack of control
	Well understood	Ambiguous concept
	Occurs at all levels in the organization	Occurs mostly in upper levels
Consequences	Behavioral outcomes	Cognitive outcomes
Examples	Institutionalized formal rules	New missions and statements of strategic intent
	Changes in management systems	Agenda setting for management
	Problem solving skills	Problem defining skills

This table comes from work by Fiol and Lyles (1985) (see note 22) and Snyder and Nason (1992) (see note 21).

a. *Organizational Learning* (Reading, Mass.: Addison-Wesley).
b. "Organizational Learning," *Annual Review of Sociology* 14: 319–340.
c. "How Organizations Learn and Unlearn?" in *Handbook of Organizational Design*, ed. P. C. Nystrom and W. H. Starbuck (London: Oxford University Press), 8–27.
d. "Influence of Organizational Learning Styles on Early Development," *The Organizational Life Cycle*, ed. J. H. Kimberly and Robert H. Miles and associates (San Francisco: Jossey-Bass), 44–82.
e. "Frames of Reference Managers Use: A Study in Applied Sociology of Knowledge," in *Advances in Strategic Management*, ed. R. Lamb (Greenwich, Conn.: JAI Press), 181–182.

tions that value substantial learning, however, will spend more time on nonroutine processes, developing differentiated structures and rules that are meant to handle a lack of control and ambiguity. Substantial learners tend to *define* problems before they occur rather than simply solving them; they emphasize new missions and statements of strategic intent, setting management agendas, and cognitive outcomes, not just superficial behavioral outcomes and control over immediate tasks, rules, and structures.

The learning continuum can also be conceived of as the difference between change and the capacity for change. Managers may create change through any number of initiatives such as quality circles, total quality management, continuous improvement, or reengineering. If these initiatives only create a flurry of activity, the learning achieved is superficial at best. But when such initiatives become a means for shaping the fundamental values and culture of not only employees but the organization as a system, they lead to learning that is rich, deep, and substantial. Therefore, the ultimate goal of any learning organization is to move programs and initiatives away from superficial outcomes to substantial ones.

5. Learning Comes through Many Small Failures

Sitkin[23] has demonstrated that a regular incidence of small failures actually promotes learning. The rationale here is that constant success fosters restricted information search, complacency, risk aversion, homogeneity, and even the illusion of invulnerability, one of the hallmarks of "group-think"; frequent small failures, however, provide the variety necessary for learning to occur. Counterintuitive as this may seem, some failures can have a positive influence on long-term performance by increasing risk tolerance, information search, problem recognition, deeper information processing, and the motivation to adapt. 3M's early experience with failure is just one real-world example.

Of course, not all failures are useful to a company, especially when they're catastrophic or when no learning is involved. Sitkin defines "intelligent" failures as containing five aspects: (1) they result from thoughtfully planned actions that (2) have uncertain outcomes, (3) are of modest scale, (4) are executed and responded to with alacrity, and (5) take place in a domain familiar enough to permit effective learning.

The implication of this work is that managers need to create an intelligent failure rationale in their organizations; in other words, the ability to take informed risks is rewarded rather than punished. When GE sank a lot of money into its new Profile refrigerator, a minor design flaw resulted in product recalls. Instead of punishing the design team, executives rewarded all of them for a great concept once the problem was fixed. And again, think about 3M. This company's ability to both generate the idea for and creatively market Post-it notes was not based on an unbroken string of product successes. It was based on a management philosophy that embraces "experimental doodling."

6. Learning Often Follows a Predictable Set of Processes

Many researchers have defined the processes followed in learning. These processes represent the steps or "flow" of learning. While various authors have used different words, the processes of organizational learning may be roughly categorized as follows:

Discovery: individual learners see a gap between expectations and reality, one that indicates that new knowledge is needed.

Invention: they analyze performance gaps and develop solutions for them. In this step, individuals learners may develop skills to address this new need; they do this through research, the advice of consultants, or education.

Implementation: learners implement solutions.

Diffusion: the organization integrates what's been learned so that it is broadly available and can be generalized to new situations.

From the perspective of $g \times g$, discovery and invention are related to idea generation, while implementation and diffusion are related to generalization. This basic sequence illustrates how successful learning moves from the discovery of new ideas to diffusion of those ideas. What's more, these processes occur sequentially; somebody has to acquire or discover an idea before it can become institutionalized.[24] Note that this process approach to learning is related to the process analysis found in reengineering and continuous improvement efforts.

7. Organizations Learn through Two Basic Sources: Direct Experience and the Experience of Others

The two sources of learning direct and through others, cover a lot of ground, but this basic dichotomy indicates why companies end up adopting different learning styles. Each source is important and has organizational payoffs. First, and most obviously, organizations learn from direct experience—that is, they acquire knowledge and develop insights through their own actions and reflections. Many writers cite examples of learning by direct experience. Nonaka and Takeuchi and Dutton and Freedman[25] focus on trial-and-error experimentation; Ulrich and Greenfield[26] discuss "action research," which means learning from structured, real-time experience rather than classroom lectures.

By directly performing a set of activities, and then reflecting on their action-outcome relationships, managers and employees can gain knowledge and expertise for improving performance over time.[27] For instance, Epple, Argote, and Devadas' research in experienced-based learning curves demonstrates that "as organizations produce more of a product, the unit cost of production typically decreases at a decreasing rate."[28] Moreover, such cost advantage can to some extent be institutionalized and transferred across time, geographical regions, and organizational boundaries. Similarly, studies by Imai and McDuffie and Krafcik[29] in continuous improvement illustrate that organizations can continuously upgrade the quality of their products and processes when organizational members engage in iterative problem-solving cycles (for example, a "plan–do–check–act" cycle).

But relying on direct experience can also be costly, depending on the business context and a company's competitive strategy. The second basic source of organizational learning is the experience of others—that is, organizations acquire knowledge without having to perform given tasks or operations on their own. Examples of learning from the experience of others include vicarious learning or learning by observation; "grafting" through acquisition and recruitment; and the diffusion of knowledge through consultants, educational institutions, and professional associations.[30] By observing, scanning, benchmarking, and imitating the successful products, processes, and practices of other organizations, management and employees can gain insights into and develop ideas about their own products and processes. Samsung Electronics' success is an obvious example of capitalizing on this kind of learning. Studies by DiMaggio and Powell and Meyer and Rowan[31] indicate other reasons for why companies may focus on learning from others: management can minimize sanctions from various stakeholders and build legitimacy for their own actions.

As many researchers have shown, the organizational choice of one learning method over another varies. Table 2.4 suggests some contextual considerations that influence the organizational choice of learning method. Bourgeois and Eisenhart[32] emphasize contextual factors like speed of environmental change; Dutton and Freedman[32] focus on competitive strategy and the level of what they call "slack"— or abundant—resources; others cite the current success of an organization and ambiguity of the technology involved as important factors in determining how organizations learn.

In general, organizations are more likely to learn from direct experience if their environments are changing rapidly, if they compete through product innovation and differentiation, and if they have sufficient slack resources, satisfactory performance levels, and technology

Table 2.4   Some Contextual Considerations in the
Choice of Learning Methods

Contextual characteristics	Learning from direct experience	Learning from the experience of others
Speed of environmental change	More likely if environment changes rapidly. Not useful to learn from others	Only useful if environment does not change too rapidly so that the experience of others is still relevant
Competitive strategy	Compete through product innovation and differentiation	Compete through cost/price
Slack resources	More abundant	More limited
Current success of organization	More likely to learn from direct experience if the organization is successful	More likely to learn from others if the organization's performance is not satisfactory
Ambiguity of technology	Less ambiguous, clear cause–effect relationship	Ambiguous, not sure of cause–effect relationship, imitate high profile companies to minimize sanctions

that is well understood. In contrast, organizations are more likely to learn from the experience of others if their environments are fairly stable, if they compete on a cost/commodity basis, if they have few resources for learning, and if they use less ambiguous technology (that is, technology in which input–output relationship is clearly understood and hence learning can be transferred easily from one situation to another). As we will see, this well-developed stream of research has influenced our own differentiation of learning styles.

8. Organizations Learn for Two Basic Purposes: To Explore New Turf or Exploit Existing Opportunities

Another stream of research focuses on the goals or purposes of organizational learning. In this case, the two basic purposes—to explore new turf or exploit existing opportunities—are clearly at odds with each other. James March, one of the influential Carnegie School scholars and a Stanford professor, explains this tension in an influential 1991 article. He notes that "A central concern of studies of adaptive processes is the relation between the exploration of new possibilities and the exploitation of old certainties. . . . Both exploration and exploitation are essential for organizations, but they compete for scarce resources."[33]

Exploration refers to experimentation with new competencies, technologies, and paradigms. It occurs when organizations attempt to create a competitive advantage through major breakthroughs in products, processes, and practices. It aims to achieve what Tushman and Anderson[34] refer to as "competency-destroying" innovations. In contrast, *exploitation* involves the refinement and extension of existing competencies, technologies, and paradigms. It occurs when organizations seek to leverage existing products, processes, and practices. For more progressive companies, exploitation may aim to create an order-of-magnitude improvement over existing products that build on existing know-how. Most companies, however, simply attempt to use existing knowledge in some productive way—and when the primary goal is to leverage existing knowledge, organizational learning tends to be more disciplined, systematic, and structured.

Both exploration and exploitation affect organizational survival and prosperity—but, just as March notes, they require and compete for resources that are scarce. A number of researchers have argued that managers often make strategic choices between the two, depending on various environmental characteristics—industry life cycle, technological trajectory, and competitive strategy—as well as the potential payoff from both learning orientations.[35] Table 2.5 summarizes all these factors. Organizations are more likely to explore new possibilities when their industry is young, major technological discontinuities are occurring, and competitive advantage is derived from technological leadership rather than cost leadership. While such organizations may ultimately enjoy huge payoffs as first movers, they also require substantial resource commitment, and returns on investment can be slow or even at risk.

A company's choice of one or the other orientation may evolve over time and differ across organizational units, depending on the learning need, resource availability, and competitive requirements. Once again, detailing the purposes of organizational learning—and the managerial decisions implied by exploration or exploitation—underpins our own work.

A New Typology: Four Learning Styles

Just as individuals learn in different ways, we believe there are different styles of organizational learning. This is the most critical and significant assertion we will make in this book. Most previous orga-

Table 2.5   Organizational Choice of Exploration versus Exploitation Learning Orientation

Characteristics	Exploration	Exploitation
Contextual Factors		
Industry life cycle	Young industry, competing for dominant design	Mature industry, refining dominant design
Technological trajectory	Develop competency-destroying innovations	Develop competency-enhancement, innovations
Competitive strategy	Differentiation strategy, technological leadership	Cost competitive strategy, cost leadership
Decision-making factors		
Potential Payoff	Huge, first movers	Comparatively smaller as follower
Resource commitment	High	Low
Certainty of return	Low	High
Temporal proximity of return	Slow	Quick
Spatial proximity of return	Remote	Close
Potential liability	Over-reliance of exploration strategy can result in too many undeveloped/underdeveloped ideas	Over-reliance of exploitation strategy can result in suboptimal stable equilibra and low adaptability

nizational learning work that addresses what managers should do has attempted to identify the "characteristics" of the learning organization. It assumes that organizations or managers that build in these characteristics will consequently create something that is higher on a "learning organization" scale. These characteristics then become a check-off list or a scorecard to measure just how much farther they need to go to become a learning organization. But while identifying what constitutes the ideal learning organization is important, we believe emphasizing the different ways that learning happens will matter more to managers, who operate in a real world of diverse businesses, organizational structures, strategies, and individual employees. The research to date, including our own, demonstrates that organizations approach learning differently, whether as explorers or exploiters—or as experimenters like 3M or benchmarkers like Samsung Electronics. For us, multiple types of learning capability exist.

We have already noted some of the reasons that companies develop different learning styles, such as great variation in industry characteristics, business strategy, business culture, and technology. Companies may need, or choose, to learn differently given the time, resources, histories, and competitive constraints they face. 3M primarily learns by experimentation because of its unique history, culture, and strategy. Samsung Electronics learns through benchmarking because of its lack of technological know-how, particular competitive strategies, and national cultural values.

Our learning styles typology (see figure 2.1) also builds on parallel work on individual personality. Recent studies have categorized the types of personalities that might exist.[36] For example, the Myers-Briggs Type Indicator, a popular test often administered by career counselors, identifies four dimensions on which personalities can be assessed: introversion/extroversion; intuitive/sensing; thinking/feeling; judging/perceiving. (These dimensions have their own roots in Jungian personality theory.) Based on how an individual scores along each of the four dimensions, a "profile" of personality type is derived. Clearly, there aren't just four kinds of personalities, and everybody is a mix of these dimensions; the appeal of the Myers-Briggs' test is that the four types make sense to just about everyone in terms of how people take in information and subsequently use it to solve problems.

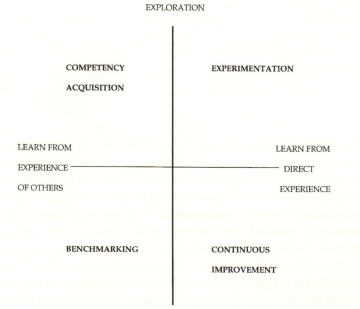

Figure 2.1   Typology of Organizational Learning Types

A similar logic can be applied to learning capability. To that end, our learning styles typology can characterize an organization—that is, we can identify "learning capability profiles." These profiles represent ways in which organizations generate ideas with impact. Once developed, learning capability profiles can be used to describe how learning occurs and what changes in learning might help a firm become more competitive. Creating a learning action plan or "blueprint" for a company will be detailed in chapter 7.

For now, let's consider what constitutes the four basic learning styles we've identified empirically: experimentation, competency acquisition, benchmarking, and continuous improvement. Note that our learning typology, as shown in Figure 1, also incorporates the dimensions of direct experience vs. the experience of others and of exploration vs. exploitation.

Learning Style 1: Experimentation

Organizations learn by trying many new ideas and being receptive to experimentation with new products and processes. The primary sources of learning are their customers and employees (direct experience). They primarily achieve organizational learning through controlled experimentation, from both inside and outside, rather than through exploiting the experience of others. 3M, Sony, Hewlett-Packard, and Rubbermaid are companies known for their experimentation strategies.

Learning Style 2: Competency Acquisition

Organizations learn by encouraging individuals and teams to acquire new competencies. Learning is a critical aspect of business strategy; it focuses on both the experience of others and an exploration of new possibilities. Common competency acquisition strategies include buying competency through recruitment, building competency through investment in training and development activities, borrowing competency through strategic alliances, and creative work arrangement with "idea places" like universities and consulting firms. The intention is to help organizational members acquire state-of-the-art competencies, which may enable and accelerate their subsequent creation of new ideas and development of innovative products and processes. Motorola and GE are well-known for their competency acquisition strategies.

Learning Style 3: Benchmarking

Organizations learn by discovering how others operate and then trying to adopt and adapt this knowledge into their own organizations. Learning comes from organizations that have demonstrated excellent performance or developed the best practices in specific processes. Benchmarking companies primarily learn from the experience of others and exploit successful technologies and practices that already exist. Samsung Electronics, Xerox, and Milliken all emphasize benchmarking.

Learning Style 4: Continuous Improvement

Organizations learn by constantly improving on what has been done before and mastering each step before moving on to new steps in a process. They often emphasize a high degree of employee involvement (such as through quality control circles, problem solving groups, or self managed work teams) to resolve issues identified by internal and external customers. These are organizations that rely on both learning through direct experience and the exploitation of existing practices. Toyota, Honda, Xerox, and Motorola are continuous improvement companies.

Our Survey of Companies: Strength of Each Learning Style

These four styles represent ideal types only. Just as individuals never conform to just one personality type, companies—especially large corporations with diverse businesses like GE and Motorola—seldom engage exclusively in just one learning style. Typically, organizations mix all four (as individuals do on the Myers-Briggs), but in different combinations and to varying degrees. We want to emphasize here that we're not merely advocating these learning styles; rather, they are the styles we've seen in action. Theorists can create learning typologies out of thin air, advocating what they think will work best. But the strength of our research is that it has an empirical basis. In addition, learning capability profiles can change over time within organizations, depending on particular situations. The research challenge for us has been to understand how contextual factors affect and contribute to each learning style, an issue we delve into more thoroughly in the next chapter.

These qualifications aside, a review of past research and our own large-scale survey of companies support this typology. Culled from a database of over 1,500 managers from 460 businesses in 411 companies, the results of our worldwide survey verifies the existence of these four learning styles through multivariate statistical techniques, confirmatory factor analyses, and reliability analyses. For those interested in the details, appendix 1 discusses our research methodology and lists the companies that participated.

To date, this is the largest sample of businesses ever studied in the context of organizational learning. Respondents came from more than 40 countries, diverse industries, and companies (although the majority were from larger companies in mature businesses). They were generally middle managers who had been with the business a good 16 years—people with the experience to have accurate perceptions of learning processes in their companies. Appendix 2 includes the questionnaire we administered, which involved queries about the kind of learning in their organizations, industry/business contexts, business culture, and organizational disabilities observed.

In general, our survey indicates that competency acquisition and continuous improvement are the most popular learning styles, followed by experimentation and benchmarking. On a five-point scale, the extent to which our sample companies focused on the four styles runs as follows:

Learning Style	Mean Score	Standard Deviation
Competency acquisition	3.58	.84
Continuous improvement	3.53	.77
Experimentation	3.11	.80
Benchmarking	2.94	.84

If we classify businesses based on their dominant learning style (the one that receives the most emphasis in organizational structure and action) here's the breakdown:

Dominant Learning Style	No. of Businesses	Percentage of the Sample
Continuous improvement	104	40
Competency acquisition	95	37
Benchmarking	33	13
Experimentation	25	10

The results make sense, given the very strong emphasis on total quality management in the 1980s, as well as the traditional association between learning and training in many corporations. But while most of the sample companies didn't emphasize experimentation, our research indicates that it *is* the most effective style for enhancing business performance, as measured by organizational competitiveness (a composite measure of fifteen items, including human resource practices, customer relations, and globalization), organizational innovativeness (a composite measure of four items, such as willingness to experiment and reputation as an innovator), and new product introduction (the percentage of sales based on products introduced in the last three years). Competency acquisition also positively affected all three performance outcomes, but not as strongly as experimentation. Companies that emphasized continuous improvement appeared to have more trouble with new product introduction, while benchmarking didn't significantly correlate with any performance outcomes.

This means for a company like 3M, which relies on new ideas and new products, experimentation has paid off—even if most large corporations operate differently. It's in the generation of ideas that the different learning styles really manifest themselves. They represent a part of the overall learning process, or the first building block, although the styles don't have much impact on idea generalization. For Samsung Electronics, our premier benchmarker, the ability to generalize ideas may play the bigger role. Chapter 3 revisits the learning styles, particularly in their effect on idea generation. The next chapter also presents a model for organizational learning capability, accounting for the ways in which business performance and context influence how companies learn.

CHAPTER THREE

A Model for Organizational Learning Capability

The Three Building Blocks

In the early 1990s, General Motors established a pocket of excellence through its new Saturn division and manufacturing site in Springfield, Tennessee. After years of falling behind Japanese automobile manufacturers like Toyota and Honda, GM rightly decided on an about-face in business strategy. Saturn was conceived, created, and brought on-line to show how new manufacturing techniques—complete with automation, high-performing teams, inventory control, and labor/ management cooperation—could transform the company. To some extent, they have. Saturn has exceeded all expectations in terms of sales, productivity, and morale. Employees have become empowered; new technologies have changed how they approach and do work; products have been created faster and with better quality; contracts with dealers limit negotiation of sales price, restricting vendor competition but ultimately making more money for GM. And a sophisticated marketing plan has built strong brand image for Saturn: warm-and-fuzzy cars made by dedicated American workers—driven by nice, regular people—and sold by nice, low-pressure dealers who don't try to chisel you on the lot.

Declared a success, the Saturn division is now considered an example of best practice for those inside and outside General Motors. Yet years after the start of production, lessons from Saturn have not been moved into other GM manufacturing sites around the world. The Saturn story, like so many other incomplete successes at so many other companies, indicates why all three building blocks of organizational learning capability—generation of ideas, generalization of those ideas, and identification of learning disabilities—matter.

In GM's case, the company created a pocket of excellence that *generated* many ideas with impact: they led to Saturn as we know it today. These ideas, however, have not been *generalized* across a number of important corporate boundaries: internal, external, and geographical, to name a few. Moreover, this lack of generalization is due to *learning disabilities* at GM that have yet to be identified by management.

By simultaneously strengthening enhancements to learning and removing barriers, managers can create a much more effective learning organization. In this chapter, we will further define the building blocks, summarizing associated management practices. Then we'll present an integrated model of organizational learning capability. The model serves as the conceptual framework for our worldwide survey of companies and for various case studies, which are detailed in subsequent chapters.

The First Building Block: Generating Ideas with Impact

Any discussion of organizational learning has to begin with what sparks ideas and their many diverse sources. In practical terms, the typology of learning styles introduced in chapter 2 provides the best frame for understanding idea generation. A company's approach to generating new ideas—becoming an expert or an experimenter, a skill acquirer or a copier—shows its true learning colors.

In short, the four learning styles reflect four different ways to generate ideas, although experimentation and competency acquisition most strongly encourage originality, innovation, and uniqueness. While our research findings reveal that most firms rely primarily on competency acquisition and continuous improvement to generate ideas, it's the experimenters—the companies focusing on new products, services, and concepts—that most positively affect business performance. But exactly why various companies adopt different approaches to idea generation is complicated by many factors. After all, firms that copy and benchmark what others have done are still generating ideas, and they may have good business reasons for exploiting what's out there rather than brainstorming new possibilities on their own.

Let's reframe the four learning styles—experimentation, competency acquisition, benchmarking, and continuous improvement—this time with a focus on idea generation (table 3.1.).

Reframing the styles indicates which companies will generate more

Table 3.1   Idea Generation in Four Learning Styles

Learning Style	Type of Idea Generation
1. Experimenters/Innovators	We constantly seek new ideas, even before old ones are fully implemented. We constantly seek new ways to do work. We try a lot of new ideas; we want to be known as experimenters within our industry. We want to be the first in the market with a new idea or concept.
2. Competent Workers / Skill Acquirers	We encourage individuals to acquire new competencies. We encourage teams to acquire new competencies. We learn by hiring people from other companies who have skills we need. Learning is a critical part of our business strategy.
3. Copiers/Benchmarkers	We learn from others, entering a product or applying a process only after it has been fully tested. We learn by broadly scanning what other companies do. We learn by focusing our scanning on specific activities done by other companies. We primarily benchmark the competition, measuring our progress against competitors' performance.
4. Experts / Continuous Improvers	We master new ideas before moving on to the next round. We upgrade the way we do existing work until we have it right. We want to be known as the best technical experts in our industry. We primarily benchmark ourselves, measuring progress against our previous performance.

new ideas within their own walls and which will look to outside sources and existing practices. In general, we have found that when companies focus on product differentiation through product innovation as a strategy, they tend to be experimenters and/or skill acquirers. Even in an industry that manufactures mundane products like buckets and laundry baskets, for instance, Rubbermaid differentiates itself through continuous product innovation and experimentation. "We introduce some four hundred new products every year," claims Wolfgang Schmit, Chairman and CEO. "Each of our [5,000] products reflects several generations of innovation, and innovation is what distinguishes Rubbermaid from a sea of competitors."[1]

The real question is, how has this company created a learning environment that drives continuous product innovation? Rubbermaid has done so through a powerful combination of the five "Ts": trends (anticipation of consumer needs), teams (for sharing information and expertise), training (opportunities for continuous education), technology (internal networks for sharing information and knowledge, which take advantage of computer-aided processes to speed up work), and creative tension (formation of cross-functional teams with diverse members). Clearly, Rubbermaid's product innovation capability did not evolve by accident. Through both experimentation and competency acquisition, this company has carefully cultivated a learning environment in which new and diverse ideas are generated, shared, developed, and transformed into new products that meet the emerging needs of customers.

On the other hand, some firms capitalize on existing ideas through continuous improvement and benchmarking to deliver products/services at more affordable prices. The game of competition is not always won by being new; being cheaper and better in everything a company does can also win. Taiwan Semiconductor Manufacturing Company (TSMC), one of the fastest growing companies in Taiwan, is an interesting example. Within 10 years, TSMC has achieved more than US$1 billion in annual sales revenue. Between 1991 and 1994, the net income of the company grew 28-fold and sales revenue six fold. In 1995, its gross margin was 52%, indicating a highly profitable business. Yet TSMC does not design or experiment with any new products. It manufactures semiconductors for major players like Texas Instruments, Motorola, and Siemens. This company has gained its competitive edge by manufacturing chips cheaper, better, and faster than other leading semiconductor firms. By continuously improving its processes and practices, then, TSMC has built a learning capability that meshes very well with its business strategy.

The Second Building Block: Generalizing Ideas with Impact

In our work with companies, we find time and again that many more firms generate innovative ideas than generalize them. In fact, when we ask managers what makes a learning organization or how to enhance learning within an organization, most emphasize coming up with new ideas through benchmarking, continuous improvement, competency acquisition, or experimentation—one or all of the four learning styles we've just discussed. But from the learning capability perspective, it's not enough to be awash in new ideas. The second building block—generalization—forms the other crucial half of our expression "$g \times g$." For generalization of ideas, *implementation* of what has been learned is essential.

While many companies have succeeded in creating pockets of excellence, such as GM's Saturn, best practices often fail to transfer across boundaries to the rest of the corporation. Colgate Palmolive, for instance, has piloted and implemented many creative marketing programs in Australia. These programs have been quite successful: the market share of selected product lines in Australia has grown 25%. Yet even with visible managerial excitement about Colgate Palmolive's Australian success, the lessons from this marketing center of excellence haven't reached the larger European and U.S. markets of Colgate-Palmolive. Thus, at Colgate Palmolive, GM, and dozens of other companies we find a similar theme: with great fanfare and enthusiasm, managers celebrate successful experiments in marketing, human resources, or manufacturing. The challenge of creating these innovations is great; but transferring innovations across boundaries is far more difficult.

Learning does not occur just because a new idea is created. Generalization is necessary, and this may happen when an employee moves from one location to another to share how work should get done—or when technology allows managers to transfer knowledge from one unit or individual to another quickly and simply. Generalization also happens when best-practice forums are created to codify and disseminate lessons from one site to another. In each case, an idea has moved across a boundary and created a change in behavior.

Managers build learning capability, therefore, not only by generating ideas but also by sharing them within—and even beyond—the organization. We want to emphasize that organizational learning capability is less an academic exercise and experience than a focused set of management actions. The primary managerial task in generalizing ideas is to create an infrastructure that moves ideas across boundaries. Later chapters of this book will detail a manager's tool kit for generalization and discuss how to build a "learning architecture." Here we give five principles for idea generalization, culled from our research and that of others.

Principle 1. Generalization Requires Recognition That Boundaries Exist, Can Be Specified, and Can Be Negotiated

In almost all situations, long-term learning that affects business performance will not happen if knowledge isn't shared. For that reason, boundary recognition and negotiation is the most important principle of generalization. Moving ideas across boundaries is an integral part of learning and takes many forms. Consider the possibilities when any of the boundaries below are crossed and the managerial challenges that such sharing presents.

Time Boundaries Ideas can and should be shared over time. Ideas outlive individuals, and they can become part of an organization's fabric or culture. Every new manager or team shouldn't have to reinvent the wheel. One professional association, for instance, held annual conferences for years with the president elect as the conference chair. Each year, the new president had to rediscover the elements of running the conference, such as creating an agenda, scheduling, and advertising. In essence, knowledge was not generalized over time, resulting in annual planning difficulties. This association overcame the time boundary by selecting co-conference chairs; each held the assignment for two years, and their terms overlapped. Every year one of the two chairs had worked on the previous conference and could share what he or she had learned in planning the current year's conference.

Vertical Boundaries Ideas can be shared up and down the organizational hierarchy. Ideas then move beyond one level, perhaps all the way from the factory floor to the executive suite. In General Electric's WorkOut program, front-line employees are invited to simplify, reduce, and eliminate the unnecessary rules, procedures, approvals, and meetings required to perform their work. By involving employees during an off-site meeting, in which they can make recommendations, senior management at GE can capture many useful ideas from different levels of the company. In Sears's "town hall" meetings, employees also meet with supervisors to share ideas up and down the hierarchy, thus removing this boundary.

Horizontal Boundaries Ideas can be shared across functional or product units. Experiments in one unit then become best practice and are shared with another unit. In GM's case, top management created the Saturn plant not only to produce a competitive small car but also to be an experimental site for innovative management practices. GM's challenge now is to move its successful Saturn ideas across horizontal boundaries, to other factories and product lines.

External Boundaries Ideas can even be shared across the supplier–firm–customer value chain. Basically, these boundaries involve stakeholders outside the firm. Forming alliances, using study groups, attending workshops, benchmarking best practices, and continually scanning emerging technologies are ways of crossing such boundaries. Samsung Electronics, for instance, learned about flexible manufacturing systems by benchmarking best practices at other companies; Motorola uses its corporate university to share its expertise with suppliers and customers; senior management at Baxter Healthcare offers free consulting/training workshops to key customers to share its expertise and to better understand what customers want.

Geographic Boundaries   Finally, ideas can be shared across geographic locations, as management practices in one location are used by others. Many consulting firms, such as Anderson Consulting and McKinsey, are building best-practice data banks so that associates in other parts of the world can gain immediate access to how other colleagues have handled similar issues or industries. In emphasizing global growth strategies, many companies are developing infrastructure and systems so that technical and managerial know-how can be rapidly transferred from mature markets to emerging ones.

Principle 2. Generalization Requires Ideas That Are Tied to Strategy

Sorting out which ideas to generalize across boundaries is often difficult. In a meeting one of us conducted with a group of senior executives at Boeing, for example, the executives seemed impressed by all the innovative work being done at the company but also felt overwhelmed. For them, deciding which of twelve good ideas to support and pay attention to was far more difficult than finding those twelve ideas. Generation without priority-setting at the top can lead to a quagmire of ideas, each becoming a quicksand "sink" for managerial energy. The challenge for Boeing executives and others is to filter the array of ideas generated in an innovative company, thus obtaining a vital few that can then be generalized across boundaries. A consideration of the following four basic questions—which every manager knows by heart but in the heat of the moment sometimes overlooks—can help act as an initial filter for screening out ideas that will not be generalized:

- Is the idea central to our customer requirements? Will customers see us differently from competitors if we implement this idea?
- Is the idea aligned with our strategy? Will the strategic direction we have taken be more likely to happen with this idea?

- Is the idea likely to have financial impact? Will it meet the economic criteria we use to make investment decisions?
- Is the idea doable with the resources available? If not, how much energy will we have to expend acquiring those resources?

Principle 3. Generalization Requires Contingent Thinking

To make full use of what we've learned, we need not only to behave differently but also to figure out why something good has happened and then make it happen again. Organizations that are good at generalization emphasize contingent thinking; managers know how to delineate all the contextual factors that may influence a best practice or process, whether that practice originates in-house or has been copied from another company. Important contingencies can involve anything from business strategy or culture to timing of a product roll-out, the introduction of a new computer system, the arrival of a new executive, the commitment and influence of the CEO, or the challenges faced in the external business environment.

Contingent thinking matters, because many firms adopt ideas but don't adapt them to current conditions. Effective generalization requires adaptation, not adoption, and contingent thinking focuses more on the "if" of the "if/then" statement. Too often, learning in organizations amounts to sharing the "then," meaning that best-practice studies proliferate without providing any context in which the original practice occurred. Hence the prevalence of mindless benchmarking or best-practice sharing, which has little impact on business performance.

True generalization is based on a series of "if's." For example, many executives have tried to copy the General Electric WorkOut program. They read about the GE experience, visit a GE site, interview GE employees, and then try to mimic what GE did in their own company. Small surprise that they usually fail. These executives focus on the "then" (the GE WorkOut program), not the "if" (the actual conditions that made this program a success). In the WorkOut program's case, the contingent conditions included a committed CEO (Jack Welch); a history of managerial innovation; incentives (both financial and nonfinancial) to participate; and the use of internal and external consultants, who adapted the program to local conditions.

Principle 4. Generalization Requires That Organizations Master Capabilities Beyond Single Experiments

Generalization occurs not only when single ideas are moved but also when the entire process of moving ideas becomes institutionalized within an organization. Stephen Covey distinguishes between production and production *capability*: the golden egg versus the capacity to create the golden egg.[2] Firms often focus on the production of a new product or the development of a new process—the golden egg. But what matters more is the process of generalization; once this process is embedded in a firm, a series of new products can be created, not just one golden egg. The capability of generalizing ideas consistently is far more important than one or two isolated successes. In chapter 5, we introduce a wide range of tools that can help companies institutionalize such generalization processes.

Principle 5. Generalization Requires That Shared Ideas Have Impact

Obvious as this sounds, ideas will have little or no impact on business performance if they don't change behavior. In an organizational context, behavior generally refers to how individual employees spend their time or how a process is carried out. But it's not enough to tell people to change or to send out documentation describing a new process. In a world of relatively free technology, ideas and knowledge are readily available. Using internet searches, trade association data bases, and best-practice studies from consulting firms, it's relatively easy to generate a working knowledge of a topic. It's much more difficult to ensure that knowledge leads to action. As Chris Argyris has said, "inquiry without action is not learning."[3] Generalization requires a holistic approach (including reward systems, training, empowerment, information sharing) to translate ideas into actions and to generalize insights across boundaries.

Again, the notion that ideas must have impact is linked to "$g \times g$." When companies can both generate and generalize ideas, they have strong learning organizations. Problems with either of the "g's" usually stem from learning disabilities—the focus of the third and final building block of organizational learning capability.

The Third Building Block: Identifying Learning Disabilities

Even if many top executives now talk about the importance of learning, exhorting their employees to ever higher levels of "knowledge management" and "change," not all organizations have equally high learning capability. That's because organizational learning disabilities can hinder generation and generalization of ideas. For managers, identifying these disabilities is an important first step, followed by appropriate intervention.

Below we list seven of the most common learning disabilities, which are drawn from our own survey of companies, as well as past research on physical and psychological disability. The first four disabilities limit companies from generating new ideas, while the latter three hinder generalization of ideas across boundaries. We are particularly indebted to William Snyder for his help in identifying many of these disabilities.[4]

Disability 1. Blindness

The first step in generating ideas involves identifying potential problems or opportunities; managers need to contrast the organization's goals with the current situation. The resulting gap between the actual and the desired states of the organization, or between the current reality and the vision, produces what Senge calls a "creative tension" that can "trigger" the learning process. The identification of these performance gaps is often what motivates later stages of both idea generation and idea generalization. Difficulties in perceiving these gaps are a learning disability we call blindness. More specifically, blindness refers to an inability to perceive accurately the organization's environment, such as through poor scanning processes.

Disability 2. Simplemindedness

Generation of new ideas entails both the analysis of problems and opportunities that have surfaced and the invention of solutions to address them. Many firms use elaborate and sophisticated analytical procedures, routines, and programs for analysis and solution generation. Unfortunately, many others don't. In fact, many organizations have no formal and even few informal methods for developing responses to opportunities or threats. We refer to this disability as organizational simplemindedness. Such a learning disability crops up when simple heuristics or rules of thumb are applied to complex situations without careful analysis. There's a tendency in organizations that suffer from this to rely on easy answers to hard questions, to overemphasize one cause among many, and to fail to consider the organization as a complex system with multiple feedback loops.

Disability 3. Homogeneity

One perspective or source of information is no longer sufficient to address the complex issues facing businesses in today's dynamic environment. It's necessary to have a variety of skills, ideas, and values in an organization. While the sheer quantity of information available throughout the organization is important, it is more important that information comes from different sources and perspectives. George Huber argues that the greater the number of different interpretations that are developed within an organization, the greater the organizational learning, and that this is particularly true the more complex the environment is.[5] We consider homogeneity in ideas and approach a definite learning disability.

The disabilities of simplemindedness and homogeneity are related yet distinct. Simplemindedness refers to the way in which information is insufficiently or inaccurately analyzed, but it doesn't indicate how much information is present. Homogeneity deals with the variety of information and perspectives available in the firm, but it doesn't refer to how well the information is analyzed. In short, simplemindedness concerns the quality of analysis, while homogeneity indicates the quantity and variety of information present.

Disability 4. Tight Coupling

Tightly coupled organizations are firms in which different departments and subunits are so tightly controlled that there's little differentiation between policies and procedures in the various units. Rigid hierarchical structures, highly centralized decision making, and highly formalized rules and procedures all cause tight coupling. Karl Weick points out that tightly coupled organizations, by presenting a uniform analysis and response to complex situations, are extremely inflexible and unadaptive.[6]

Loosely coupled organizations, on the other hand, allow departments and subunits some autonomy to deal with their own unique circumstances but maintain a degree of oversight and compatibility with the whole. In a loosely coupled firm, each strategic business unit may try different variations of the standard procedures, technologies, or strategies. Some variations will provide improvements, others not. But the variations that work are retained in the unit where they originated; more important, since there are ties to the rest of the organization, successful variations are communicated and eventually implemented in other areas of the company.

Disability 5. Paralysis

As the CEO of a Fortune 100 company said, "The competitive difference is not in deciding what to do, but in how to do it. Execution becomes paramount." For the purposes of generalization, the solutions generated to organizational problems and opportunities must be implemented; the whole point is to turn good ideas into concrete actions, procedures, or structural changes—in other words, an idealistic vision is translated into action and real, tangible change.

Paralysis, of course, is the physical inability to act, and organizational paralysis refers to an inability of the organization, for whatever reason, to take action or implement new procedures. Paralysis can occur when an organization holds on to the "tried and proven ways of doing things"[7] long after their usefulness has expired. Hornstein describes this as the "rule of repeated action": when companies face situations that are doubtful, they tend to do what they did yesterday. If it isn't working, they do it twice as hard, twice as fast, and twice as carefully.[8]

When a company suffers from paralysis, great ideas and solutions may abound, but they aren't translated into action, and there's little change. Reward systems that reinforce old behaviors will hinder change. Rigid rules, procedures, role expectations, or organizational cultures can all result in the inability of managers to take new actions. Conflicting goals, a weak vision, and apathy will also retard action. Organizations in which failure is heavily punished are prone to inaction, since employees are hesitant to take risks or to make any change for fear of the consequences.[9] In paralysis situations, analysis outweighs action, and organizations spend more time imagining than doing.

Disability 6. Superstitious Learning

Idea generalization also occurs when organizational experience and results are evaluated, encoded into the organizational memory, and diffused to all relevant areas. But organizations, like individuals, can be superstitious when they misinterpret the meaning of experience, whether they use limited data, fabricated meanings, or irrational mythologies. We call the inability to interpret accurately the meaning of experience superstitious learning. In firms with this learning disability, connections between organizational actions and outcomes are misspecified. This is often caused by turbulent environments or a great deal of ambiguity; such ambiguity can result in a lack of clarity in the relationship between an organization's actions and its environment.

Causal relationships are perceived to exist without much support and without a consideration of other explanations, particularly in strong positive or negative environments. As a result, wrong ideas are generalized. For instance, construction companies in Hong Kong used to suffer from a high rate of industrial accidents because of poor safety precautions. But even in the 1990s, instead of linking the industrial accidents to safety policies, many traditional Chinese companies attributed such problems to offending the gods who protect the earth. As a result, it became an industrial practice among construction workers to worship all kinds of gods before they started work on a construction site. Industrial safety has now improved because of education and government regulation, but construction companies still believe that such a ritual is critical to the well-being of their workers. As this example illustrates, superstitious learning can be a difficult disability to cure when it is deeply internalized.

Disability 7. Diffusion Deficiency

Encoding previous learning into the organizational memory can occur via new routines, policies, procedures, conceptual maps, behavioral norms, and organizational culture, as well as through paper documentation and computer data. But this is not enough. What has been learned must be diffused to all relevant areas of the organization. Such diffusion occurs through the communication system, computer network, training, socialization, and cross-functional teams. We call the inability to do this diffusion deficiency. This learning disability can develop when learning occurs in an individual or unit of the organization but is never spread to other portions of the firm. Political fiefdoms and power dynamics can restrict the diffusion of ideas and procedures across the organization, as can rigid pyramidal organizational structures.

The seven learning disabilities highlighted here are clearly not exclusive, but they indicate the ways in which individual learning and organizational learning capability can be impaired. We believe that learning disabilities are related to the culture and business strategy of a company. For instance, companies that have a clan-based culture, particularly many successful firms like traditional IBM and NEC, may face the risk of becoming too inwardly focused and blind to environmental changes. Hierarchical companies may be risk averse and suffer paralysis. Firms that have market-oriented cultures may attempt to develop consistency in service standards and processes and end up with tight coupling. And high-tech companies, which tend to emphasize ad hoc systems and organizational approaches, while they are often spontaneous in many kinds of activities, can suffer from diffusion deficiency.

We have found that the presence of any one of these learning disabilities is enough to block the learning process. For example, a firm may do a great job generating ideas, but if it suffers from organizational paralysis and cannot implement those ideas, it will stagnate. Likewise, even if the firm generates ideas and implements them effectively, if it can not diffuse the learning to all relevant areas of the organization, the firm as a whole will not learn. Conversely, if a firm is great at generalizing ideas with impact, but suffers from homogeneity or simplemindedness, the learning will fail. In other words, the ability to implement and diffuse bad or simplistic solutions will retard, not promote, organizational learning. Since any one of the learning disabilities alone can bring learning to a screeching halt, great vigilance must be taken to avoid all of them. We will discuss each of these learning disabilities in greater detail in chapter 6 and illustrate them with detailed examples from our research in the health care and electronics industries.

Pulling It All Together: An Integrated Model

Of course, it would be absurd to argue that all companies should be experimenters, or that benchmarking is always an inferior learning style—or that companies suffering from paralysis are never successful. In the real world, any number of variables can affect why corporations choose particular business strategies, why individual managers make certain decisions, or why a firm triples its revenue in two years rather than shutting down. Once again, consider General Motors. The company's business context in the late 1980s—increased competition in the world automobile industry, eroding market share, and an out-of-step hierarchical culture—mobilized management to learn. In turn, GM developed some learning capability by creating the Saturn division. But GM's failure to generalize what was learned in this "pocket" has affected its overall business performance—that is, General Motors as a whole is still not as competitive or innovative as it could be.

To understand how these various factors drive organizational learning capability, we've developed a model that pulls them all together. Our model integrates the three building blocks with the business context that influences the development of such a capability—for example, industry characteristics or business culture—and the performance consequences that occur if an organization has a greater learning capability, a particular style of learning, and/or a set of learning disabilities.

Figure 3.1 graphically represents the logic of these relationships. It captures the flow of our research, identifies the concepts we have studied, proposes how they fit together, and suggests the relationships among them. Indeed, figure 3.1 specifies three kinds of relationships: (1) those among the building blocks of learning capability;

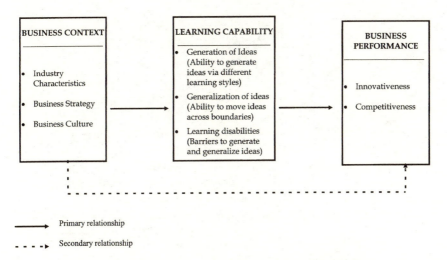

Figure 3.1   Model of Organizational Learning Capability

(2) those between business context and learning capability; and (3) those between learning capability and business performance. What this means in practice is that business context affects learning capability, and that an organization's learning capability ultimately affects performance. (Business context and performance are also related, but that relationship is of secondary interest here.) Below we describe the various components of our model; in our survey, we studied most of these items and the possible links among them. While our results, which we'll detail in chapters 4 and 6, don't indicate strong connections between every one of the items and organizational learning, some interesting insights are found, and the conceptual model encompasses the most important learning elements.

Business Context

In the box on the left of figure 3.1, we list contextual variables that may influence how and why companies learn. These variables are industry characteristics, business strategy, and business culture. These are the antecedents of learning capability.

Industry Characteristics   The industry a company is in—be it automobiles, computers, or financial services—may affect how learning happens. For our worldwide survey of companies, we identified six industry characteristics: market concentration, customer relationships, supplier relationships, technological interdependence, environmental predictability, and industry type. Table 3.2 indicates how we

Table 3.2   Measures of Industry Characteristics:
Questions to Sample Companies

Characteristic	Question
1. Market concentration	"What percentage of the market is accounted for by your four largest competitors?"
2. Customer relationship	"To what extent do the customers of your business try to maintain a long-term working relationship you?"
3. Supplier relationship	"To what extent does your business work to maintain a long-term relationship with your key suppliers?"
4. Technological interdependence	"To what extent does the major work within your business require interdependence among the employees?"
5. Environmental predictability	"To what extent are the changes predictable for the market in which you will operate over the next three years?"
6. Industry type	"What is the SIC code that most closely represents your business?"

asked respondents about these characteristics. The pace of business change and uncertainty in the industry can also affect learning.

Business Strategy   When a firm's top managers choose to emphasize, for instance, product differentiation (through product innovation or quality) over cost reduction, the business strategy selected will impact organizational learning. Based on the work of Michael Porter and others,[10] we identified and measured fifteen business strategies. These include a focus on quality of products or services, providing specialized services, building employee commitment, and controlling channels of distribution. To compete successfully, a business strategy can focus on

1. Advertising
2. Brand identification
3. Building employee commitment
4. Competitive pricing
5. Controlling channels of distribution
6. Cost reduction
7. Developing operating technology
8. Developing/refining existing products

9. Differentiating products or services from those of competitors
10. Improving relationships with customers
11. Innovation in marketing techniques and methods
12. New products or services development
13. Operating efficiency
14. Providing specialized products or services
15. Quality of products or services

Business Culture   The influence of culture on learning has received much attention in the literature. For our work, we adapted a framework of cultural types developed by Bob Quinn and his colleagues.[11] They identify four culture types based on two dimensions (loose control versus tight control; internal focus versus external focus): (1) clan cultures (loose/internal) value human commitment, morale, participation, and openness; (2) adhocracy cultures (loose/external) emphasize adaptability, growth, and innovation; (3) hierarchy cultures (tight/internal) focus on stability, control, and management of the existing bureaucracy; and (4) market cultures (tight/external) emphasize output, production, efficiency, and goal clarity. (See table 3.3 for a list of practices that characterize each culture.)

Table 3.3   Measures of Business Culture

Organization culture	Value

The following statements describe types of operating values that may exist in your business. Please indicate whether they do, and please indicate also the extent to which each item is valued.

1. Clan culture	Empowerment of employees to act
	Participation, open discussion
	Assessing employee concerns and ideas
	Human relations, teamwork, cohesion
2. Adhocracy culture	Flexibility, decentralization
	Innovation and change
	Expansion, growth, and development
	Creative problem solving processes
3. Hierarchical culture	Control, centralization
	Predictable performance outcomes
	Stability, continuity, order
	Routinization, formalization, structure
4. Market culture	Task focus, accomplishment, goal achievement
	Efficiency, productivity, profitability
	Outcome, excellence, quality
	Direction, objective setting, goal clarity

Business Performance

In the box on the right of figure 3.1, the model shows the two main consequences of a company's ability to learn: innovativeness and competitiveness. While we recognize that other consequences exist—for example, morale and commitment of employees, customer satisfaction, market share—our research focuses on these two key measures because they are related to the short-and long-term performance of a firm.

For our purposes, *competitiveness* is the ability of a business to compete in its niche or market position. We identified and measured fifteen relevant components of a company's competitiveness, including its human resource practices, production capability, and financial performance in the last three years. *Innovativeness* refers to an organization's willingness to experiment and take risks, and we broke this down into four components. (See table 3.4 for a full list of the components of competitiveness and innovativeness.) In some of our analyses, we also included new product introduction, defined as the

Table 3.4   Measures of Business Performance

Competitiveness	Innovativeness
How does your business compare to competitors for each of the following functions or activities? (1 = much worse; 5 = much better)	*Compared to your major competitor, how would you rank yourself on: (1 = much worse; 5 = much better)*
Financial performance in the last three years	Willingness to experiment
Computer/management information system	Willing to take risks
Customer buying criteria	Reputation as an innovator
Customer relations	Cycle time for innovation
Distribution channels	
Divestitures	
Financial management	
Globalization	
Government relations	
Human resource practices	
Marketing and sales	
Mergers/acquisitions	
Organizational structure	
Production capability	
Research and development	

percentage of sales based on products introduced in the last three years, as another indicator of organizational innovativeness.

Learning Capability

Finally, we place learning capability in the middle of our model because it is both influenced by context and an influence on performance. As such, it is the linchpin for managerial action. Our basic definition runs as follows: organizational learning capability is the capacity to generate and generalize ideas with impact, across multiple organizational boundaries, through specific management initiatives and practices. Learning capability is therefore based on the three building blocks: generation of ideas, generalization of ideas, and identification of learning disabilities.

Another way to think of learning capability is through $g \times g$—a company's ability to learn comes down to generation of ideas with impact multiplied by generalization of ideas with impact. Organizations with high learning capability, such as 3M and Matsushita, would therefore score high. But organizations with lower learning capability, like General Motors, are probably saddled with disabilities that interfere with $g \times g$.

Let's revisit GM one more time. If we look at individual divisions within GM like Cadillac or Saturn, we see that the company definitely contains some pockets of excellence. Cadillac has won the renowned Malcolm Baldrige Quality Award and excels at continuous improvement. And by benchmarking with NUMMI (a joint venture between Toyota and GM), Saturn has implemented many innovative ideas and practices, such as employee involvement, extensive use of teams, an egalitarian culture, and collaboration between management and the union. Looking at GM as a whole, however, it's clear the company's learning capability is hindered because of its limited ability to generalize ideas across horizontal boundaries (that is, across different businesses). GM appears to suffer from paralysis and diffusion deficiency, among other learning disabilities.

To compete in today's rapidly changing environment, corporations need to strengthen their learning capability by simultaneously managing all three building blocks. Excelling in one or two blocks, as General Motors has done, is insufficient. In the next chapter, we'll begin a detailed analysis of the first building block—idea generation—including the results of our worldwide survey, as well as case studies of several exemplary companies.

CHAPTER FOUR

Generating Ideas with Impact

3M, HP, and Other "Idea Machines"

In the industrial society of the mid-twentieth century, corporations competed through the efficient use of physical assets. Coming up with innovative products certainly mattered to many businesses of the 1950s and 1960s, but efficiency was the key criterion for success. But in the current postindustrial or knowledge society, corporations compete with their intellectual assets, and new ideas form the basis of today's competition. Corporations that fail to generate new ideas rapidly enough to meet customers' demands, that don't keep abreast of deep and radical technological changes, or that are unable to respond to all kinds of challenges posed by traditional and unconventional competitors will die. It's that urgent and that final. Consider what some top executives say about the new business game.

Southwood J. Morcott, CEO of the Dana Corporation: "The only way to improve your margins today is by improving your product. . . . Through our ideas generation program, we expect people to have two new ideas each month. And we expect management to implement 80 percent of these ideas."

Marsh Fisher, co-founder of Century 21 Real Estate Corporation: "The real true source of power in any company today is ideas— the rest is housekeeping. . . . Ideas are the DNA of everything that is worthwhile."

Jack Welch, Chairman and CEO of the General Electric Company: "My job is to listen to, search for, think of, and spread ideas, to expose people to good ideas and role models. . . . When self-confident people see a good idea, they love it."[1]

Of course everybody loves a good idea, and dreaming up new inventions and businesses sounds fun. But when these executives talk about searching for new ideas and encouraging their employees to do so, they mean ideas that influence the bottom line, not just creativity for creativity's sake. From the quotations given, we can tease out at least two common themes: (1) corporations are working hard to generate new ideas from all sources—both internally and externally, from the top and the bottom, from existing practices and brand-new thinking; (2) generating ideas is critical for business success but not good enough by itself; ideas must be used. In fact, generating ideas with impact—the first building block of learning capability—comes down to more than brainstorming sessions with one's colleagues or staring soulfully into space. The notion of impact is crucial when discussing idea generation and learning capability, because impact means a new idea has affected customers, financial performance, and/or employee performance.

So how do companies become effective "idea machines"? Based on our research, it's clear that business culture and strategy, not to mention particular competitive contexts, influence how new ideas are sparked. In addition, the four learning styles systematically differentiate how new ideas are generated. This chapter begins with key findings from our worldwide survey and then moves on to case studies of four idea machines—3M, HP, Motorola, and Alcatel Bell—to illustrate how companies employ different learning styles to good effect.

Survey Results: Experimenters Are High Performers

Even at a very early stage of our research, we were convinced that organizations generate new ideas differently because of the business contexts in which they operate. In turn, we believed, and have found, that different organizational learning styles lead to different performance outcomes. Although styles often overlap in real organizations, it's clear successful companies develop capability in at least one type of learning in order to grow, evolve, and adapt to changing business environments.

In chapter 2, we introduced our worldwide survey of companies. With a sample of more than 400 firms, we verified the existence of four learning styles: experimentation, competency acquisition, benchmarking, and continuous improvement. We also measured how much each of the four learning styles dominated in our sample. Those results bear repeating here. When we classify businesses by their dominant learning style (the one that receives the strongest emphasis in a company), we find:

Dominant Learning Style	No. of Businesses	Percentage of the Sample
Experimentation	25	10
Competency acquisition	95	37
Benchmarking	33	13
Continuous improvement	104	40

The results of our survey indicate that companies rely more on competency acquisition and continuous improvement to generate new ideas than on experimentation and benchmarking. Since we also established connections among styles, business performances, and contexts, here's where the research reveals the most interesting possibilities for managerial change. The style most suited to a company that wants to emphasize product innovation, for instance, may not be the one embraced by its culture. Let's begin with the connection between business context and idea generation.

How Business Context Influences Learning Style

We assumed from the beginning that industry characteristics, business strategy, and business culture would all affect learning capability and the different learning styles. However, the survey results point to business strategy and culture as being the strongest contextual variables. Based on our sample, the different learning styles don't appear to be significantly shaped by industry characteristics, such as supplier relationships, market concentration, or technological interdependence in the work process.

Strategy, however, does influence style of idea generation. Companies with a product differentiation strategy, for example, are most likely to be experimenters, continuous improvers, or skill acquirers (see table 4.1). That's because firms can differentiate products by continuously upgrading and refining the features of existing products, or by seeking to develop new products through experimentation and competency acquisition. Needless to say, benchmarkers—those that copy ideas from others rather than generate them on their own—don't shine in this arena.

Yet being a copier can have strategic advantages. Companies that embrace a cost competitiveness strategy, rather than product innovation or differentiation, tend to generate new ideas through continuous improvement and benchmarking. That's because learning geared

Table 4.1   Correlation between Business Strategy and Learning Styles

Learning styles	Product differentiation strategy	Cost competitiveness strategy
Experimentation	.186**	.096
Competency acquisition	.262**	.096
Benchmarking	.023	.140*
Continuous improvement	.266**	.145*

*Correlation significant at .05 level

**Correlations significant at .01 level

toward exploiting outside sources and existing possibilities is more cost-effective; it requires less investment than exploring radically new products and processes.

Then there's the influence of culture on idea generation. The most obvious finding from our research is that organizations with a hierarchical culture are rarely experimenters (see table 4.2). If a hierarchical organization wants to become an innovator, it may need to either change its overall business culture or create a new organization under its corporate umbrella that has a different culture. The latter approach was taken by General Motors with the creation of its Saturn division.

Clan cultures value long-term relationships and organizational cohesion; these kinds of companies—Japanese firms are the most renowned—are more likely to learn through competency acquisition, experimentation, and continuous improvement. Indeed, companies with a strong clan culture are willing to invest heavily in competency acquisition, because they assume their investment in human capital will pay off in the long run. Strong clan-oriented companies may also be experimenters, because they offer job security to employees and

Table 4.2   Correlation between Business Cultures and Learning Styles

Learning styles	Clan culture	Adhocracy culture	Hierarchical culture	Market culture
Experimentation	.330**	.388**	−.259**	.208**
Competency acquisition	.488**	.401**	−.120	.301**
Benchmarking	.073	.086	−.036	.034
Continuous improvement	.303**	.219**	.020	.257**

**Correlations significant at .01 level.

provide a safety net for taking risks. Finally, clan-oriented firms easily become continuous improvers because of their emphasis on team-work and organizational commitment.

Organizations with an "adhocracy" culture are explorers and in-novators and are therefore more likely to generate new ideas through competency acquisition and experimentation. Many high-tech firms in Silicon Valley have adhocracy cultures, and they learn primarily through experimentation and self-directed learning (that is, seminars, magazines, university faculty, consultants). In our survey, we also found that strong adhocracy firms could be continuous improvers, since they still need to exploit known technologies.

Finally, companies with a market culture—that is, they are cus-tomer-driven—learn by competency acquisition, continuous improve-ment, and experimentation. In this case, competency acquisition might involve key customers in employee training programs; experi-mentation might occur through responding to customer requests or challenges; and continuous improvement happens through feedback from customers. Service-industry companies such as Nordstrom, Dis-neyland, and Marriott are very likely to employ these learning styles to generate new ideas.

An interesting geographical note: in our sample, we found no sig-nificant difference in the level of experimentation as a learning style among businesses in North America, Western Europe, and Asia (see table 4.3). But without exception, Asian businesses scored highest on competency acquisition, benchmarking, and continuous improve-ment. The finding is striking in two regards. First, while North Amer-ican and Western European businesses are generally thought of as being more creative than Asian ones, these three groups don't appear

Table 4.3　Learning Styles of Companies in Different Geographical Regions

Learning styles	North American businesses (N = 199)	Western European businesses (N = 17)	Asian businesses (N = 39)	Significance level
Experimentation	3.09	3.14	3.22	N.S.
Competency acquisition	3.50	3.51	4.07	>.001
Benchmarking	2.91	2.79	3.25	>.05
Continuous improvement	3.50	3.25	3.85	>.05
Overall learning	3.25	3.20	3.59	>.001

Learning styles are scored on a five-point scale, 1 = "to very little extent" and 5 = "to a very large extent."

to differ in their use of experimentation to generate new ideas. Second, the emphasis Asian businesses have placed on learning in recent years may partly explain their competitiveness. Regardless of how "creative" Westerners believe they are, it's a reminder to North American and Western European firms that revitalizing their learning capability may be necessary to compete in the global marketplace.

How Learning Style Affects Business Performance

As we've already reported, experimentation was the least popular of learning styles among our sample companies. Yet our results indicate it's the most effective way to enhance business performance, as measured by competitiveness, innovativeness, and new product introduction (i.e., percentage of sales revenue generated by new products introduced in the last three years) (see table 4.4). When we divided our sample into high-, medium-, and low-performing businesses based on these two performance outcomes, we found that experimentation was the only learning style that significantly differentiated the high and low performers in *all three areas* (tables 4.5–4.7).

If experimentation is the most effective learning style, why is it then the least popular one? A more detailed analysis of the data revealed that while experimentation has a long-term positive impact on business performance, it may temporarily detract from competitiveness in the short term. This makes sense, since experiments are often expensive and time-consuming, and they often don't start producing returns for several years. Ironically, the data suggest that the learning style with the strongest effect on long-term performance also has significant short-term costs and risk. These short-term costs help explain why a

Table 4.4   Correlation between Learning Styles and
Organizational Performance

Learning styles	Organizational competitiveness	Organizational innovativeness	New product introduction[a]
Experimentation	.248**	.360**	.181**
Competency acquisition	.245**	.275**	.180**
Benchmarking	.046	.023	.030
Continuous improvement	.229**	.224	.083
Overall learning	.281**	.322**	.172**

a. New product introduction is measured by the percentage of sales revenue accounted for by new products introduced in the last three years.

**Correlations significant at .01 level.

Table 4.5 Learning Styles and Organizational Competitiveness

Learning styles	Lowly competitive businesses (N = 93)	Highly competitive businesses (N = 80)	Difference in mean scores	Significance level
Experimentation	2.90	3.35	0.45	>.001
Competency acquisition	3.38	3.69	0.31	>.05
Benchmarking	2.91	2.95	0.04	N.S.
Continuous improvement	3.36	3.68	0.32	>.01
Overall learning	3.13	3.42	0.29	>.01

Learning styles are scored on a five-point scale, 1 = "to a very small extent," 5 = "to a very large extent."

Table 4.6 Learning Styles and Organizational Innovativeness

Learning styles	Lowly innovative businesses (N = 93)	Highly innovative businesses (N = 80)	Difference in mean scores	Significance level
Experimentation	2.84	3.47	0.63	>.001
Competency acquisition	3.29	3.90	0.61	>.001
Benchmarking	2.93	3.01	0.08	N.S.
Continuous improvement	3.33	3.74	0.41	>.001
Overall learning	3.09	3.53	0.44	>.001

Learning styles are scored on a five-point scale, 1 = "to very little extent," 5 = "to a very large extent."

Table 4.7 Learning Styles and New Product Introduction

Learning styles	Lowly innovative businesses (N = 93)	Highly innovative businesses (N = 80)	Differences in mean scores	Significance level
Experimentation	2.86	3.38	0.52	>.01
Competency acquisition	3.49	3.77	0.28	N.S.
Benchmarking	3.01	3.05	0.04	N.S.
Continuous improvement	3.39	3.61	0.22	N.S.
Overall Learning	3.18	3.45	0.27	>.05

Learning styles are scored on a five-point scale, 1 = "to very little extent," 5 = "to a very large extent."

New product introduction is measured by the percentage of sales revenue accounted for by new products introduced in the last three years.

lot of firms don't embrace experimentation as a learning style. Instead the companies in our sample generally opted for competency acquisition and continuous improvement, styles that appear to help with competitiveness and innovativeness but don't significantly affect new product introduction.

In table 4.4, we also show the correlation between a company's overall learning (the average of its four learning style scores) with these three performance outcomes. Perhaps not surprisingly, the higher the overall learning score, the higher a company's score on competitiveness, innovativeness, and new product introduction. This is an important finding, one that past theorists and executives have often assumed but rarely tested empirically. But once again, it's not a firm's strength in overall learning but its emphasis on experimentation that is most strongly associated with innovativeness and new product introduction. The finding indicates there is certainly a fit between learning style and specific performance outcome. And while many companies focus on competency acquisition and continuous improvement to generate new ideas, experimentation is a powerful learning style—the one most likely to be associated with high performance.

Interestingly, benchmarking was not emphasized as the dominant learning style by as many companies as we first believed it would be. With the exception of a very few high performers like Samsung Electronics, the firms in our sample did not systematically scan what other companies were doing, either broadly or narrowly. Although high-performing businesses tended to focus more on benchmarking activities, their scores weren't significantly different from those of low performers in all three performance outcomes. It appears that benchmarking as a stand-alone learning style is not very useful for generating new ideas. In addition, most companies don't use benchmarking strategically and systematically, which results in little performance impact. More often than not, companies we work with simply copy the practices of others rather than understanding the reasons that such practices are successful. "Blind" benchmarking, then, may account for the weak association we found between this learning style and performance.

Managers should take heed. When asked how to get new ideas, executives often send out best-practice or benchmarking teams to learn what others are doing. Yet our research suggests that such common approaches may not yield good results. It's possible that while the team may acquire good ideas from other companies, they won't be transferred or adopted successfully by their own firm. Benchmarking may be a good academic exercise, but it's generally not as helpful in generating ideas as the other learning styles.

Exemplary Companies: Idea Machines in Action

Based on our survey, most organizations generate ideas in a number of ways, although one or two learning styles usually dominate. Experimentation seems to be the most effective style, especially for companies interested in product innovation and differentiation, but even that assumption doesn't play out neatly in the real world. The case studies that follow offer additional insights about how companies learn differently; how their learning styles are related to particular business strategies and cultures; and, finally, how learning styles make a difference in business performance. These company stories put flesh on the bones of our research findings and provide a feeling for how ideas are generated in the rough-and tumble-business environment.

3M: A True Experimenter

Without a doubt, 3M is the prototype of the idea machine. Since 1902, this company has successfully invented and introduced more than 60,000 products into the marketplace—an average of 600 products a year—not to mention the other products that have failed. 3M's success is largely due to its unique approach to generating ideas with impact; here is a company that actually encourages employees to experiment with all kinds of new ideas, to test them with customers, to cultivate those that work, and to fix or discard those that don't. A three-step process of variation, selection, and retention is the 3M formula for creating products as diverse as masking tape, Post-it notes, overhead projection systems, and bioelectronic ears.

This company's core values and management practices are the key to its strong capability in idea generation. We've already referred to 3M's success in previous chapters, as well as the gamble its founders took on a failed idea: the extraction of corundum as an abrasive agent to export to grinding-wheel manufacturers. As a result of initial mishaps, 3M could not afford to pay its president, Edgar Ober, a salary during the first few years. Now we'll detail some of the elements that have made this company's experimental learning style so effective. Note that we are indebted to *Built to Last* by James Collins and Jerry Porras for much of this case study.[2]

The 3M Culture   The first thing any observer notices about the workings of 3M is that new ideas are welcomed. The most important article of corporate faith emphasizes original ideas that address a demonstrable human need. Even if some ideas seem absurd, they'll be given careful attention; everyone understands that such "absurdities" can grow into big businesses. As discussed in a 1989 *Business Week* article,[3] products like Post-it notes would never exist as a commercial product if 3M didn't have such an experimental/tolerant culture; in fact, initial market surveys indicated that the product would fail. As early as 1925, this mind-set was developed and firmly stated in 3M's technical guidance manual: "Every idea evolved should have a chance to prove its worth, and this is true for two reasons: (1) if it is good, we want it; (2) if it is not good, we will have purchased our insurance and peace of mind when we have proved it impractical."[4]

As a result, phrases like "Give it a try—and quick" or "Let people run with an idea" are more than slogans; they are guiding organizational values. 3Mers subscribe to a simple principle: "No market, no end product is so small as to be scorned."[5] The fact is, no one can accurately predict how new products will evolve. And even if a new product stumbles, 3M allows failures. As ex-CEO Richard Carlton said in 1950, "Our company has, indeed, stumbled onto some of its new products. But never forget that you can only stumble if you're moving."[6] Occasional failures are inevitable if the experimenting organization wants to succeed.

3M's Management Practices   A company's culture can certainly be a powerful motivating force, but management must implement those values if they are to have any currency. Like other experimenting companies, such as Honda[7] and Sony, 3M's learning style is strongly influenced by its corporate culture, which in turn was imprinted by its founders and early history. Yet that corporate culture has been translated into a set of real management practices that encourage risk-taking and experimentation. Most important, 3M provides a safety net for experimenting with new ideas: nobody is fired for merely championing an idea that failed, and employees are often rewarded for their innovation and originality. While many other companies pay lip service to the importance of creativity and experimentation, 3M is one of the few that does what it says.

Reward System.   In addition to allowing failures, 3M has developed a reward system to encourage experimentation with new ideas by research scientists, division managers, and other employees. Research scientists who make outstanding and original contributions within 3M are inducted into the prestigious Carlton Society. Named after the outstanding director of research and later CEO, Richard Carlton, this technical honor society comprises the best and brightest 3Mers, those who enjoy tremendous autonomy, resources, and discretion to pursue their favorite research. And if scientists develop a new technology and successfully share it with other divisions, they receive technology sharing awards. The primary goal is to encourage not only generation but generalization of good ideas.

Division managers are also motivated to champion and support new ideas. The 30 percent rule—that is, 30 percent of divisional sales revenue must be generated from products introduced in the last four years—affects the annual bonus that division managers receive. Moreover, 3Mers who successfully develop a new product will get the opportunity to own it as his or her own project, department, or division, depending on sales levels of the product—a good route to promotion. And if a new venture fails, that engineer or manager will be reinstated in his or her previous position with the same salary. At 3M, intelligent failures are not punished. Among those new business ventures developed, 3M also grants "Golden Step" awards to the most successful ventures every year. The ultimate purpose of these reward systems is to encourage both divisional managers and technical scientists to come up with successful new products that will sell in the market.

Finally, employees are all tied to the financial performance of the corporation through its profit-sharing program. Since the culture emphasizes that 3M's success is linked with the company's ability to generate new products continuously, 3M employees have a shared interest in cultivating new ideas.

Resource Support.   The company offers its technical people the time and the autonomy to foster new ideas via experimental "doodling: they can spend up to 15 percent of their time on personal projects (the 15 percent rule). In addition, Genesis Grants of up to $50,000 are available for developing prototypes and market tests of brand-new products.

Communications.   To generate new ideas, 3M creates ample opportunities such as forums so that its employees can learn from customers and colleagues inside and outside their own divisions. Because the 3M culture values new ideas that are grounded in a demonstrable human need, understanding what customers want and the kinds of problems they've encountered is essential. For instance, the invention of masking tape by a young 3M employee named Dick Drew was sparked by his visit to a customer in the 1920s. When he dropped by an auto paint shop that worked on two-tone auto paint jobs, he found the technicians there were frustrated with existing adhesive tapes and improvised glues that failed to separate the two colors, leaving behind ugly blotches and uneven lines. "Can't anyone give us something that will work?" yelled the paint man. "We can!" Drew responded and started to experiment back in the lab.[8] To encourage customer-based innovation, 3M now regularly sends small teams of technical personnel called problem-solving missions to customer sites to study and resolve customer problems. Ideally, understanding these problems will eventually stimulate 3Mers to come up with innovative solutions.

To share new ideas quickly within the corporation, 3M regularly sponsors technical forums in which research scientists and other interested employees can exchange new ideas and findings. The corporate goal is to use new ideas and technology across a wide spectrum of applications. 3M also organizes new product forums, presenting the latest products developed within different 3M divisions. Indeed, what distinguishes this idea machine from other companies is that 3Mers also generalize new ideas with impact. 3M's technology sharing awards, technical forums, and new product forums are all examples of how it creates a real learning environment, one in which an astonishing number of new ideas are not only generated but also shared across organizational boundaries. And it's hard to argue with the results: founded on an idea that failed, 3M has become one of the most respected companies in the world, with a large portfolio of successful products.

HP's Video Communications: Reinvented Overnight

While 3M is the prototypical experimenter, Hewlett-Packard's Video Communications Division (VCD) has relied on competency acquisition as well as experimentation to explore new technology and develop new products. Based on our interviews and research at HP, the following case study about VCD vividly illustrates how a business engages in exploration-oriented learning in the midst of a rapidly emerging technology.

At Telecomm '91 in Geneva, the huge gathering of world telecommunication executives every four years, Hewlett-Packard's CEO John Young and TMO (Test and Measurement Organization) sector manager Ned Barnholt observed the rapid market changes and growth in video technologies.[9] Determined to enter the video communications market, Young chose HP's Stanford Park Division to lead the company in this emerging technology, renewing that division in the process. The journey was truly amazing; it reflected this company's capacity to adapt to fast-changing business environments and the value of competency acquisition as a learning style in this business context.

Members of one of the oldest divisions within the Test and Measurement Organization, employees at the Stanford Park Division were typically electrical engineers with long tenures (often more than 15 years). Since its opening in the 1970s, the Stanford Park Division had created many new products in testing and measurement. The employees there had developed a strong sense of ownership in those products. By 1991, the division had a staff of more than 600. While still profitable, it was not performing as well as other HP divisions.

After receiving their marching orders from John Young, the division's top managers immediately changed its name to the Video Communications Division; transferred all existing products to other divisions; and, most dramatically, reclassified all electrical engineers as video engineers. HP committed itself to providing resources and management support to these engineers, but video technology was just emerging at the time, and few training resources were available. Instead, the division's engineers learned by working closely with customers to address their needs and by continuously retraining themselves through reading and attending seminars.

Of course, the rapid transformation of the Stanford Park Division into the Video Communications Division had its share of problems. The management committee, for example, was concerned that some employees could not meet the new technological requirements in the video communications industry. In one instance, the committee talked to an engineer about their concern and offered to find him another job. During the meeting, the engineer was so upset that he left the facility immediately. In the next two weeks, he didn't return to work, nor did he talk to anybody. But three weeks later, he suddenly came to a staff meeting and showed the general manager a newly invented product that the division had been struggling to develop. Even after an emotionally rocky start, this engineer demonstrated to senior management his will and competency in adapting to the new business requirements. Indeed, pride, technical contribution, and hard work are some characteristics of what became the learning culture at VCD.

Through a combination of experimentation and learning through customer interaction, these electrical engineers became experts in video technology virtually overnight. Without hiring any outside people, the Video Communications Division introduced 14 new products within 18 months of its inception. At the National Association of Broadcasting '93 Show, the HP QA 100 Quality Advisor, which is capable of catching and correcting illegal colors on 4:2:2 serial digital data, even won one of the ten best product awards. Other HP video products that have hooked media attention include Broadcast Video Server, Media Stream Server, Video Printer, and Digital Set-tops, all making services like interactive TV and video on-demand technologically feasible. The Video Communications Division is now able to serve major clients such as Pacific Telesis, Bell South, TCI, Time Warner, and CBS, strengthening their capabilities in video communications technology.

By understanding customer needs and challenges, HP engineers experiment with solutions that address their clients' system inefficiencies. But the question remains: how did they learn so quickly in a new technical field? In our field interview with her, Deihleen Claffey, TMO Human Resource Manager, attributed such a heightened learning environment to three key factors:

The HP Culture   This company values technical contributions, so much so that employees feel good if they can make such a contribution. In fact, if we return to our survey distinction between business cultures, HP's is one of the best examples of combined adhocracy and clan culture. When the engineers at the old Stanford Park Division were challenged to make a technical contribution in the emerging video technologies, many of them felt excited rather than worried; for the most part, they didn't balk at the change.

VCD's Business Context   Engineers at the Stanford Park Division understood that the division as a whole was not performing up to expectation. If the situation persisted, they believed it would be closed down, and that they would be redeployed to other businesses or states. When top management asked them to go after an emerging market with the help of a lot of resources, they were highly motivated to make the transition a success.

Employee Characteristics   HP has a strong reputation of hiring the best and the brightest talent. The engineers at the division are technologists who are interested in learning the latest trends in their fields and are self-driven. As long as the company provides them with a direction, a rationale, and resources, they're willing to learn continually.

In brief, HP's culture, the particular business context at the time, and the general competency of this company's engineers allowed for rapid organizational learning in its new Video Communications Division. Human resources manager Claffey emphasizes that the major benefit of being a learning organization is "the flexibility of people's ability to shift contribution quickly." Given that the business environment will continue to change ever more rapidly, learning organizations that enable employees to become more flexible will certainly have a competitive edge.

Motorola: Building Your Own School

Since its inception in 1928, Motorola has continuously anticipated changes and renewed itself, adapting to new business environments through product and process innovations. Starting as a battery elim- inator business, Motorola has since ventured into car radios, two-way radios, transistors, semiconductors, cellular telephones, pagers, and, most recently, satellite communications systems. It has pioneered many management innovations, including six-sigma quality, total cycle time reduction, total customer satisfaction, empowerment, globaliza- tion, and developing new core competency in software.[10]

Motorola, well positioned in the fiercely competitive and rapidly changing electronics industry, is considered a leading learning orga- nization by many business experts. What enables the company to keep moving into new market turf and innovative product areas? Our re- search reveals that one important reason is its extraordinary ability to generate new ideas through corporate education and learning activi- ties. These activities expose its leaders to future trends and diverse sources of information beyond their daily interactions; hence, Moto- rola stretches its leaders to think creatively and proactively about the new opportunities. Such a learning style—competency acquisition— fits perfectly with its business strategy and culture.

Motorola's strategy is clearly product differentiation with a com- petitive emphasis on quality, customer satisfaction, and innovation. Its strategic emphases are revealed through the company's history of major initiatives and continued changes in product/market mix. From our perspective, Motorola is one of the most successful non-Asian clan-based cultures. The company's top executives believe in the stra- tegic importance of people. Its culture emphasizes "making ordinary people do extraordinary things."[11] Employees who make long-term contributions and demonstrate a commitment to the company are strongly valued, which makes a good cultural foundation for compe- tency acquisition as a learning style.

Indeed, ever since Motorola was founded by Paul Galvin, the im- portance of learning and education has been deeply rooted in its cul- ture. Galvin believed in investing in people. As described by Harry Mark Petrakis, his biographer in *The Founder's Touch*, "He was not an inventor, but a builder whose blueprints were people."[12] Accord- ing to his son Bob Galvin, who later served as Motorola's CEO from 1956 to 1988, "My father urged us to reach out . . . to people—to all the people—for their leadership contribution, yes their creative lead- ership contribution."[13] It's no wonder that Bob Galvin approved the establishment of Motorola University in 1980 with a five-year plan and a $35 million budget.

Now Motorola spends approximately $120 million annually on training and development. From the top of the hierarchy to the bottom, every employee is required to spend at least 40 hours a year in training. All training programs offered at Motorola University, which now offers classes through 27 offices in 17 countries, are designed either to generate or to generalize new business initiatives and strategies. Envisioned as "a major headlight for change," this well-known company university has spearheaded many learning initiatives to accelerate both organizational and management development.[14]

Motorola trains its managers by constantly challenging them and exposing them to a diversity of opinions. Consider the following creative approach to generating new ideas. In order to help leaders think about future opportunities, Motorola has arranged for them to meet 16- and 17-year-old students.[15] What do these kids think about the future? What products will they buy? The meetings have focused on such questions, and as a result Motorola recently discovered a large untapped market for cellular phones and pagers among teenagers. According to the kids, however, the designs of these products to date have been too dull and boring. Therefore, Motorola is now developing a "new generation" of cellular phones and pagers.

Motorola University is also renowned for mixing employees with customers and suppliers in its training programs. By including customers and suppliers in its own programs, Motorola has created a learning environment that not only shapes the mind-set of customers and suppliers but also helps Motorolans understand more deeply their needs and challenges. Through such interactive discussions, useful new ideas are often generated that lead to productive changes in products, services, and processes.

Similarly, when Motorola enters into emerging markets, its emphasis on education and training helps Motorolans learn about the cultures and business environment of a host country.[16] In turn, Motorola has often contributed, in a substantial way, to the economic development of that country. In the People's Republic of China, for instance, the Cultural Revolution prevented many Chinese from obtaining the work experience necessary for middle-management work. When Motorola wanted to enter Chinese telecommunications markets in 1987, it collaborated with the Chinese Ministry of Telecommunications Industry in offering high-quality training programs to over 10,000 Chinese managers. Motorola was able not only to learn about the business cultures and practices of China in this fashion but also to build valuable relationships with important government officials there. This is competency acquisition at a very sophisticated level.

And Motorola has developed a unique process for preparing its future global leaders. The leadership development process is called GOLD (Global Organization Leadership Development).[17] The mission of GOLD is to develop a cadre of leaders that are future focused and change oriented. The GOLD process includes 20 to 25 participants at a time. Targeted participants are typically 30 to 35 years old, both men and women, and are drawn from different functions and countries. In addition to classroom training, job rotations, overseas assignments, and mentorship, GOLD participants are formed into teams to study key issues of the business. Each team's assignment is to study, analyze, and make recommendations to senior management about *changing (or breaking) whatever is well established* in the process. The goal is to stimulate participants to think differently about ways of doing business and creating the future of the company. During the GOLD team sessions, minority viewpoints are intentionally championed, since top management believes that such viewpoints can lead to a paradigm shift (or continual renewal) in Motorola's business.

As Ken Hansen, Director of Strategic Education at Motorola University, has said, "Unlike many training and education activities in other corporations, our University is more than a Human Resources function, it is an integral part of our marketing and business effort. . . . There is a direct alignment between the education we provide and the corporate business initiatives. Our major charter is to develop and implement training and education that supports the achievement of Motorola's business initiatives."[18] It is through its educational activities that Motorola develops new products, enters into new markets, prepares future leaders, and constantly renews its organization and business. As noted by former CEO George Fisher, "I am very much a believer that our training program is perhaps one of the most important elements of the drive that Motorola made in quality over the years and, in fact, the most important element of a cultural transition in the company."[19]

The following results dramatically reveal the impact of Motorola's learning culture and its emphasis on competency acquisition:

- In 1988, Motorola won the first Malcolm Baldrige Quality Award.
- From 1987 to 1993, Motorola was able to cut costs by $3.3 billion, not by layoffs but by retraining workers to simplify processes, reduce wastes, and improve quality.
- By the early 1990s, manufacturing cycle time had been reduced from weeks to hours.

- China has become one of Motorola's fastest growing markets, doubling its sales revenue every year from $50 million in 1990 to $2.8 billion in 1995.

Motorola's story illustrates how a company can both generate and generalize ideas through a corporate-wide dedication to education. By encouraging employees and teams to acquire new ideas from potential customers, existing customers, suppliers, and other unconventional sources—taking competency acquisition as a learning style to a new level—Motorola has delivered impressive business results.

Alcatel Bell: Reaping Low-hanging Fruits

Founded in 1882, Alcatel Bell (AB) was the largest Belgian supplier of telecommunications equipment in 1992. It had sales revenues of about a $1 billion (U.S. dollars) in 1990. The company is a subsidiary of Alcatel, the largest telecommunications group in the world, even ahead of AT&T. This interpretation of the AB story, based on a case study written by Todd Jick, a member of our research team, looks at how business context can radically affect the ways a company learns. AB's position in the rocky arena of telecommunications forced it to make key changes, even more than in HP's case with an emerging technology, but not all at once or through a radical reorganization. The Alcatel Bell case indicates how continuous improvement as a learning style can help an organization adapt to the most unstable of business environments.

Here we'll highlight an unusual technique, the use of what AB top management called "In Charge of Change" projects. This case covers how AB generated new ideas through this program from 1990 to 1992. The primary learning style involved was continuous improvement—specifically, the simultaneous engagement of multiple continuous improvement initiatives. In 1991, some 1,000 managers undertook various change initiatives in quality, cost effectiveness, and innovation to accelerate AB's transformation into a "continuous change learning organization."[20] In Charge of Change aimed to move AB from a traditional bureaucratic, hierarchical, command-and-control culture to one of empowerment, speed, and continual innovation.

Throughout the early 1990s, the telecommunications industry was in the throes of revolutionary technological change. In particular, the ascendancy of digitized switching (telephone exchanges) and transmission networks (copper or optical fiber cables, satellites, and microwave) pushed the telecommunications, consumer electronics, and computer industries to integrate services far beyond the traditional dial tone. This revolution required escalating investment in R&D, which could only be amortized through global markets. Consequently, telecommunications manufacturers, formerly constrained by national boundaries and protection, began globalizing their activities through mergers, acquisitions, and alliances. Such was the strategy of major players like Alcatel, AT&T, Northern Telecom, Siemens, and Ericsson. In the case of Alcatel, top managers felt that if its AB subsidiary didn't make major changes in culture, make productivity improvements through technology, and retrain the work force, the company could eventually lose out to the competition.

In December 1990, CEO John Goossens invited the top 1,200 managers of Alcatel Bell to conceive of and implement a change project within their own professional or political networks. Rather than calling for large-scale change or trumpeting an abstract notion of new values, he was interested in smaller, more realistic initiatives. Goossens asked these managers to come up with

> A project for which you have the necessary resources or for which you can get the resources from your boss or colleagues. Not projects costing millions, but projects supporting our mission: customer orientation; open management style; innovation and cost effectiveness; teamwork; and quality. Select your change project, discuss it with whomever you think you'll need: your boss, your colleagues, your subordinates. Organize a team around it. Inspire your team![21]

At AB, then, the targets of change efforts became those "low-hanging fruits" that could help the company perform better—continuous, incremental initiatives that might eventually lead to mass mobilization but did not require radical change all at once. In this way, Alcatel Bell became a continuous improver, focusing its learning efforts on the managers and employees who worked at the company every day.

To prepare managers, Goossens personally invited the top three executive levels to attend a two-day seminar in September of 1990. The primary message of his In Charge of Change (ICC) training program was empowerment and personal responsibility. Before the program, every participant received a copy of *The Empowered Manager: Positive Political Skills at Work* by Peter Block.[22] It sent a signal to the participants that these seminars would discuss tough, pervasive, and sensitive issues like the politics inside AB. The program began with lectures on getting things done in an organization, covering concepts like empowering oneself and others, as well as negotiating with allies and adversaries. Participants were then asked to apply these ideas to what they were currently working on. The initial training programs were well-received; lower levels of managers and forepeople also participated in an abbreviated version of the training. In the ICC programs, models for organizational change were presented, and participants were invited to discuss their own cases of change.

Because of the momentum created by the ICC training programs, the immediate response to Goossens' innovative call for action in December 1990 was positive and overwhelming. Within a month, a thousand managers had sent him proposals describing their change projects. Julien De Wilde, Director of Strategy and Services, explained the strategy behind these projects:

> Goossens' top priority was delegation of authority and ICC projects pushed responsibility for change downward. Secondly, ICC suggested change should be projects that managers could execute themselves without major investments or expenses. Everyone could participate. Thirdly, we wanted to give people visibility who took the responsibility to change their environments. The contradiction which some people felt was that we started a change process in a company that never had been doing better. Why? Because we knew that our markets and the external environment would change. We wanted to adapt proactively, but some people asked: why change a winning team?[23]

Asking individual managers to conceive of and implement change projects meant that the types of projects, as well as the speed and success of implementation, varied widely. "Our goal for the ICC projects," said Chris Verougstraete, former manager of Industrial Relations and Internal Communications, "was culture change. However, more than 50 percent of the change efforts were technology driven."[24] Another executive provided the following estimates: approximately 80 percent of the ICC projects were extensions of what people were already doing; 15 percent of the projects were new and useful; and 5 percent amounted to new but impractical ideas. Others noted that most projects were individually conceived and implemented; teams of managers developed only a small number of ICC projects.

Some managers like Marcel Van Osselaer began their change projects immediately, and success followed quickly. Van Osselaer, production manager of printed circuit boards in AB's Gent plant, restructured his work, cross-trained workers, and provided visual feedback to employees on quality and speed of production through the use of large bulletin boards. By the end of six months, he and his team had met their original quality and delivery-time targets and set more challenging ones.

But for most AB managers, the pressures of day-to-day business made it difficult to complete their projects. In September 1991, the

Training and Education Department surveyed a sample of the 1,000 managers who had submitted ICC proposals, asking what factors had stimulated and/or hindered their completion. Lack of time was the most common answer. Others said they lacked the resources, and still others mentioned poor support within their organizations. The good news was that an overwhelming majority of respondents liked the challenge and freedom associated with ICC projects.

More important, AB's change efforts continued to be shepherded by those at the top, a rarity in most companies once such a decentralized process has begun. From the inception of In Charge of Change, Goossens and the Executive Committee paid special attention to the progress of projects. Division managers and the Executive Committee were responsible for following ICC projects and for assessing their impact. By January 1992, the Executive Committee selected 55 exemplary projects and then winnowed this group to 15 "Champions of Change." These Champions were honored in numerous ways: they presented their projects to the Executive Committee, received a gold coin, had breakfast with Goossens, and got a good deal of publicity within AB.

Eighteen months after Goossens' invitation, 40 managers presented their accomplishments to colleagues in a series of workshops called "Learning from Experience." The Training and Education Department selected these projects for their results, the processes that these managers used, and the lessons their projects might offer others. In this case, the workshops helped to generalize the good ideas that had been generated in the various areas of AB, taking them across boundaries and expanding their impact. Once again, the first two building blocks of learning capability—idea generation and generalization—go hand in hand at high-performing companies.

Still, the results for In Charge of Change were mixed. Approximately half the projects had been completed by June of 1992; others were at varying stages of development. The projects, of course, were intended to serve a purpose above and beyond solving current problems. They were to be a vehicle for "learning how to learn" through direct experience. Yet the relative success of the projects overall, as well as the value of the learning derived from them, was hotly debated within the company. Should AB generate new ideas through simultaneous, loose, and experiential initiatives like In Charge of Change, or should it focus on a more structured and centralized approach? As it happened, CEO Goossens decided on a hybrid approach. He didn't formalize a Phase II for In Charge of Change; at the same time, he endorsed the inclusion of project reviews in performance appraisals.

Such a hybrid result, of course, is typical of the practical implementations a continuous improver might come up with. And when top managers reviewed the two-year ICC program, their evaluation was generally positive in spite of the time and resources involved. One senior line manager said, "What I liked about the ICC projects was their visibility, and the quickness of implementation. Also, if we had not done the ICC projects, we may have missed some important opportunities. We would have been less open to change." One of the designers of the training programs, Jan Ginneberge, was also a strong supporter of ICC: "The success of the 40 managers who presented at the Learning from Experience workshop was spectacular." And ICC managers whose projects were showcased were very enthusiastic. As one said, "I am grateful to Goossens because he gave me the autonomy to challenge myself and the opportunity for me and my colleagues to learn and grow."[25]

In some ways, Alcatel Bell's ICC effort resembles GE's WorkOut program, which aims to jump-start a culture of constant change, generate ideas from all levels of the organization, reap low-hanging fruits, and then generalize best-practice lessons across the company. While each change effort may be small in scope, the cumulative effect of many change projects across the corporation over time can be substantial. Continuous improvement as a learning style, therefore, is not just maintaining technical expertise or fine-tuning processes; if properly applied, it can provide people with the freedom and confidence to invent something new.

The Upshot: How Companies Generate Ideas with Impact

Every company's experience is unique, but the particulars of 3M, HP, Motorola, and AB generally reflect our survey research. Of the companies in our sample, those with high learning capability mixed all four styles. But the most successful learning organizations emphasize experimentation and competency acquisition, especially if their business strategies focus on new products or product differentiation. Such a company is more likely to have a clan or adhocracy culture and will steer clear of a hierarchical mind-set. Here's a summary of essential points from our survey and the case studies:

- A company's learning style is affected by its business strategy and culture; industry characteristics appear to play a minor role, if any.
- To generate new ideas, most corporations adopt competency acquisition and continuous improvement rather than experimentation and benchmarking.

- Experimentation, however, is most strongly associated with business performance, especially in new product introduction.
- Benchmarking is not correlated with performance and may be the style least likely to generate new ideas.
- True learning organizations often have cultures that continually reinforce the importance of new ideas (3M) or emphasize learning/education (Motorola).
- Learning cultures are systematically reinforced by and aligned with a set of HR processes (3M).
- Adhocracy cultures (HP), particularly in technical businesses that employ highly educated workers, often use competency acquisition to good effect.
- With proper executive support and specific management practices, continuous improvement as a learning style (AB) can help change a company's culture over time, allowing it to face new business challenges.

There's one other general point we'd like to underscore. Idea generation rarely occurs in a vacuum, and a company that carries through a change program like Alcatel Bell's or continues to fund education like Motorola doesn't simply come up with new ideas. Organizations with high learning capability also generalize ideas with impact, the topic of our next chapter.

CHAPTER FIVE

Generalizing Ideas with Impact

The Case of Samsung Electronics

The difference between knowing what to do and doing it is like the difference between reading about being a musician and becoming one. All the reading, study of theory, and talking to musicians about what they do cannot replace the practice and effort required to play an instrument well. Knowing how to play and actually playing are separate pieces of the playing process.

The difference between generating and generalizing ideas with impact is also vast. Both are important. As we discussed in the previous chapter, generation focuses on finding ideas through a mix of the four learning styles; generalization, however, emphasizes implementing those ideas. Experimenting companies generate many new ideas, for instance, but the second building block of organizational learning capability requires acting on and learning from the experiments. Those that primarily generate ideas through competency acquisition must turn those competencies into action and results. And for benchmarkers like Samsung Electronics, while successful idea generation happens through benchmarking external practices, it is generalization that takes those outside practices inside the company.

At its simplest level, generalization means the movement of ideas or knowledge across boundaries so that visible action occurs. Knowledge can take many forms. It can be embedded and found in the ways in which organizations process information, upgrade competence, allocate rewards, make decisions, or carry out myriad other work practices. The boundaries across which such knowledge moves are temporal (from one time period to another); vertical (from the top to the bottom of an organization); horizontal (from one function, department, or business to another); external (from the company to suppliers or customers); and geographic (from one global site to another).[1]

In this chapter, we specify management practices that enable firms to generalize ideas with impact. Our aim is to expand the learning process from merely acquiring knowledge to using it—from isolated experiments to building a true learning culture—and from creating pockets of excellence to establishing general patterns of knowledge transfer. While our research on how firms generate ideas and overcome learning disabilities is underpinned by an empirical survey, our work with how firms generalize ideas is based on case studies and our own consulting practices. First we focus on Samsung Electronics, providing a detailed case of how a successful company shares ideas across many boundaries. (The Samsung story is based on our own interviews with the company's managers and its in-house literature.) Then we propose a "tool kit" for managers who want to improve generalization in their companies.

The Samsung Story: How a Benchmarker Generalizes Ideas

Samsung Electronics Company (SEC) was founded in 1938 by Lee Byung-Chull as a small trading company. The Korean War left Mr. Lee with almost no resources to rebuild his company, however, and in 1951, with savings donated by employees, he started anew. Lee was very good at spotting business opportunities in a wide range of endeavors and expanded Samsung into whatever industries presented such opportunities. The result was that Samsung became a large conglomerate of about 30 profitable but often unrelated businesses. Samsung now has a significant presence in consumer electronics, semiconductors, computers, telecommunications, shipbuilding, petrochemicals, construction, paper manufacturing, aerospace, sugar, wool, insurance, and department stores. Samsung is also on the cutting edge of many high-tech fields, including DRAM semiconductor chips, robotics, and biotechnology. But this hodge-podge of unrelated companies became increasingly difficult to coordinate over the years. In the early 1990s, Samsung underwent a thorough reorganization to provide synergy and focus in three areas: electronics, engineering, and chemicals.

Samsung Electronics Company was founded in 1969 and has grown at a rate of about 60 percent per year. The reorganization of Samsung focused SEC into four primary business divisions: consumer electronics, semiconductors, telecommunications, and computers. By 1991, it had sales of $7 billion (U.S. dollars) and 46,000 employees. While SEC began producing microwave ovens only in 1979, it now has over a fifth of both the U.S. and world market, although most of its microwaves are sold under other brand names. SEC is also the world's third largest DRAM chipmaker.

Yet at the height of this remarkable success and while still quite profitable, top management at Samsung Electronics chose to scrap its efficient production system and rebuild it literally from scratch. Here we come to the core of this case, and the business context that drove Samsung to learn and change. In the early 1990s, some customers were asking for product orders that were either too specialized or too small for SEC to fill profitably. For example, SEC already made all General Electric microwave ovens; both sides were pleased with the relationship, but to reduce inventory costs, GE asked for small batches of some models to be delivered on a just-in-time basis. Such orders were beyond SEC's abilities at the time. Since one of Samsung's guiding values had always been to meet customer needs, the failure to do so in even a few instances caused great concern at SEC. Try as they might, engineering teams could not come up with a way to meet similar future orders profitably within the constraints of their existing system.

The production system at the microwave plant in Suwon was based on traditional assembly line principles and required large production runs to be profitable. Major reasons for SEC's past success were the hard work and low pay of its employees. But by the late 1980s, Samsung Electronics could no longer base its competitiveness on cheap labor, because the average pay of Korean workers had steadily increased. In addition, SEC's business strategy had matured from a focus on low-cost, entry-level products to one that emphasized quality and reliability. Top management realized that while it was becoming more difficult to compete on cost, SEC did not have the cutting-edge technological and production systems of high-quality leaders—most notably, its Japanese competition.

As we've pointed out in earlier chapters, Samsung Electronics jump-started its successful leap to flexible manufacturing systems through benchmarking the practices of other companies. Given the nature of its competition, this wasn't an easy approach to take, but it turned out to be the right one. Yet if SEC had simply copied what it saw out there in the fiercely competitive world of consumer electronics, the company's new manufacturing system would never have taken off. The SEC story largely illustrates how ideas, benchmarked or otherwise, can be effectively generalized across boundaries. Generating ideas would not have been enough to make this organizational leap, but it was the starting point of the learning process. Let's backtrack a moment and detail how this benchmarker approached the first building block of organizational learning capability.

Generating Ideas for Flexible Manufacturing Systems

In 1990, Chairman Lee, the son of Lee Byung-Chull, fostered what he called a "total commitment program" for dealing with the problematic manufacturing system. Top managers exhorted employees to ignore SEC's large profits and to think instead as if they were in the midst of a financial crisis. Indeed, SEC made analysis of this problem its main priority. First of all, competitor practices were quickly analyzed. Teams studied various academic theories and applied them to SEC's situation. It soon became clear that its most successful competitors were Japanese firms organized around flexible manufacturing systems (FMS). For Samsung Electronics, adopting such a system, along with related programs of just-in-time management, batch production, and total quality, seemed the perfect solution. It would allow the company to meet the varied needs of its customers by producing small batches of specialized products on the same line, quickly and profitably. So SEC executives decided to restructure along FMS lines.

Unfortunately, this was easier decided than done. Flexible manufacturing was totally foreign to Korean businesses, and SEC was no exception. Not only did Samsung Electronics have no experience with FMS, but its organizational structure was antithetical to many of the basic precepts of FMS. At that time, SEC had a traditional hierarchical, "machine" bureaucracy structure. Decisions, even for relatively simple issues, were passed up the hierarchy until they reached a high-level manager or executive. Rigid rules, procedures, and authority relationships were clearly demarcated and understood. This structural rigidity was reinforced by several general cultural values of Korean society. At the risk of gross oversimplification, the Confucian values of filial piety, respect, and face, as well as the cultural value of high power–distance in Korea, translated in organizational terms into the view that employees should demonstrate respect, obedience, and dedication to their superiors and firm.[2] In addition, most of the line workers in the SEC plants were women, and most of their supervisors were men. Norms surrounding traditional gender-based role differentiation further reinforced one-way communication and structural rigidity. All these factors added up to an organization that ran smoothly with a minimum of fuss but that was also quite inflexible and bureaucratic.

Compounding the problem was that many of the top Japanese firms treated FMS as their source of competitive advantage and were not open to sharing their secrets.

Samsung Electronics took several approaches to learning more about flexible manufacturing systems, some more obvious than others. It had a good foundation to begin with, since many of its managers had received graduate degrees at universities in the United States, Japan, and Europe and therefore had some basic knowledge of FMS. These managers were asked to read everything they could about FMS in both the popular press and academic literature. Many of them were also sent overseas to study the production systems of foreign companies. The conclusion of this preliminary research was simple: SEC should focus its learning on American theories and Japanese practices. Yet its next approach to generating new ideas about flexible manufacturing systems was much less obvious and indicates why Samsung Electronics is one of the few companies to use benchmarking effectively.

SEC undertook a systematic and aggressive benchmarking initiative in three ways. First, the company created joint ventures with exemplary Japanese and U.S. firms. The goal was to learn and transfer FMS practices through cooperative arrangements, so Samsung Electronics traded some of its products for the flexible manufacturing techniques of firms like Toshiba, Toray, and Fujitsu. For example, SEC exchanged DRAM chips for Toshiba's FMS knowledge.

Second, Samsung Electronics required the transfer of FMS expertise as part of its sales agreement with targeted customers. Since SEC manufactured a wide range of products, many Japanese firms were willing to provide such expertise in order to establish a business relationship with a huge potential customer. Therefore, by leveraging its large purchasing power, SEC was often able to send its managers to Japanese plants to study their systems.

Third, SEC circumvented the resistance of large Japanese firms to sharing their production technology by fostering strategic alliances with small or mid-size foreign companies that had what SEC wanted to learn. Alliances with smaller Japanese firms like DNS, Thine, and TOWA had many advantages over those with larger ones. Small and mid-size companies were less resistant to sharing state-of-the-art information, especially when they had financial difficulties that SEC could help address by offering huge purchases of their products. Sometimes these firms had developed even more advanced technology than the big competitors; they also had a great deal of knowledge about practices in Japanese firms.

There's no doubt that Samsung Electronics generated the right ideas about FMS through a variety of means, especially clever joint ventures that allowed the company to buy and trade for what it needed. But when such a large-scale organizational change is called for, the right ideas are not enough. SEC then had to generalize the knowledge it had acquired and implement it in a new production system that would affect the company's bottom line.

Generalizing Ideas for Flexible Manufacturing Systems

Once the company had acquired FMS expertise from the Japanese and others, those in charge of planning the new SEC system integrated it with popular and academic research to form a rough set of general guidelines. This synthesized knowledge, however, posed a number of immediate problems. It had been acquired from a variety of sources and was based on many different products ranging from telecommunications equipment to computer chips. Managers weren't sure how to apply this knowledge to other products, especially SEC's products. Their conclusions were largely untested within Samsung Electronics itself, so it was unclear how the unique business context and culture of Samsung would affect the learning process.

Since the microwave plant had been the catalyst for exploring flexible manufacturing systems, executives decided to implement FMS there first, work out the bugs, and only then apply it to other product lines. To ensure the success of the program, a total commitment was made to what SEC calls the 3 Ms—that is, the necessary money, manpower, and machinery. These were provided without question. The job of translating a general knowledge of flexible manufacturing to microwave production was assigned to groups of cross-functional and cross-level teams. They developed specific plans for building FMS and were given carte blanche to build the new line. Work proceeded around the clock. The building of the new FMS microwave line and the reorganization of the plant occurred primarily through a system of trial and error. A prototype line was built, its performance was analyzed, and modifications were made. Then there was further analysis, and so on.

In fact, the methods SEC used to generate ideas also helped generalize them. Through the company's joint ventures and buying capability, managers, engineers, and supervisors from Japanese plants were brought in to analyze SEC's early attempts. Samsung Electronics also hired foreign technical assistants (primarily retired Japanese and American managers and engineers) to provide assistance with the implementation.

The new manufacturing system that resulted—up and running within six months—radically differed from the old. The old production line of 605.7 meters had been reduced to 64.9 meters. The lead time for each product was reduced from 181.5 minutes to 25.3 minutes with FMS. The new system made it possible, in the course of a day, to switch each line over to produce four or five different products. In this case, a radical change occurred through benchmarking outside practices rather than through in-house experiments or continuous improvements. What is remarkable is that this happened so effectively in a process that involved transferring knowledge across many boundaries, as well as changing the company's organization and culture.

Education and training at SEC are crucial supports for the new manufacturing system. In 1992, the company paid for relevant university courses both in Korea and overseas for more than a thousand employees. SEC's own training and vocational programs are even more extensive. A typical training regimen for new engineers includes one month of lectures about the company, three months of general skill or technological training related to their jobs, and nine months of on-the-job training. Samsung Electronics has also recently completed a U.S. $200 million center that provides its researchers and engineers with training in the latest technological advancements. Perhaps most important of all is continuous on-the-job training. Since the production line is always changing and problems are constantly surfacing, employees have to adapt. Some of this learning is accomplished through SEC's vocational programs, but more of it occurs from working with fellow employees on teams and through job rotations. In fact, a supervisor's primary role is to facilitate learning for his or her employees.

In addition, FMS could not work at Samsung Electronics without empowerment. Two major factors contributed to the shift from top-down hierarchical management to the empowerment approach that is essential for FMS. First, the extensive overseas educational program took place during the time when empowerment was a big fad in the West. Many of Samsung's managers returned convinced that employee empowerment was the latest business advance. Second, the Japanese firms that were brought in to implement FMS emphasized, with an almost religious zeal, that employee involvement at all levels of the design and operation of FMS was critical. As a result, even top executives now believe that a greater number of important decisions should be made by lower-level managers and line workers. Many decisions actually begin with such employees. When a lower-level manager or worker has an idea, they are encouraged to form a project team on their own to develop it. The team then reports the recommendations to its superior. The recommendation is either implemented or passed up the hierarchy for approval. Only very rarely will mid- or upper management veto an idea that's based on shop-floor experience, and most ideas are at least given a try.

This vertical boundary-crossing is reflected in SEC's top down–bottom up leadership style: top executives, as is usual, make general decisions that are clarified and operationalized as they move down the organization, but ideas are also often generated and implemented by those at the bottom. The ideas then move up the organization for approval and generalization throughout the firm. Progressively higher levels of management usually choose between existing modifications rather than making new changes. Only if such changes are made does the process start all over again. Such an approach is a radical departure from the old Samsung way, in which executives came up with ideas and solutions, then passed them down to managers to figure out how to implement them. These managers, in turn, issued orders that employees were expected to follow and execute. Now SEC is working on flattening its organizational structure. In general, "slim" organizations move faster because there are fewer layers of management for decisions and information to pass through, and decisions are made closer to where they will be implemented.

As with so many learning organizations, the different programs and practices at SEC were all interconnected and dependent on each other. Nothing really develops in a vacuum. For example, FMS requires highly versatile and skilled workers who are able to spot problems and are empowered to solve them. SEC's extensive training and education programs provide the skills employees need to do this. And empowerment only works to the benefit of the firm if semiautonomous workers use their freedom to pursue organizational goals. The strong SEC culture and trust of management helped assure that individual and organizational actions and goals were aligned. In addition, top management's support of the 3 M's—whatever money, manpower, and machinery it takes—provided the necessary material conditions for FMS.

The new flexible manufacturing system was initially implemented only in SEC's microwave plant. But once it was proven successful there, its lessons were analyzed and spread to other areas of Samsung Electronics, including the VCR plant in the Suwon plant complex. Much of the same process that the microwave plant went through—conceptually learning about FMS, then figuring out how to apply it to specific product lines—is now being repeated by other plants such as the VCR facility. Yet the process flows more smoothly at these plants, since the knowledge is now internal to SEC, and the microwave plant's experience provides a blueprint for how to proceed.

Samsung Electronics and the Five Principles of Generalization

In chapter 3, we laid out five principles for idea generalization, based on our work with a number of companies. The story of Samsung Electronics, our generalization champion, shows all five of the principles in action. Let's consider the principles with SEC in mind.

Principle 1: Generalization Requires Recognition That Boundaries Exist, Can Be Specified, and Can Be Negotiated   In SEC's case, four boundaries were crossed: external, vertical, horizontal, and temporal. External boundaries focus on stakeholders outside the firm. Forming alliances, using study groups, attending workshops, benchmarking best practices, and continually scanning emerging technologies are ways of crossing external boundaries. SEC did much of this, since its leaders realized they had to learn from outside sources. Its customers created the need to change; competitors and venture partners were sources of insight on how to do FMS; and the academic literature provided the processes of FMS.

Vertical boundaries, on the other hand, exist where knowledge or ideas need to be shared from top to bottom within an organization. Within SEC, vertical boundaries were crossed when leaders made sure that the concepts of FMS were fully deployed from the top to the bottom of the through teams, empowerment, and shared decision making. Horizontal boundaries also involve the inner workings of the organization, and they can be jumped over when information is moved from side to side within the firm. This sideways movement of ideas may occur across businesses, functions, or manufacturing facilities. The FMS work was first implemented, through extensive trial and error, at a microwave plant within SEC and then designed to be moved throughout all of Samsung by sharing information on FMS across units. Finally, boundaries exist across time. By capturing the know-how of FMS through rules, procedures, manuals, computer programs, and individual knowledge, Samsung has been able to transfer such knowledge to new employees.

Principle 2: Generalization Requires Ideas That Are Tied to Strategy   By the late 1980s, SEC executives knew that their cycle times would eventually hinder the company's business success in microwave ovens and other consumer electronics. For Samsung Electronics, FMS was not a trivial or faddish activity but a core part of achieving the right business results. Customers like General Electric demanded such production changes; investors would be well served by implementing them; and the Samsung corporate office used SEC's experience with implementing flexible manufacturing as a test for the rest of the firm.

Principle 3: Generalization Requires Contingent Thinking   Adaptive, contingent thinking involves delineating key contextual factors. SEC was able to draw on the academic and practical experience of many companies; but more important, it synthesized and integrated this knowledge into specific requirements that matched contingencies like the organization's culture and country of origin. The goal was not for a Korean firm to master Japanese best practices but to learn from them and create *Korean* best practices in FMS.

Principle 4: Generalization Requires That Organizations Master Capabilities Beyond Single Experiments   By implementing FMS in very specific ways, Samsung Electronics engaged employees through meetings, built relationships with both customers and competitors, turned customer requests into action, and ultimately implemented technological innovations in manufacturing across the company. The use of FMS at the microwave plant did not remain an isolated experience, and one of the most crucial by-products of this process was an organizational capacity to adapt and change. While flexible manufacturing has yet to move across the entire organization, it's a pretty safe bet that SEC has already created organizational learning capability through the FMS experience; and the more this process is replicated, the more new management techniques will be identified and implemented in the firm. When this happens, SEC will achieve its goal by becoming more agile, flexible, innovative, and dynamic.

Principle 5: Generalization Requires That Shared Ideas Have Impact   At Samsung Electronics, the FMS was not merely knowledge in the abstract. It changed how work was organized with measurable results. The ideas shared had clear impact as measured by cycle times, flexibility of operations, and profitability. With the reduction of the production line from 605.7 meters to 64.9 meters, the lead time for each product was reduced from 181.5 minutes to 25.3 minutes. Moreover, each line can now be switched to produce four or five different products. The organization itself changed, from the way the microwave plant was laid out, to the commitment of its employees, to the decisions made by those employees. An emphasis on flexible manufacturing systems led to a series of pragmatic actions that changed both how the organization operated and how individuals within the organization behaved.

A Manager's Tool Kit For Generalization

Samsung Electronics is a company with high learning capability, and its story indicates why generalizing ideas matters so much to business performance. But what if you're the manager of a small paper-goods factory, or you run a food services organization, or you oversee a large pharmaceutical corporation? How do we take the specifics of this case and apply them to other kinds of firms? As we emphasize throughout this book, a number of factors influence how particular companies learn—business strategy, context, culture, and organizational structure, to name but a few. While the lessons SEC learned about flexible manufacturing systems aren't relevant to every industry and business, the generalization principles can be recast as a series of management practices. We call this a tool kit for generalizing ideas with impact, one that includes seven tools that executives and human resources managers at different types of companies can try.

Tool 1. Create a Generalization Culture

Culture represents the identity of the firm as perceived by both its customers and its employees. As such, it is embedded in how a firm gets work done, allocates rewards, shares information, and manages people. For example, Continental Airlines executives realized in the early 1990s that their culture, or identity, was awful. The company's most frequent business travelers identified Continental with bad service, late flights, and poor employee attitude. Consequently, its new executive team, under the direction of CEO Gordon Bethune, put together the Go Forward Plan, the goal of which was to create a fundamentally new culture within Continental. The plan focused on four factors: "fly to win" (improve revenue); "fund the future" (reduce debt); "make reliability a reality" (increase customer service measures); and "work together" (create a work environment of dignity and respect). Central to the Go Forward Plan was a new culture in which ideas generated from one experience could be shared throughout the organization. For example, suggestions on how gate agents might board flights more quickly and thus be on time were shared across airports and among gate agents.[3]

Executives at almost any company will say that a learning culture is important to them, but it really is critical for some firms. Learning—

constant, fast, and substantive—matters most in industries where technological change is rapid; customers have the ability to change suppliers; new competition is emerging; knowledge and service are the product rather than physical items; competitors can match product and price; and customers have high expectations. The computer and biotech industries are just two examples. For firms operating in these market and industrial conditions, learning becomes critical to competitiveness.

Many of these companies have the classic adhocracy cultures of Silicon Valley (HP, Apple, Oracle, 3-Com, Quantum, Sun Microsystems), in which highly educated workers are motivated to learn new subject areas on their own. They may have a vested (material and/or emotional) interest in the company and be good at working autonomously. Indeed, many firms like this wear their cultures on their sleeves, trumpeting their origins as start-ups and hacker-run anarchies. Yet just because a culture is firmly established doesn't mean it is still effective. Correctly identifying the culture of your organization—and then making sure it aligns with the larger business strategy and context—is the way real learning happens. Woe betide the start-up that has failed to shift with a changing market or with organizational expansion, not to mention behemoths that cling to old-fashioned hierarchies.

As with so many good ideas, generalization is the key. Whether you have a service culture or an adhocracy, a market-oriented culture or one that emphasizes efficiency and cost-cutting, you'll want to maximize idea generalization. Above all else, your organization should have a *learning culture*. Once you've identified your culture, and assuming it's the right one for your company, take a hard look at how ideas are shared within and beyond the organization. The assessment items in worksheet 5.1 may be useful, especially for managers in companies where learning is critical to business strategy and performance. The items have been drawn from a number of studies of learning culture[4] and may help you to assess the extent to which ideas are generalized in your company.

Tool 2. Ensure the Individual Competencies Necessary for Generalization

Competencies represent the knowledge, skill, and ability of individuals within an organization. As in the case of Samsung Electronics, most organizations that generalize ideas at a high level employ individuals with similar abilities. In their work on Career Architect, a tool for identifying leadership competencies, Eichinger and Lombardo have identified 68 competencies individuals might demonstrate. These competencies are based on dozens of studies and content analyses of myriad competence models.[5] In their work, they have identified some of the competencies of individuals who are central to helping organizations learn by generalizing ideas across boundaries: Conflict Management; Learning on the Fly; Informing; Listening; Motivating Others; Perspective; Political Savvy; Problem Solving.

To develop these competencies, companies can either "buy" outsiders that have them or "build" from within. A buy strategy for competencies involves bringing in outside talent, either full-time as new employees or part-time through some form of contracting (such as consultants or through outsourcing partnerships). Buy strategies generally imply that internal talent doesn't exist or can be sourced externally more effectively. Although this may be the current reality at a company, looking outside for help is not always the best long-term solution or good for morale. Alternative ways to staff the talent required for sharing ideas are summarized in worksheet 5.2's checklist.

A build strategy for competencies occurs when management invests in the training and/or development of existing employees. Build implies that with appropriate nurturing, current employees can acquire the competencies required for sharing knowledge. Moving talent across units within an organization is a common practice for sharing knowledge. A succession planning system, in which employees have the opportunity to apply for jobs throughout an organization, increases the likelihood of ideas being shared. Using training events as forums for sharing ideas and for turning ideas into action also facilitates the generalization process. Again, these and other "staffing tools" are listed in worksheet 5.2.

In the late 1980s through the mid-1990s, many firms focused on buying new blood. When Larry Bossidy became CEO of AlliedSignal, for example, he changed 90 of the top 120 positions in his first year. However, as the economy has strengthened, it's now become more difficult to buy talent in this fashion. By the mid-1990s, the pool of highly skilled people shrank to the point that key jobs might remain open as long as four months. AlliedSignal did not face this problem alone; other companies have had trouble filling key jobs as quickly as they did in the early 1990s. The lack of outside talent meant that more effort shifted to helping existing employees acquire new competencies, through training and other in-house programs. From a generalization point of view, building your talent from within probably has the bigger payoff in any case, since it helps with sharing ideas across time, organizational units, and geographic boundaries.

Tool 3. Provide the Right Incentives for Generalization

The old adage, "People do what they are rewarded for," is at least half true. Without doubt, incentives change behavior. But incentives only work when they're based on clear and explicit standards. Without clear standards linked to rewards, rewards may be haphazard and not focused on actual employee behavior. A better adage might be, "People do what they are rewarded for—if they know *why* they got the reward."[6]

For those interested in generalizing ideas, these standards and incentives must also be linked with learning. The first step is to measure the extent to which learning occurs and to build this measurement system into a firm's performance management system. A number of successful companies demonstrate that performance appraisals with measures and standards specifically tied to learning increase learning in the company. 3M uses a "vitality index" that measures the percentage of revenue in a business from products introduced in the last four years. Such a measure reflects both idea generation and idea generalization. 3M's vitality index encourages experimentation, risk taking, and sharing of ideas, but other measures of learning, especially those that reinforce generalization, might include the number of good "postmortems" conducted for both mistakes and successes, how much a unit or manager relies on multiple appraisers; and the extent to which customers are involved in the appraisal and reward process.

Once standards and measures are established, rewards for meeting those standards can be allocated. Some rewards are financial (base pay, bonus, stock options); others are nonfinancial (for example, special recognition awards to managers who anticipate competency needs and learning strategies). In either case, as long as rewards are tied to the measures of learning, accountability for learning increases. From a generalization standpoint, of course, such measures of learning and innovation should be conducted at all levels of the organization.

Tool 4. Organize Work for Generalization

Governance of the organization and how people work together can be modified through three strategies: teamwork, work-process improvement, and an overall focus on the capacity for change. *Teamwork* within and across organizational boundaries ensures that people work together for a common purpose.[7] Teams take many forms: project focused, using resources throughout an organization to support a specific project; consulting focused, when a firm creates centers of expertise that become internal consultants to a business; management focused, in which a firm forms a leadership team to integrate and govern the enterprise. Teams may be formed for a short-term, specific task or work together for the long term in order to govern tasks over time. Their members may be drawn from a specific unit or from across multiple units and may sometimes even include suppliers and customers. Regardless of the form, teamwork facilitates idea generalization. When individuals from different units or perspectives join forces, different ideas and approaches are shared and exchanged.

Work-process improvement helps share ideas by committing to continuous improvement. Continuous improvement comes from constantly seeking new and improved ways to manage a process, then experimenting with and implementing those innovations. In general, reengineering efforts, which systematically assess and improve how work is done, depend on learning. Ideas from employees, other companies, customers, suppliers, and consultants can be imported into the firm to improve the flow of work.

As for *capacity for change*, this overall strategy goes by many names: agility, transformation, flexibility.[8] Regardless of the name, the challenge is to increase an organization's ability to change. A company's capacity certainly influences the ability to generalize ideas. Some practices for increasing capacity for change include

- Reject business you can't learn from and walk away from bad clients.
- Build more flexible information systems.
- Establish a physical setting that encourages sharing (for example, small conference rooms, nonwalled offices).
- Build relationships with "idea places" like universities.
- Develop a disciplined process for managing change.

Tool 5. Create Information Tools for Generalization

Developing information tools that help generalize ideas doesn't necessarily involve fancy new computers; a useful information tool can be a new staff position, an electronic system, or informal communication practices within your company. Collectively, formal and informal processes for communicating ideas can be a great tool for sharing information across boundaries, as long as they work toward the same business goals.

Most of the large professional service firms have created the position of "director of knowledge transfer," whose primary responsibility is to move information across units. In other cases, all of a firm's professionals are expected to transfer knowledge in specific ways. Arthur Andersen, for instance, leverages technology through the work of its consultants, who move best practices from one site to another. On completing an assignment, an Andersen consultant is expected to answer some basic questions: What was the presenting problem? What were the methods used to deal with the problem? What were the results? What were the lessons learned? These answers then merge into an ever-evolving data set that other consultants may draw on for their consulting practices. Andersen consultants all over the world therefore share information with each other across many boundaries. A consultant is as likely to retrieve information from Europe, Asia, or North America when accessing the Andersen data base. In this case, the information becomes a carrier of the values of the firm.

To be sure, technology-based tools like the Andersen data base or work-sharing software can be a real boon for idea generalization. User-friendly information systems like Lotus Notes can create the infrastructure for sharing ideas. And one company used technology to generalize the knowledge gained from a training experience. Managers there had originally designed the five-day event as a series of modules. In each module (which generally lasted a half or full day), concepts were taught and illustrated, and traditional tools like cases, worksheets, checklists, and handouts provided for turning concepts into action. The intent of the training program shifted, however, when technology was applied. The five-day event now focused on how to access a computer-based data set that included three levels of information.

At the heart of the data set was information summarizing the concepts taught in each of the five modules. The second level contained the appropriate tools, exercises, and worksheets. The third level was made up of examples of applications (much like Arthur Andersen's consultant data set), in which experiences with the tools were shared and stored. After the five-day program, participants were allowed access to the material over the next 12 months. Eight or nine months after the training, for example, a participant might face a business issue covered in the original five-day event. By accessing the data base, she could quickly review the concept, pick the tools most useful for the specific problem, and review how others have applied those tools. Once she had resolved the issue, this participant would be expected to provide a short synopsis of how she adapted the tool, thus adding to the data set.

In addition to creating staff positions and/or technology that emphasizes information-sharing, a number of less formal communication practices encourage idea generalization. If organizational learning is your focus, one of your first tasks will be identifying the communication patterns in your company and determining which informal practices hinder and which help generalization. In our consulting work, we have observed that companies are good at sharing ideas when they have at least some of the following:

- Easy communication, great informality
- An organization-wide campaign that links learning to training and education
- Honest and public assessments of learning dysfunctions
- An open flow of information
- Lots of informal, face-to-face meetings
- Information that skips levels rather then flowing along hierarchical lines
- "Sensing" meetings from below, in which employees from many levels of an organization share information with each other
- External benchmarking and communication
- A system for sharing information and successes

Tool 6. Develop Leaders Who Generalize Ideas

Although getting company leaders on board may seem obvious, it's one of the most crucial managerial tools for encouraging knowledge sharing across boundaries. In organizations with high learning capability, leaders at all levels model and encourage the sharing of ideas. The leadership assessment in worksheet 5.3 highlights some of the behaviors and abilities of executives who facilitate learning, through both generating and generalizing ideas. The total score of these twelve abilities—or the learning leader index—can provide rough estimates of how well particular executives move ideas across boundaries.

Tool 7. Diagnose Your Generalization Pattern by Creating a Learning Matrix

Lastly, here's a more specific technique that can help identify how, or whether, generalization is happening in your organization. One challenge of generalizing ideas within a large company is to identify where good ideas are housed and then find out how to share them. At General Electric, Steve Kerr, Chief Learning Officer and Vice President of Management Development, has created a *learning matrix* that identifies the source of good ideas for sharing across geographic, functional, or business boundaries.[9] To sketch a matrix for your company, follow these five steps.

Step 1   Answer the question: "To be world class at X, we must. . . ." X can be anything the corporation is committed to doing well, such as service, quality, customer focus, cycle time, training. The outcome of this step should be identification of 10 to 12 critical factors that will help a corporate initiative to succeed. Arriving at this outcome might involve a small research team, task force, or other group to define these critical success factors. These answers become the columns in worksheet 5.4.

Step 2 Answer the question, "What are the units (functions, businesses, or territories) where the critical success factors can be demonstrated?" Your answers here form the rows in worksheet 5.4.

Step 3 On a scale of 0 to 5, score each cell of the matrix: 0 = not applicable; 1 = not good at all; 2= sort of good; 3= average; 4 = we think we are good; 5 = others think we are good (that is, we've been certified by someone outside the business as "world class" in this particular area). This assessment should be done by either an organizational unit leader or a rating team external to the unit (such as a corporate group that inspects the unit or an outside rating agency). Scores of 0 to 4 can be provided by members of the unit, but a score of 5 must come from someone outside the unit.

Step 4 Combine the individual assessments by row into an overall learning matrix. The information provided by each organizational unit now forms a general pattern for a particular initiative (X). This matrix can help pinpoint pockets of excellence and provides an overall corporate score on any initiative. The overall score may provide feedback for a corporate staff person assigned to pursue initiative X. And the matrix itself indicates the baseline for how ideas are generalized across these different units.

Step 5 Create processes for sharing ideas and knowledge based on the high-score cells in each column and apply them to the lower score cells. This is where the rubber meets the road. The beauty of Kerr's learning matrix is that it highlights specific problem areas or "breaks" in the generalization pattern. As we've already noted in the discussion of the other tools, there are a number of mechanisms for generalizing knowledge and experience from one cell to another.

- Make the high-score cells best practice sites where others can learn.
- Create case studies from the higher score cells for others to draw on.
- Move talent from higher to lower score cells.

- Create an incentive system for those in high-score cells for sharing knowledge.
- Assign someone from corporate headquarters to oversee the entire matrix process, ensuring that a larger percentage of cells achieve scores of 5 each successive year.

The Upshot: Sharing Ideas Is More Important Than Ever

In the current economy, generalizing ideas with impact—the second building block of organizational learning capability—has become critical to overall learning. It's not enough to be a fountain of creativity; companies must match new ideas to particular business strategies and contexts and then implement them in a practical, effective manner. And once a good idea has been implemented, the organization must retain the knowledge gained, sharing it across as many boundaries as possible.

Generalizing ideas with impact comes down to effective implementation and boundary crossing. It may not be easy to move knowledge across years, countries, or diverse businesses under one corporate umbrella, but as our case study of Samsung Electronics well illustrates, idea generalization is the key to making organizational learning competitive. That's why today's managers, particularly those involved in human resources and organizational design, need their own version of a generalization tool kit—one that includes specific practices and assessments that encourage sharing ideas across boundaries.

Consider, once again, the difference between a musician and someone who has lots of ideas about how to play a violin. The idea person may try plucking the strings or observe how others do it, but he won't be a violinist until he *implements* his knowledge through practice and training. As firms spend more time and money generating ideas (though experiments, competency acquisition, benchmarking best practices, and continuous improvement), the ability to generalize must increase accordingly. Simply put, organizational learning doesn't happen when generalization is low. In fact, problems with generalizing or generating ideas often reflect learning disabilities in a company—which takes us to the third and final building block of organizational learning capability.

CHAPTER SIX

Identifying Learning Disabilities

Samsung Revisited and Three Health Care Systems

It's no accident that most organizations learn poorly. As Chris Argyris and many other theorists have pointed out, the ways organizations are designed and managed, the definitions of people's jobs, and—most important—the manner in which we have all been taught to think and interact inevitably create fundamental learning disabilities.[1] The last two chapters have emphasized that successful organizational learning involves an ability to generate and generalize ideas with impact—recall our expression for learning capability, $g \times g$. Yet as any manager who has participated in learning initiatives can attest, problems soon arise that interfere with idea generation, idea generalization, or both; they may even prevent the firm from becoming a learning organization, no matter how committed the CEO, line managers, or HR staff are. These learning disabilities are generally poorly understood and hard to diagnose from within the firm, a frustrating situation for all concerned. That's why we believe that identifying learning disabilities is the third essential building block for creating a learning organization.

Consider Midwestern Health (not its real name), a hospital where one of us was a consultant. A new CEO had joined the organization about a year before our consulting team was brought on board. He was convinced that major shifts in the health care environment necessitated significant changes in how the hospital operated, and he successfully communicated this need to the rest of the organization. The CEO became very enthusiastic about the seminal book on organizational learning at the time, Peter Senge's *Fifth Discipline*. He bought 500 copies of the book and made it required reading for every manager. He also hired Senge's consulting firm to set up a two-week experiential "learning university" that all managers were required to attend. There, away from the hospital, they concentrated on systems thinking and engaged in "Microworlds" computer simulations. At the end of the two weeks, managers returned to Midwestern Health as enthusiastic as their CEO, determined to change the hospital into a "lean, mean, exciting machine."

Yet despite this initial excitement, when we visited the organization six months later nothing had changed. The CEO told us with real agony in his voice, "I did everything right and nothing happened." Managers claimed there was an "invisible force" that caused all the best ideas to fade. Many spoke of the impossibility of altering the system's "inertia." The disappointment of these managers, including the CEO, was palpable. They experienced hidden but real barriers to learning, and their negative reactions were understandable. But talking about invisible forces and inertia generally makes people feel helpless; they are unable to move forward and don't know how to frame the problems they encounter constructively. Recognizing that all organizations are prone to learning disabilities is the way to start, and identifying those disabilities, the many barriers to change and growth that exist in any company, helps reframe the learning challenge.

From the perspective of this book, we would reframe Midwestern Health's challenge this way: the new CEO did a decent job of idea generation through competency acquisition. A consulting team was hired and a two-week experiential learning program was delivered to jump-start exciting new ideas. He assessed the need for change, communicated it effectively to his employees, and went to great expense to train them. But the change program did not address the generalization half of the equation. While employees came back from the training session brimming with new ideas, the application of those ideas was taken for granted. Little effort was made to change how hospital staff worked or to diffuse what had been learned throughout the organization. The reward system was not modified at all, so employees were still rewarded for old behaviors. In the new regime, managers were expected to be bold and take risks, yet they were still rewarded for playing it safe. The structure of the organization was not altered. Employees wanted to work in a lean and flexible environment, but a typical pyramidal hierarchy with dozens of layers of management remained in place.

This explains why we use a multiplicative function ($g \times g$) instead of an additive one ($g + g$) in our learning equation. In the case of

Midwestern Health, even though its generation ability is high (say, 8 out of 10 points), its generalization ability is low (3 out of 10). If we were to rely on an additive function to express learning capability, Midwestern Health would score 11 out of 20 points (55 percent of the total possible score), which doesn't sound too bad. However, when we multiply generation by generalization, this organization scores only 24 out of 100 points (or 24 percent), a miserable failure in our opinion, and a much more accurate view of its learning environment. For Midwestern Health, executive investment in competency acquisition did not lead to any behavioral or organizational changes with business impact.

This hospital's experience highlights the importance of real-world actions when it comes to organizational learning. Simply training and changing the way employees think is not enough. Learning organizations must be able both to generate and to generalize ideas, which means that most companies will have to make substantial changes in their systems, structures, and procedures. Note that the agonized CEO at Midwestern Health is not alone, since most learning efforts only include one of the factors of our expression. In this chapter, we will return to our worldwide survey of companies, reporting what we discovered about learning disabilities in our sample. Then we'll turn to Samsung Electronics and to two health care systems. These case studies will illustrate not only the ways in which learning disabilities can affect organizational learning but also how they can be effectively overcome.

Survey Results: Seven Basic Learning Disabilities

In our worldwide survey, we developed over thirty questions based on the learning disabilities we had previously identified in the literature. As we discussed in chapter 3, after conducting the analyses, we found that the 400 or more companies in our sample suffered from seven basic learning disabilities: the first four disabilities affect idea generation, and the latter three hinder idea generalization. They are outlined next and are accompanied by the relevant items we asked our survey respondents. While some of the questions were asked in a positive way, they were all converted to indicate the extent to which an organization suffers such a disability.

Because of the complexity of the relationships among the learning disabilities, context variables, and business performance variables, a more complex statistical analysis was required. We relied extensively on multiple regressions and structural equation modeling to understand learning disabilities. These techniques allowed us to examine the relationships between any two variables while simultaneously considering the relationships with all other relevant variables. For this reason, regression and path model coefficients are reported, not correlations. However, these coefficients can be interpreted as if they were correlations.

Four Learning Disabilities That Affect Generation

1. Blindness: inability to assess environmental opportunities and threats accurately
   We aren't good at scanning the external environment for opportunities and potential problems.
   We don't actively find or create new markets.
   We are bad at perceiving long-term environmental threats and opportunities.

2. Simplemindedness: deficiencies in analysis and solution generation
   We are bad at determining the causes of unexpectedly low and high levels of performance.
   We are bad at deciding on plans of action to redress performance shortfalls.
   We have difficulty generating and evaluating a wide variety of alternative solutions to performance shortfalls.

3. Homogeneity: lack of variety in skills, information, ideas, and values
   We don't ensure that all employees have access to more information than the minimum required to perform their jobs.
   We don't encourage diversity in people and ideas within our organization.
   We punish intelligent risk-taking, which results in failure.

4. Tight coupling: excessive coordination among different organizational units
   We maintain too much managerial control, which defuses multiple, competing perspectives in our organization.
   Groups and departments in this organization don't function independently unless there's a lot of integration.

Three Learning Disabilities That Affect Generalization

5. Paralysis: inability to implement new actions or procedures
   We tend to overanalyze problems before implementing ideas and thus miss opportunities for improvement.

Employees have little say in how their work is done.
We have trouble implementing new procedures.

6. Superstitious learning: inability to interpret accurately the
   meanings of experience
   The rationales we give for our performance outcomes often have
       little to do with the actual causes of these outcomes.
   The actions we take often have little effect on performance out-
       comes.
   Too much time passes between employee actions and feedback
       on those actions.

7. Diffusion deficiency: inability to share ideas with all relevant
   parts of the organization
   Learning in one group or unit doesn't spread throughout our or-
       ganization.
   Individuals here may learn, but what they learn isn't transmitted
       to others in the organization.

The companies in our sample only suffered to a modest degree from
these learning disabilities, at least as reported on our questionnaires.
Still, we found that diffusion deficiency, simplemindedness, and tight
coupling were the most common disabilities, followed by blindness,
paralysis, homogeneity, and superstitious learning. Given a five-point
scale, where 1 means low disability and 5 means high, disability,
here's how they ranked:

Learning Disability	Mean Score	Standard Deviation
Diffusion deficiency	3.08	.57
Simplemindedness	3.03	.49
Tight coupling	3.00	.62
Blindness	2.94	.48
Paralysis	2.92	.47
Homogeneity	2.79	.53
Superstitious learning	2.62	.50

In other words, the companies in our sample had the most trouble
with translating individual learning into organization-wide procedures
and knowledge, developing capability in processing complex information, and allowing different businesses and units to adapt their
practices to idiosyncratic situations. That's probably to be expected,
given the current complexity and rate of change in the global economy, which forces businesses to process ever more complex information and to be more flexible in responding to specific customer
needs. We have observed diffusion deficiency, for instance, in many

large companies like GM, in which pockets of excellence and best practices aren't shared rapidly enough with other parts of the organization. Yet all of these disabilities, together or separately, can affect the generation and generalization of ideas in a company. Business context and performance are also reflected in how these learning disabilities develop and play out. The following sections discuss the relationships between these factors.

How Business Context Influences Learning Disabilities

As with idea generation in our sample, industry characteristics such as customer and supplier relationships don't appear to have much impact on learning disabilities. But one of the most interesting results of our survey is that business strategy has a very strong effect on the learning disabilities. Companies that compete on product differentiation through innovation, speed, or quality are able to reduce all seven learning disabilities. As learning capability is critical to product differentiation strategy, a company that competes via differentiation is more effective in combating learning disabilities. Companies that compete on cost are also able to somewhat reduce learning disabilities in simplemindedness, tight coupling, and superstitious learning, but not as dramatically as companies with product differentiation strategies. Clearly, business strategy affects learning disabilities (see table 6.1).

Business culture also appears to have a strong influence on the development of learning disabilities in two ways (see table 6.2). First, regardless of the type of culture, the stronger a company culture, the

Table 6.1   Effects of Business Strategy on Learning Disabilities

Learning disability	Strategy	
	Cost competitiveness	Product differentiation
Blindness	−.06	−.36*
Simplemindedness	−.10+	−.47*
Homogeneity	−.03	−.51*
Tight coupling	−.12+	−.30*
Paralysis	.00	−.46*
Superstitious learning	−.10+	−.50*
Diffusion deficiency	−.02	−.35*

Findings reported are standardized beta based on regression analyses.
*Finding significant at <.05 level.   +Finding significant at <.10 level.

Table 6.2   Effects of Business Culture on Learning Disabilities

	Culture			
Learning disability	Clan	Market	Hierarchy	Adhocracy
Blindness	−.04	−.20*	−.23*	−.40*
Simplemindedness	−.27*	−.36*	−.18*	−.19+
Homogeneity	−.68*	−.12*	.06	−.02
Tight coupling	−.48*	−.09	−.21*	−.12
Paralysis	−.50*	−.17*	.07	.01
Superstitious learning	−.31*	−.35*	.01	−.05
Diffusion deficiency	−.46*	−.15*	−.14+	−.08

Findings reported are standardized beta based on regression analyses.
*Finding significant at <.05 level.   +Finding significant at <.10 level.

higher the ability to reduce learning disabilities. This finding is supported in that all significant relationships between business culture and learning disabilities are negative. Second, not all cultural types are equally effective in reducing learning disabilities. Cultures that focus on employees (clan culture), customers, and market competition (market culture) are most the effective in reducing learning disabilities. These two findings echoed the research findings of Kotter and Heskett, who found that companies focusing on employees, customers, and shareholders developed a stronger capacity for change and, as a result, enjoyed higher business performance[2]. Here are some further details we learned from the survey study regarding each cultural type.

A clan-based culture is characterized by loose, decentralized control with an internal focus. Clan companies emphasize human resource values like morale, involvement, cohesion, and openness. Clans foster "active" employees that are likely to be flexible and committed to the organization. These qualities result in an organizational structure that limits tight coupling, effectively implements ideas (thus limiting paralysis), and shares information (limiting homogeneity and diffusion deficiency). Yet an internal focus can result in poor environmental scanning, which leads to blindness. Overall, we found that the clan companies in our sample suffered from few of the learning disabilities, except for blindness.

Market-oriented cultures have tight controls with an external focus. This promotes a customer-oriented value system with a focus on productivity, efficiency, and market competitiveness. The external focus makes these firms particularly aware of their external environment, limiting blindness; a focus on competition, profits, and rationality ensures efficient coordination (minimizing diffusion deficiency) and promotes change once old procedures no longer positively affect the bottom line (limiting paralysis). Therefore, market-oriented cultures have few of the learning disabilities, except that they are prone to tight coupling, which means the "one size fits all" approach may lead to difficulties even though its intent is to ensure consistency in service and processes.

Companies with hierarchy cultures are effective in reducing blindness, tight coupling, and simplemindedness. While it is understandable that companies in hierarchy culture often develop elaborate processes and systems to process information (thus reducing simplemindedness), the ability of these companies to reduce blindness and tight coupling contradicts what we expected. However, companies with a hierarchical culture are prone to paralysis and homogeneity.

Companies with adhocracy cultures are least effective in combating learning disabilities. An adhocracy-based culture is characterized by loose, decentralized control and an external focus. As a result, companies with adhocracy cultures are most effective in avoiding environmental blindness. However, compared with companies with other cultures, they are less effective in reducing other learning disabilities.

In the real, messy world it is unlikely that any one kind of organizational culture will perfectly promote all aspects of organizational learning and avoid all the learning disabilities. But this is not to say that all cultures are created equal. The adhocracies in our sample had by far the highest number of learning disabilities, while clan and market cultures had the fewest. The trick, then, is for organizational leaders to be aware of which disabilities their particular culture is likely to promote and to take steps to limit their impact.

Finally, we discovered that national differences come into play with learning disabilities, just as they do for idea generation. Geographically speaking, we found systematic differences in disabilities among North American, Western European, and Asian companies (see table 6.3). Overall, the Asian firms in our sample suffered less than North American and European businesses did from the learning disabilities, though not by much. This was largely because, other things being equal, individualist cultures tend to be hindered more by learning disabilities than collectivist ones. We can surmise that Asian organizations are better than their Western counterparts at understanding their external and internal business environments, and that they do a better job of coordinating different functions and business units.

Table 6.3   Learning Disabilities across National Cultures

Learning disability	North America businesses (N = 189)	Europe businesses (N = 17)	Asia businesses (N = 38)
Blindness	3.01	2.83	2.69
Simplemindedness	3.09	2.92	2.75
Homogeneity	2.81	2.79	2.57
Tight coupling	3.07	2.98	2.66
Paralysis	2.95	2.89	2.79
Superstitious learning	2.64	2.48	2.56
Diffusion deficiency	3.17	2.90	2.75

Findings reported are the mean scores of learning disabilities on a five-point scale (1 = low disability, 5 = high disability).

How Learning Disabilities Affect Business Performance

In our survey, six of the seven learning disabilities reduced innovativeness and competitiveness (see table 6.4). This result is hardly a surprise, but it confirms that learning matters. An organization suffering from learning disabilities tends to be less innovative and competitive. In particular, homogeneity and blindness have the most negative impact on a firm's innovativeness, while superstitious learning, blindness, paralysis, and simplemindedness significantly reduce a firm's competitiveness.

Table 6.4   Effects of Learning Disabilities on Firm Performance

Learning disability	Performance	
	Innovativeness	Competitiveness
Environmental blindness	−.21*	−.12*
Simplemindedness	.07	−.11+
Homogeneity	−.24*	.20*
Tight coupling	−.19*	−.02
Paralysis	−.18*	−.11*
Superstitious learning	−.18*	−.13+
Diffusion deficiency	−.14*	−.03

Findings reported are LISREL maximum likelihood estimates.
*Finding significant at <.05 level.   +Finding significant at <.10 level.

However, one of the learning disabilities, simplemindedness, didn't affect innovativeness and had only a modest effect on competitiveness. This is one of our more interesting findings. Most researchers view the ability to analyze and develop solutions to organizational problems as the most important component of organizational learning.[3] Simplemindedness is the disability that prevents effective analysis, so it should influence what many would argue is the core of the learning process. Yet our results indicate that barriers to this process do not reduce the ability of firms to develop innovative products and services.

What we discovered about the impact of homogeneity on business performance probably explains this unexpected finding. Homogeneity and simplemindedness are related but distinct disabilities. Homogeneity refers to a restriction in the variety of information and perspectives available to the organization. Simplemindedness concerns the *quality* of analysis, while homogeneity indicates the *quantity* of information present. In our worldwide survey, homogeneity had the strongest negative impact on innovativeness of any of the learning disabilities. This indicates that different perspectives are more important in developing and implementing solutions to organizational problems than the ability to analyze limited information well. For instance, Sitkin[4] found that firms which punish failures have restricted perspectives on cause-and-effect relationships. An acceptance of "intelligent" failures results in a much greater variety of information concerning such relationships. The bottom line is that sophisticated analytical systems that use limited information, or information from only one paradigm, won't produce effective results. As the old adage goes, "garbage in, garbage out."

Another one of our findings indicated on table 6.5 is perhaps even more provocative: homogeneity most significantly *increases* competitiveness. In other words, homogeneity is a double-edged sword. It often decreases innovativeness, but it may actually help with a firm's competitiveness. There are several possible reasons for this. Since homogeneity implies there's less organizational demand for multiple and conflicting sources of information, executives may focus more on implementation of decisions based on consistent sources of information. In some business situations, not having to wrestle with information generated from all over the map and under the sun may in fact help companies move faster. And there's another more practical reason for why homogeneity can positively influence the bottom line: when companies rely on homogeneous sources of information, executives can reduce the cost of acquiring a large variety of information and improve cycle time in decision making. Either reason can improve organizational competitiveness in the market, at least in the short term.

This finding presents a dilemma for corporations: is homogeneity a learning disability or an advantage? We don't have a simple answer to this question. However, we believe corporations may want to encourage varying degrees of homogeneity in different parts of their organizations. In R&D and marketing departments, homogeneity will probably hinder idea generation and look more like a learning disability. Given the complexity and rapid rate of change in today's global markets, senior executives should also take in and analyze as much information as possible. But production and middle to lower level employees will probably work more efficiently if they only have to contend with a few consistent sources of information. Other researchers have come to similar conclusions. For instance, Nonaka argues that the process of variety amplification, followed by reduction, is at the heart of Japanese approaches to organizational learning.[5]

The Learning Disabilities in Action

To illustrate how learning disabilities can influence the capacity of organizations to generate and generalize ideas with impact, we'll now focus on what specific companies have done with their learning problems. In the first case study, we'll revisit Samsung Electronics, our premier benchmarker, focusing on its successful efforts to combat organizational learning disabilities. The second case builds on our opening story about Midwestern Health, adding two other health care organizations that, unfortunately, displayed classic examples of learning disabilities once a change process had begun. We hope this contrast between a company that has few learning disabilities and those that have many will indicate why the final building block matters so much to business performance.

Samsung Electronics: Confronting Performance Shortfalls

As detailed in the last chapter, Samsung Electronics Company (SEC) has become highly successful in the last few decades. Yet despite its impressive business performance, in the early 1990s SEC completely revamped its production system along flexible manufacturing lines, largely through a sophisticated use of benchmarking. Here we focus on how SEC was able to overcome various learning disabilities to launch such a radical change.

How SEC Approached the Generation Disabilities   Since the company's microwave business was so profitable in the 1980s, it would have been easy for SEC to rest on its laurels and not pay much attention to the rapidly evolving competitive environment. Had it done so, SEC would have suffered from the all too common disability of blindness. Yet Samsung's strong cultural emphasis on meeting customer needs made SEC managers aware early on that the company was having difficulty responding to some customers' requests—namely, small and specialized orders on a just-in-time basis. These managers began delving into why Samsung Electronics could not profitably fill small and/or customized orders, and they discovered an outdated production system based on the traditional assembly line that required large production runs to be profitable. Clearly, Samsung was quite effective at preventing the disability of blindness. Even while SEC remained profitable, its cultural values emphasizing total satisfaction of customer needs made the company hypersensitive to the changing environment.

Once executives were aware of the problem, SEC went to great lengths to prevent homogeneity by deliberately fostering a variety of ideas and perspectives from which a solution could be drawn. To summarize, SEC acquired diverse knowledge about flexible manufacturing systems (FMS) through a variety of mechanisms, including analyzing competitors; study abroad in Europe, Japan, and the U.S.; "academic" research; and the transfer of knowledge from exemplars of FMS through joint ventures, buying, and trading. Learning was acquired from three continents, from competitors, and from various academic theories, so that not only a wealth of information was gathered but also many different paradigms were considered. In all, SEC is a corporate exemplar in creating variety and minimizing homogeneity.

Another way that SEC limited homogeneity was through tolerating failures. Top executives realized that when failures were punished, this stifled creativity and risk taking. The subsequent lenient treatment of failure, combined with generous rewards for success at SEC, resulted in a strong "go getter" attitude among employees. Managers, R&D researchers, and engineers want to take on "impossible" projects or projects that others think are impossible. Many employees have attributed the success SEC has had in developing products, especially when no one thought they could be done, to this enthusiasm for great challenges and the "can do" spirit of Korean workers. Failures, when they do occur, are treated as positive contributions in that they provide opportunities to learn. At Samsung Electronics, a failure is thoroughly analyzed by managers and employees to determine why it happened so that similar problems can be prevented in the future.

How SEC Handled the Generalization Disabilities   Employees originally involved in the monumental change to a flexible manufacturing system at the microwave plant are now leading teams in other plants with other product lines, again helping to generalize these ideas and minimizing diffusion deficiency. Compare this systematic approach with Midwestern Health's "invisible forces" and "inertia."

Paralysis at SEC has also been reduced by involving employees. When switchovers to other products occur on the line, it is SEC workers who break down and rebuild their stations. This differs substantially from the typical American practice, in which management decides on the switch; industrial engineers redesign the line; other engineers "build" the new line; and, finally, workers are trained for (or often just placed on) the new line. At Samsung Electronics, most of these steps have been eliminated by having the line workers themselves participate in the redesign analysis; they actually build the new stations themselves. This eliminates the need for training an employee to work on someone else's design, since the SEC worker is already the expert on her own station. And because workers have participated in the design, they are unlikely to resist the changes. The result is an organization that's leaner, more dynamic, and filled with experts at every level.

The methods used to acquire knowledge of flexible manufacturing were also used to help implement it. For example, through joint ventures and buying clout, managers, engineers, and supervisors from Japanese FMS plants were brought in to analyze SEC's early attempts. SEC also hired foreign technical assistants (primarily retired Japanese and U.S. managers and engineers) to provide assistance with the implementation. With their practical know-how, these outside experts were able to offer guidance with particularly difficult problems that might otherwise have resulted in paralysis.

As we've already noted, FMS was initially implemented only in the microwave plant. Now that it has proven successful, the lessons are being analyzed and spread to other areas of SEC. Much of the same process that the microwave plant went through in learning about FMS and then figuring out how to apply it to specific product lines is being repeated by other plants, such as Samsung's VCR facility. It is much easier for these others, however, since the knowledge is now internal to SEC. Indeed, the experience of its microwave plant has provided a blueprint for other plants.

All learning and problems are almost instantly documented, which has reduced both diffusion deficiency and superstitious learning. For example, every worker can shut down the whole line if a problem surfaces. At the head of each line are four clocks and four different colored lights that resemble police sirens. Each light and associated clock record the reason and the time the line is shut down. If a worker notices a quality problem, she shuts down the line by pulling one of the hanging levers that is located periodically along the line. For a quality problem, the red light flashes and a chime sounds. The light and chime can be heard all over the plant, and they signal the appropriate supervisor to come. The quality clock records the length of time the line was down due to this problem. Other sets of lights/clocks/chimes are for equipment failures, lack of materials, and temporary line shutdowns. The monitors display every type of problem so the appropriate supervisor can handle it; records of all types of problems are automatically made.

Let us reiterate that any employee can stop the line. Employees are even encouraged to stop it and are rewarded for stopping it. It's considered part of their job to search for and discover problems. In fact, if not enough problems are discovered over a given period of time, managers assume the system isn't working properly. Most problems are solved quickly by the worker or the worker and the supervisor together. More substantial problems are solved by teams of workers and managers, and the first hour or two of each shift is devoted to such team-based problem solving. Rapid documentation and problem solving reduce superstitious learning, which involves an inability to see correct cause-and-effect relationships. Since feedback and accurate information are generated instantaneously, cause-and-effect relationships are much clearer than they otherwise would be.

Samsung Electronics, then, successfully moved through each stage of organizational learning: idea generation, idea generalization, and identification of learning disabilities. More to the point of this case, SEC overcame such common disabilities as blindness, homogeneity, diffusion deficiency, paralysis, and superstitious learning, which explains its high organizational learning capability. All employees that we spoke with seemed to have a clear idea of what these disabilities were and spent a great deal of time trying to ensure that they didn't develop at SEC.

Here we have a company with the rare ability to generate and generalize ideas with impact; yet even with a strong market/clan culture and the commitment of top managers, the radical change to a new manufacturing system required enormous company resources and preparation. It's easy to see why so many other organizations falter when faced with learning disabilities. Rome wasn't built in a day; and as the next case shows, neither are most HMOs.

Health Care Systems: When Good Ideas Fall Apart

The trials and tribulations of Midwestern Health opened this chapter; now we'll present brief accounts of two other health care systems with similar problems. These two have been selected from a consortium of six health care systems with centers in Minneapolis, Seattle, Northern California, Columbus, Portland, and San Antonio. (Due to issues of confidentiality, we'll refer to the two organizations highlighted here only by city or region.) Each system was made up of several hospitals, HMOs, and/or other types of insurance providers; each was attempting to implement organizational learning to change its operations. One of us observed these efforts roughly a year after they had begun, as the following stories show.

Seattle Health   This organization was less successful than Midwestern Health, in generating new ideas and had several pronounced learning disabilities. Seattle Health's management recognized the great changes facing their industry, but that was hardly surprising given the national debate on health care going on at the time and the proliferation of HMOs with radically different approaches to health. As always, recognizing problems is the first step toward building learning capability. But when the rubber hit the road, Seattle Health had trouble developing solutions to their problems.

While Seattle Health did little benchmarking of competitors, it was quite adept at assessing the local environment. Each of its branches (distributed in major population centers throughout the state of Washington) had a "community team." These teams were made up of 9 to 15 individuals from the local community and other major stakeholder groups. A team typically consisted of five individuals who had been patients within the last year, a doctor, a primary care nurse, a representative from the business community, and an administrative staff manager. They were responsible for telling management what the community wanted in health care. Team members were unpaid but took their positions seriously and felt they were making a positive contribution. Seattle Health's management took the teams seriously as well, and relied on them as their primary source of information. Even though this method for assessing the environment was quite simple and didn't rely on sophisticated procedures, it worked remarkably well. For this organization, blindness was not the problem.

Unfortunately, while Seattle Health had an excellent ability to discover problems, other aspects of organizational learning were not so effective there. When the community teams informed management of specific problems with health care delivery or new programs they would like to see implemented, the decision about what to do with this information was the responsibility of only one senior manager at each branch. Seattle Health's hierarchical culture reinforced the notion that branch managers were the only legitimate source for developing solutions or new procedures. One branch manager even jokingly remarked that the community team had "the gall" to suggest a new procedure, "like they have any idea how to run a hospital." But when only one person, even an expert, is engaged in generating solutions, the variety of ideas and perspectives considered is greatly reduced. This is a good example of homogeneity wreaking havoc. Like a strangle hold, Seattle Health's culture, structure, and decision making practices severely restricted the range of ideas and perspectives that would even be considered, let alone acted on.

When a senior manager did develop a solution to a community team's "problem," the branches were fairly effective in implementing it. Unfortunately, the solutions tended to be of limited use and were often discarded after a trial period. For example, the senior manager at one branch read a glowing article in a popular magazine about self-managed work teams. This seemed to be a good idea, since staff motivation wasn't high and innovative ideas were few; self-managed teams were supposed to result in dramatic increases in both areas. When the manager presented the idea at a monthly staff meeting, it was warmly received. After all, who wouldn't want more control over their own job? Each new team was created with a mix of employees from different areas and according to a list of the "five core procedures" for team functioning, such as positive interdependence, personal responsibility and accountability, and interactive skills. However, within a week, there was chaos. Experts in their own field (like radiology) had a tough enough time consulting with secretaries to make decisions, but when it became clear that pay was determined partially by performance appraisals of peers and lower level colleagues, there was a revolt.

The problem here was that the senior manager used only one source of information, the magazine article, and so didn't realize how difficult it was to create self-managed teams and how much training was required for them to be effective. The situation was made worse because the solutions were generated by one individual, so that the number of perspectives that could be brought to bear in analyzing the problem and identifying possible solutions was limited. Ironically, this cycle reinforced the belief that having a really "sharp" branch head was the key; few people questioned the system itself or identified the learning disability—homogeneity—that had hindered generating ideas or generalizing them beyond a short time period.

Thus, Seattle Health made some headway with organizational learning, primarily in the realm of community-building and input; but it was not nearly as effective at generating new programs as it could have been.

Northern California Health In contrast, Northern California Health could generate and implement ideas quite successfully, but it was weak when it came to generalizing them across the organization. This system had a charismatic CEO and a strong top management team that mobilized employees to create a learning organization. These managers kept close touch with the latest market changes through actively benchmarking health care exemplars and forming cooperative learning systems with them, such as joining a consortium of health care systems to exchange knowledge and foster research. They also instituted a "participative restructuring" process that helped develop and implement new procedures through the use of employee teams. These teams adapted general restructuring principles to their specific units.

This all sounds both practical and well focused, so where did Northern California Health fall down? For one thing, the organization didn't keep records of its solutions and changes, which resulted in a great deal of learning being continually lost or needlessly repeated—in other words, this organization suffered from diffusion deficiency. The only records were in people's heads, so turnover disrupted continuity.

For another, Northern California Health had no formal structures for diffusing learning across the organization. One local hospital, for instance, attempted to implement a captivated care system in which payments were on a per-person basis as opposed to the traditional fee-for-service basis. This was a significant change that affected nearly all aspects of the hospital's functioning and had all sorts of unanticipated consequences. Six months later, the head administrator found out that the crosstown affiliate had implemented a similar system successfully, but these results had not been diffused throughout the organization. Had the learning from the affiliate been diffused to the local hospital undergoing the change, that hospital would have been warned of potential costly problems. And it would not have had to repeat the same mistakes the affiliate wrestled with.

In other words, this health care system had trouble generalizing its good ideas and efforts. While Northern California Health made progress through the use of employee teams and specific initiatives, it failed to transfer this knowledge of best practices and processes throughout the organization.

The Upshot: How Companies Overcome Learning Disabilities

As the struggles of these health care systems indicate, the presence of even one disability can be enough to reduce substantially, and often block completely, overall learning. Our survey research shows that learning disabilities have a major impact on business performance and are related to business strategies, business cultures, and national origin. While Samsung Electronics successfully circumvented the learning disabilities inherent in its out-of-date competitive situation and organizational structure, Midwestern Health, Seattle Health, and Northern California Health all had a tougher time with generating or generalizing ideas with impact.

Based on our survey results, companies should be concerned with all the disabilities. But homogeneity, in particular, may be tough to modulate. The importance of having a requisite variety of ideas on tap is often overlooked by managers, even if homogeneity had the strongest negative impact on innovativeness in our worldwide survey. At the same time, homogeneity may positively affect competitiveness, especially in business situations where consistent sources of information help a company take action.

In general, companies with high learning capability will continually scan the external environment, picking up long-term threats and new opportunities before the competition; yet they will also coordinate actions between different groups, increasing communication and idea sharing. Such organizations typically focus on product differentiation strategy with strong clan and market cultures. Here's a summary of what the survey and case studies reveal about learning disabilities:

- There are seven basic learning disabilities: environmental blindness, simplemindedness, homogeneity, tight coupling, paralysis, superstitious learning, and diffusion deficiency.
- Of these seven disabilities, the first four affect idea generation and the latter three influence idea generalization.
- The presence of only one or two of the learning disabilities can block organizational learning.
- Lack of variety and quantity of ideas in an organization (homo-

geneity) has much more of a negative impact on business performance than unsophisticated analytical procedures (simplemindedness).

- Firms with product differentiation strategy appear to be better at minimizing the disabilities than firms with cost competitiveness strategy.
- Strong clan and market cultures are most effective in reducing learning disabilities; adhocracy cultures are strong in combating environmental blindness but prone to suffer many other disabilities; hierarchical cultures are hindered by superstitious learning, homogeneity, and paralysis.
- Strong market/clan culture, top management commitment, and employee involvement—when done well—can overcome most disabilities (Samsung Electronics).
- Homogeneity can become a real problem if idea generation is only limited to one or a few managers (Seattle Health).
- Companies suffer from diffusion deficiency when they don't rapidly and systematically document new procedures and solutions (Northern California Health).

In the next chapter, we'll extend these findings by outlining what managers can do to improve learning capability in their organizations. Both our survey research and our case studies indicate why most organizations combine learning styles, and how the complexities of any business environment shape a company's particular learning profile. Now we'll lay out some practical steps for how learning architects— the many managers and HR staff concerned with improving company operations—can create a blueprint for organizational learning.

CHAPTER SEVEN

Building Organizational Learning Capability

A Blueprint for Learning Architects

Consider the following scenario.

You are a member of your company's top management team. Performance indicators suggest that the firm's sales performance in your home country is softening due to market maturity and stiff competition from overseas competitors. After years of downsizing and cost-cutting efforts, it's clear the company can only grow by increasing its presence in emerging markets like China and India. Active participation in these emerging economies could help the company gain access to huge and rapidly growing markets in Asia, establish low-cost manufacturing bases, and serve existing customers globally.

Unfortunately, when several of your company's businesses started to establish manufacturing and sales operations through strategic alliances and wholly owned subsidiaries in China and India, they met with various degrees of success. While some found the right partners and negotiated the appropriate terms of cooperation, others ran into difficulty right from the beginning. Moreover, even though it isn't difficult to build state-of-the-art manufacturing facilities in China and India, transferring the management and technical know-how necessary to run these facilities from your home country has been quite challenging.

Your top management team has taken at least one crucial step: it has recognized that the company needs to develop its learning capability to support global growth. You understand that it's imperative for the company to learn in the shortest possible time to operate effectively in these emerging economies, where the rules of the game are radically different from those in your home country. You know that different businesses must capture and share their experiences in order to avoid making costly mistakes over and over again. Your company must also transfer its management and technical know-how from the home country to these new operations. Your managerial challenge is how to make this happen.

This globalization scenario is one of many familiar situations in which top executives recognize that learning capability is critical to implementing their company's business strategy, yet they still wrestle with the very real difficulties of creating a true learning organization. Other common learning scenarios arise when companies try to achieve a breakthrough in productivity improvement, cycle-time reduction, customer service, technological innovation, or the creation of new business opportunities.

Our work to date, including empirical research, case studies, and consulting insights, all addresses one overall question: How can companies build organizational learning capability—the capacity to generate and generalize ideas with impact, across multiple boundaries, through specific management initiatives? The ultimate test of our ability to answer this question, of course, is the extent to which we can add value to management practice. We believe, along with many others, that building organizational learning capability will become ever more crucial to companies in the evolving global economy, but that doesn't mean the process is easy, or that creating a learning organization will be a snap once top managers "get it." As earlier chapters have emphasized, there's a lot of talk about "learning" and "culture change" in the current business arena, but few executives go beyond enthusiastic speeches. If nothing else, the last chapter on learning disabilities demonstrates why even good companies suffer from them, and how hard they are to overcome.

In this chapter, we get down to specifics, drawing on the work presented thus far to help managers approach the real challenges of building organizational learning capability. Here we offer a practicum for the learning architects of any company, all those with the authority, expertise, and potential to make the many changes necessary. Even if you're a forceful CEO, you'll need more than vague promises and value statements; you'll need a blueprint of specific actions that includes a sequence for how to proceed.

True learning organizations, such as 3M, Samsung Electronics, Matsushita, HP, or Motorola, explicitly or implicitly include all three building blocks in their blueprints: (1) generating ideas; (2) generalizing ideas; and (3) identifying learning disabilities. These companies have particular business strategies, cultures, and competitive contexts, but high learning capability still comes down to the ability to generate and generalize ideas with impact, or $g \times g$. Based on this, the following four-step process should help managers to assess the current learning capability of their organizations and to formulate action plans to enhance it. The four steps are

> *Step 1.* Assess the need for learning capability: Why should we focus on learning capability?
>
> *Step 2.* Audit existing and future learning capability: How well do we currently learn?
>
> *Step 3.* Identify management choices for improving learning capability: What should we do?
>
> *Step 4.* Implement actions for building learning capability: How do we make it happen?

The rest of this chapter details the four steps and presents worksheets to help executives or management teams begin the process. To help illustrate what a real company might do, we'll discuss General Electric's learning progress at many of the steps. As consultants, we have gone through these steps with a number of other companies—AlliedSignal, AT&T, Boeing, Banc One, BellSouth, Canada Life, Champion, Columbia Gas, Coca-Cola, Hallmark, Harley-Davidson, Honeywell, General Electric, Lucent, Marriott, Motorola, Praxair, Rockwell, Royal Bank, Sony, Southern Company, TRW, Union Carbide, and *USA Today*—and our experience with this process has been positive. Managers who had previously considered the "learning organization" a set of abstract ideals have been able to translate these ideals into actions.

For example, Lucent, a spin-off of AT&T that produces the components and technology required for the telecommunications industry, focused its learning efforts on "breakthrough" projects rather than skills training. By going through the four-step process, Lucent managers found that when they dedicated a team of individuals to a specific business problem, such as doing business in India, they not only generated innovative solutions but also were able to use them. The key action taken here was that the teams usually included managers who were accountable for implementing team recommendations.

A dynamic CEO like GE's Jack Welch is generally the sponsor and prime mover behind a true learning organization. Yet the day-to-day learning champion in a company is often somebody explicitly charged with responsibility for making learning happen. Indeed, General Electric was the first company to have a "chief learning officer" or CLO, a special position dedicated to designing and delivering training and to shaping GE's learning culture. Since then, many firms have defined chief learning officers as those individuals who integrate business, learning, and change. They are responsible for making the case for learning, for building learning processes, and for making learning a reality.

Of course not every firm has taken this tack, let alone hired a CLO. We fully acknowledge that building learning capability is a difficult task, especially if you're a middle manager or HR director in a company that hasn't really embraced learning as an explicit goal or cultural value. But completing even a few of the worksheets here will help managers get their feet wet and perhaps lead to an increased organizational commitment to change.

Step 1. Assess the Need for Learning Capability

We believe that building learning capability will help any company. Yet it's also true that this capability is more important to some business strategies than to others. Before an organization jumps onto the bandwagon of organizational learning, its managers need to answer two basic questions:

1. Why Is Learning Capability Critical to Business Success?

During this first assessment step, executives should look long and hard at whether the resource commitment required for increasing learning capability will bring real benefits to the company. Subsidiary questions that managers should discuss are these: Is learning capability aligned with our strategy? Will the strategic direction we have taken be more likely to happen with the building of learning capability? Is learning capability central to our customer requirements? Will it help us serve customers better and faster? Is learning capability likely to differentiate us from competitors? Is learning capability likely to have financial impact? Will it meet the economic criteria we use to make investment decisions?

Worksheet 7.1 provides a quick diagnostic tool for creating a dialogue among senior executives. In fact, an open and honest discussion of these issues is critical to the development of a learning agenda. Unless the top management team is emotionally and intellectually committed to the building of learning capability, it will just become another fad of the month.

At GE, Jack Welch believes in learning as a means for competitive differentiation: "GE is unique in that it is . . . a very large, multi-business company with a learning culture that has transformed the diversity of its businesses and its size—from what is sometimes perceived as a handicap—into a tremendous competitive advantage. GE is a widely diverse array of 250 business segments. . . . What sets it apart is a culture that uses this wide diversity as a limitless source of learning opportunities, a storehouse of ideas whose breadth and richness is unmatched in world business. At the heart of this culture is an understanding that an organization's ability to learn, and translate that learning into action rapidly, is the ultimate competitive business advantage."[1] Indeed, the openness of GE employees to new ideas from any source is important to its emphasis on speed, six-sigma quality, and agility.

2. What Are the Critical Ideas We Need to Generate and Generalize?

The answer to this question should help pinpoint the specific areas of learning that are critical to business competitiveness. Subsidiary questions that managers should discuss are these: Which ideas should be generated and generalized quickly in order to maintain the competitive edge of our company? Are these ideas related to new ways of doing businesses in emerging economies? Are they related to product innovation? To new ways of serving and delighting customers? To new technological breakthroughs? Will these ideas affect the speed of new product introduction (cycle time)?

GE's learning focus evolved over time. Starting with its WorkOut program in the late 1980s, GE emphasized ideas from employees that reduced bureaucracy. Then it looked outside the company, focusing on best processes and practices that are being deployed by some best-in-class companies. Later still, it has focused on process improvement, change acceleration, six key strategic initiatives, and, most recently, six-sigma quality. Clearly, GE has built its learning capability with specific initiatives through a phased implementation approach. If managers don't identify specific critical learning areas that are central to business competitiveness, their companies may confuse employees with a wide range of uncoordinated initiatives.

Step 2. Audit Existing and Future Learning Capability

Once the strategic focus of learning capability is determined, managers can proceed to auditing existing and future learning capability by answering the following three sets of questions. Note that the auditing step accounts for all three building blocks of learning capability.

1. *Auditing Idea Generation Capability (Worksheet 7.2)*
   Current effectiveness: How well do we generate new ideas in the critical learning areas through experimentation, competency acquisition, benchmarking, and continuous improvement?
   Required effectiveness: In order to accomplish our business strategy, how well should we generate new ideas in the critical learning areas through experimentation, benchmarking, continuous improvement, and competency acquisition?
   Gap analysis: What are some areas where we could improve in the four learning styles?

2. *Auditing Idea Generalization Capability (Worksheet 7.3)*
   Current effectiveness: How well do we generalize new ideas in the critical learning areas across time and across vertical, horizontal, external, and geographic boundaries?
   Required effectiveness: In order to accomplish our business strategy, how well should we generalize new ideas in the critical learning areas across time and across vertical, horizontal, external, and geographic boundaries?
   Gap analysis: What are some areas where we could improve vis-à-vis the five boundaries?

3. *Auditing Organizational Learning Disabilities (Worksheet 7.4)*
   Current effectiveness: How seriously do we suffer from each of the key learning disabilities?
   Required effectiveness: In order to accomplish our business strategies, how much do we need to reduce our learning disabilities?
   Gap analysis: What are some areas where we could improve for each of the seven learning disabilities?

If a company is serious about building learning capability, this process must first be conducted by the senior management team. But the same audit can also be conducted at various levels and units within an organization to add to the pool of information about what learning currently looks like and how it might evolve in the future. By getting honest thoughts and reactions down on paper, Worksheets 7.2, 7.3, and 7.4 should help managers assess an organization's ability to generate and generalize new ideas with impact. Note that the goal of this audit should be firm answers to the questions above, including the $g \times g$ and other scores derived from the worksheets.

1. *Our organization's current learning capability:* This score is calculated by multiplying the current effectiveness scores in idea generation capability (column 2 in Worksheet 7.2) and idea generalization capability (column 2 in Worksheet 7.3).

2. *The learning capability we require in the next 5 to 10 years:* This score is calculated by multiplying the required effectiveness scores in idea generation capability (column 3 in Worksheet 7.2) and idea generalization capability (column 3 in Worksheet 7.3).

3. *Key leverage areas for improving learning capability:* These can be compiled from the "Areas of improvement" columns on the worksheets. After the audit, you should have a clear sense of whether idea generation or generalization needs to be improved, which learning styles could be strengthened, and which organizational boundaries require better management to facilitate learning. Since most firms have limited resources and time, we suggest identifying only two or three key leverage areas.

4. *Key learning disabilities that hinder learning within our organization:* Worksheet 2C should help to uncover these. But even with the worksheet to stimulate discussion, identifying learning disabilities in any organization is never easy. It often involves direct observation and honest discussion of problems. You may need to call in outsiders to help with this part of the audit, either consultants or staff members outside your organization.

Step 3. Identify Management Choices for Improving Learning Capability

Once managers understand where organizations should focus their resources, the next step is to formulate some actions that address the identified gaps and learning disabilities. Here's where our "learning architecture" may help guide companies.[2] It provides a systematic and holistic approach to the choices managers can make to improve learning capability.

Many models of organizations exist that provide an architecture for organizational assessment and improvement, such as the 7-S model (Phillips and Kennedy), organizational alignment (Nadler and Tushman), and the star model (Galbraith).[3] Each model highlights management choices for changing organizations. The 7-S model, for instance, suggests that seven components in an organization (strategy, structure, system, style, shared values, skills, and superordinate goals) need to be aligned and integrated. In an organization that works effectively, the theory goes, change in any one component will result in a change in the other systems. When a business strategy changes—say, top managers decide to focus more on cost—other organizational systems will need to adapt. You can also think of organizational alignment as the equivalent of adjusting TV color knobs. A change in any one color dimension must be balanced by a change in the others for the overall color to be picture-perfect.

For our purposes, the learning architecture shows general areas for change in any company, and how these areas are aligned with one another. By applying this framework to a specific firm, executives can begin developing a blueprint of their own that identifies appropriate management choices.

Elements of a Learning Architecture

The architecture we use for assessing learning capability is presented in table 7.1. The framework is divided into three general parts. First, culture provides the organizational "ceiling"—the overarching values within a firm that link management practices and business strategy. Next, four "pillars" represent four critical areas—competence, consequence, governance, and capacity to change—that an organization must develop in order to live its culture and execute strategy. Finally, leadership has to be the foundation of the firm. How leaders spend time, focus attention, and share responsibility for action is the bedrock on which any learning architecture is built. On this basis, let's consider in more detail six domains of management action that affect learning capability.

Culture   A number of researchers and theorists have defined business culture as the shared values within a firm.[4] As we've discussed in other chapters, you can also think of culture as a company's mind-set, represented by what employees inside the organization and stakeholders outside it (suppliers, customers, competitors) believe about the organization as a whole. Key cultural values range from an emphasis on customer service, quality, or cost to "We believe in social responsibility" or "We are the hottest hackers in our field." If top management wants to build learning capability, however, a commitment to learning has to be central to a company's mind-set. And to ensure that learning capability is a central part of the organization's culture, management practices that are directly linked to creating, sustaining, or changing a culture in general may be applied to creating a culture focused on learning capability in particular. Of course, when learning is emphasized, a "one size fits all" approach won't work. Managers who want

Table 7.1 Building a Learning Capability: A Management Architecture
Management Practices to Generate and Generalize Ideas

CULTURE			
To what extent is our culture/mind-set focused on learning?			
COMPETENCE	CONSEQUENCE	GOVERNANCE	CAPACITY FOR CHANGE
To what extent do we have individual, team, and organizational competencies for learning?	To what extent does our performance management system encourage learning for individuals, teams, and processes?	To what extent do our organization structure and communication processes encourage learning?	THROUGH WORK PROCESS & SYSTEMS To what extent do our work process and systems encourage learning?
STAFFING	APPRAISAL	ORGANIZATION DESIGN	CHANGE INITIATIVES
TRAINING/DEVELOPMENT	REWARDS	COMMUNICATION	WORK PROCESS & SYSTEMS
LEADERSHIP			
To what extent do leaders throughout the organization demonstrate a commitment to learning?			

to create a learning culture should encourage individual workers to learn from one another, and they might try the following practices:

- Welcoming inquiry and analysis of all decisions
- Supporting failures that are the result of overreach
- Encouraging a norm of reciprocity
- Building dialogue into the organizational decision making process
- Believing that better solutions always exist

The slogan for GE's learning culture, for example, is "Finding a Better Way Every Day." This translates into a set of core values that directly encourage learning. In more practical terms, GE leaders are measured, trained, and rewarded if they "are open to ideas from anywhere," "have the self-confidence to involve everyone and behave in a boundaryless fashion," "have a passion for excellence and hate bureaucracy," and "see change as opportunity not threat."

Competence   This term has been widely used in the past few years.[5] In its original meaning, competence represents the knowledge, skill, and abilities of individuals or teams within the organization. Needless to say, if learning capability is an important goal of management, then competencies must be acquired or developed that foster learning. Such competencies might include inquiry, reflection, systems thinking, mental modeling, conflict management, ability to make data-based recommendations, networking, risk taking, creativity, or tolerance for ambiguity. As we've discussed earlier, ensuring that these competencies reside in individuals and teams comes through staffing and development systems that buy and/or build them. Indeed, competency acquisition is one of the most popular and effective learning styles; and by moving people around an organization through cross-training, ideas in one unit can be generalized to others. Rather than randomly building competence by hiring "good" people, managers committed to learning capability systematically build *learning* competencies. Specific actions managers might take to build learning competencies include these:

- Instituting job rotations and assignments across divisions
- Hiring outsiders with new ideas into key positions
- Hiring and/or promoting people who are known as learners and who have demonstrated a capacity to learn
- Removing nonlearners from key positions and telling people about it
- Building training programs to share best practices and requiring all to attend ongoing education experiences

- Using a "postmortem" format to learn from experience: what did you learn? What will you do differently as a result?

General Electric has systematically built employee competence in learning through both classroom training in Crotonville (GE's corporate university) and ongoing opportunities to participate in WorkOut sessions or other project teams to improve processes. All these opportunities help employees to learn and share with each other in finding better solutions in daily business operations. Specifically, Crotonville is renowned for courses that disseminate best practices and facilitate change. In addition, based on a clear set of leadership competencies, only GE leaders who demonstrate learning capability are promoted or retained.

Consequences   People generally act out of self-interest. Given a choice, they'll generally spend more energy on activities that result in favorable outcomes rather than no outcome or an unfavorable outcome. Establishing consequences for good and bad behavior simply means that when good behavior is exhibited, good things happen (a raise, company-wide recognition, a pat on the back); when bad behavior is exhibited, bad things happen (a demotion, a dressing-down). To ensure the right consequences for learning capability, managers need to do two things. First, they should identify the behaviors that are consistent with learning, such as generating new ideas, sharing them with others, and collaborating effectively in a team. Second, they must design effective consequences.

To have any impact, consequences must be instilled throughout the organization via the performance management system. Performance management systems set standards (for individuals and/or teams) through performance appraisals. When these standards are met, the reward system ensures positive financial and psychic outcomes, which reinforce the value of the standard; but when they aren't met, the system corrects and disciplines employees. Once again, managers who want to build learning capability must link reward systems to specific learning behaviors. They might try the following practices:

- Changing performance appraisals to include learning actions and outcomes
- Using multiple stakeholders for appraisal (such as peers, subordinates, or customers)
- Rewarding good postmortems of mistakes and successes
- Rewarding people for sharing ideas and best practices with others

- Giving special recognition awards to managers who anticipate competency needs and learning strategies
- Encouraging and rewarding experimentation
- Tying the bonus/incentive system to learning
- Holding people accountable but not punishing mistakes

When Jack Welch fired five senior executives in 1993, he sent a powerful message to all employees: achieving the numbers cannot guarantee a job or future success at General Electric. GE leaders and employees must walk the talk, practicing good learning behaviors in everyday activities. A "360-degree assessment" takes into account such leadership behavior, and the result of this assessment affects not only an individual's development plan but also his or her future career opportunities at GE.

Governance   Governance involves how the organization is structured, decisions are made, and information is shared. In fact, these three management "decision points" indicate how behavior is governed within an organization. To build a governance system that encourages learning capability, therefore, the organization's structure, decision-making processes, and information systems need to encourage the generation and generalization of ideas with impact. Note that traditional hierarchical organizations may impair learning, while "virtual" team organizations can support and sustain it.[6] Learning architects should bear in mind that more fluid organizational structures generally reinforce sharing rather than stockpiling of ideas. Managers can take the following specific actions to improve learning through governance:

- Building a boundaryless organization with no respect for divisional barriers
- Building a network organization that is fluid, flexible, and adaptive;
- Using ad hoc cross-functional teams
- Establishing centers of excellence, with job rotation in and out of a center
- Working with subcontractors, suppliers, and other outsiders in a fluid, informal fashion
- Creating an organizational learning campaign that emphasizes how learning is different from but linked to training and education
- Publishing learning dysfunctions openly
- Allowing information to skip levels rather than move hierarchically
- Encouraging external benchmarking and communication
- Sharing information and successes throughout the organization

GE, for instance, has used councils extensively to share best practices and learning, communicate new developments, identify cross-business and cross-regional opportunities, and drive functional and corporate initiatives. Such councils started from the very top and have moved all the way down to regional and business levels. As described by Welch:

> Every quarter, about 30 of us hold a 48-hour meeting in Crotonville. Each person—the Network president, the Power Systems president—gets up and talks about generic ideas. When we leave there after 48 hours, we may not be the smartest people in the world, but we are the most knowledgeable at that moment because we have been exposed to all these relevant topics. What's happening in China? What's happening in this business or that business? For 48 hours people share ideas, all knowing that everything counts towards the whole.[7]

Capacity for Change through Work Systems and Processes   The ways in which work is allocated and accomplished may encourage learning. Even more important, designing and structuring these work systems can continuously reinforce an organization's overall capacity for change. Involving customers in work decisions, rejecting bad clients, and forming alliances with "idea places" are all examples of how work can encourage learning. Companies with higher capacity for change are more likely to innovate, to do effective project or program management, and to be seen as "doers." Creating capacity for change requires the discipline of turning managers' knowledge about how to change into how work is actually done. As such, they might take these specific actions:

- Involving customers in the design and development of products
- Accepting product challenges that cannot yet be performed, demanding a stretch from workers
- Building more flexible and current information systems
- Establishing a physical setting that encourages sharing

GE has created various forums and vehicles through which new learning can be generated. Its WorkOut program has allowed employees to think creatively in a safe environment without being concerned about the attitudes of those higher up in the hierarchy. General Electric has also used WorkOut to create a vehicle to learn from key suppliers and customers in improving the value-chain partnership. Welch has attributed GE's learning culture and the appetite for ideas to WorkOut, which allowed the company and employees to see the power of learning. In addition, GE uses what it calls Corporate

Audit, Corporate Business Development (an internal management consultant), its Corporate Training Institute (Crotonville), and Corporate R&D to capture good ideas that are scattered around the company and to serve as catalysts for change for other businesses and regions.

Generalization of ideas across boundaries can be observed in other ways at General Electric. Welch notes:

> Our Medical Systems business, for instance, is a world leader in remote diagnostics, which means an installed GE CT scanner can be remotely monitored by our service people as it operates in a hospital. They can detect and repair an impending malfunction, sometimes on-line, sometimes before the customer even perceives there is a problem. Medical Systems has shared this technology with our jet engine business, with locomotives, with Motors and Industrial Systems, and with Power Systems, enabling them to monitor the performance of jet engines in flight, of locomotives pulling freight, of running paper mills, and of turbines in operation in customer power plants. This is one of the capabilities that give us the opportunity to create a multi-billion dollar service business by upgrading the installed GE equipment operating around the world.[8]

Leadership   Last but not least, as most authors who discuss learning organizations point out, leaders are critical to building learning capability.[9] The ultimate test of learning capability is the extent to which leaders demonstrate through their actions a commitment to generating and generalizing ideas. Leaders who pay attention to learning, value it, spend time learning themselves, and encourage others to do the same will communicate the importance of building a learning organization. In fact, an organization's culture often reflects the personality of its leaders: consider GE, Samsung, Motorola, Lucent, HP, and 3M. Still, many company leaders can engage in activities that model the act of learning itself, which will help build learning capability beyond their personal commitment. These leaders might try

- Coaching other managers and employees
- Facilitating meetings and disputes
- Teaching special seminars on their areas of expertise
- Communicating a vision
- Walking the talk: asking questions, reading new materials, attending executive training, spending time on learning

Jack Welch personally commits himself to attending Crotonville seminars every month to discuss and debate with new managers at GE. Welch also urges every manager and employee to look at business as it is—not as what they hope it is. As we've already noted, GE managers cannot succeed without demonstrating the leadership behaviors that demonstrate learning in a boundaryless fashion. At this exemplary company, candor and reality testing at the highest levels form the foundation of learning.

If you've noticed some common themes in these six learning domains, you're on target. Many of the specific actions managers can take to improve organizational learning involve rewarding the right behaviors—experimentation, idea sharing, teamwork, and competency acquisition—and communicating to everyone what learning means and when it happens, openly addressing an organization's problems and building the commitment of top management. Our learning architecture distinguishes between these domains to demonstrate the many areas that learning encompasses in a company, but an individual blueprint for change will certainly include management actions that affect more than one domain and cross plenty of organizational boundaries.

More Specifics: Identifying Your Management Choices

With the learning architecture firmly in mind, managers create their own blueprints by identifying actions to take within the six domains. To help with this somewhat daunting task, we have compiled over a hundred specific management activities that can be used to improve learning capability (see table 7.2). This list includes some of the possibilities already suggested and has been taken from the literature on learning organizations, from our case studies of Samsung, HP, Motorola, 3M, and Alcatel Bell, from additional research we've conducted with other companies, and from our worldwide survey. While these aren't the only management actions that can improve learning capability, we're confident that table 7.2 includes a majority of what has been identified and used in many companies.

When consulting with various firms, we've used the extensive list of activities in two ways. First, we ask managers to identify two or three management actions in each of the six domains that they could implement in their organizations, thereby addressing the areas of possible improvement already uncovered during the audit step. These items are then written down in the appropriate slots on worksheet 7.5. Managers, working individually or in teams, generally find it helpful to have a list of specific choices in front of them. In our experience, they then implicitly (or explicitly) rate their own behavior for each of the hundred actions. In fact, many learn by going through this exercise that they're already engaging in some of the actions. The exer-

Focus

I. Culture: *To what extent is our culture/mind-set focused on learning?*

Building a learning culture
We often:
Maintain a bias toward action.
Value dialogue more than discussion.
Make learning part of cultural values.
Welcome open inquiry and self-analysis.
Are as playful as well as have a serious approach to the work endeavor
(work is fun).
Perceive any change as an opportunity, not a threat.
Encourage the capacity to be continually aware of internal processes and
the external environment.
Anticipate future demands rather than rest on past successes.
Maintain a long-term focus.
Ensure trust.
Believe that knowledge is more important than job title.
Have a shared culture.
Encourage the norm of reciprocity.
Build a shared vision throughout the organization.
Have customers participate in the shared mind-set or vision of the
company.
Ensure that a commitment to learning is in all formal strategic documents.

II. Competency: *To what extent do we have individual, team, and
organizational competencies for learning?*

Staffing: Ensuring the right people are hired in, promoted through, and moved
out of the organization.
We often:
Hire outside expert.
Look to acquire new competencies.
Hire and promote curious chiefs.
Seek fresh blood (from universities, oddball places).
Follow the whims of the stars (but insist that the stars, like all mortals,
engage in the sharing norm).
Formally recognize learning (Director of Knowledge Management at
McKinsey).
Hire people who are known as learners and who have demonstrated a
capacity to learn. Learning competencies include inquiry, reflection,
systems thinking, mental modeling, conflict management, disciplined
postmortem process, ability to make data-based recommendations,
networking.
Outplace nonlearners and tell people about it.
Promote learners, both in the hierarchy and in public recognition events.
Ensure personal mastery in all employees, i.e., a commitment to learning.

Table 7.2 (*continued*)

Focus

Leave people in jobs long enough to demonstrate learning.
Find candidates for every position from many sources.
Put people who have different backgrounds into management positions.

Training: Building learning competencies through training
We often:
Attend as teams rather than as individuals and focus on learning application rather than just knowledge acquisition.
Invest heavily in ongoing education at all levels of the organization.
Build the skill of conceptualizing and building core competencies.
Involve customers in all aspects of training.
Share ownership of training with line and HR.
Guarantee that training stretches participants, both intellectually and practically.
Use training forums to challenge work assumptions and processes.
Require systems training for all employees.
Teach skills in dealing with problems from a systems point of view to all.

Development: Developing learning competencies through real-life experience
We often:
Use postmortem format to learn from experience. What did you learn? What will you do differently as a result?
Sanction cross-functional moves.
Support learning sabbaticals.
Rotate people, allow people to move more or less as they wish, find their own way.
Encourage innovative job assignments (e.g., start up, turnaround, etc.).
Participate in task forces.
Practice external job sharing.
Assign people to special projects.
Have on-the-job apprenticeships.
Ensure that every person has a learning plan.

III. *Consequence: To what extent does our performance management system encourage learning for individuals, teams, and processes?*

Performance appraisal and rewards systems: Ensuring standards, consequences, and accountability for learning
We often:
Change performance appraisal to include Learning Actions and Outcomes.
Use peer and subordinate appraisal.
Reward for good postmortems of mistakes and successes.
Give special recognition awards to managers who anticipate competency needs and learning strategies.
Encourage and reward experimentation.
Use group and individual rewards. *(continued)*

Table 7.2   (*continued*)

Focus

Tie bonus/incentive system to learning.

Rely on multiple appraisers.

Try to create automatic ongoing measurement at all levels in critical performance areas.

Reinforce subjective evaluation that takes "rewards" for learning/sharing into account.

Use customers for appraisal and rewards.

Measure learning and innovation at all levels in organization.

Share widely the results of operational and financial metrics.

Hold people accountable, but do not punish mistakes.

IV. **Governance:** *To what extent does our organization structure and communication processes encourage learning?*

Organization design: Structuring work and process to facilitate learning
We often:

Encourage team learning: make sure people can work together in teams through dialogue not discussion.

Ensure a fluid (boundaryless) organization with no respect for divisional barriers.

Have a simple structure.

Build a network organization.

Ensure that the organization is fluid, flexible, adaptive.

Focus less on chain of command and more on learning.

Use ad hoc teams.

Establish centers of excellence.

Work with subcontractor/supplier and other outsiders in a routine/fluid, informal fashion.

Endorse cross-functional teams.

Communication: Openly and frequently share information to accelerate learning
We often:

Have easy communication, great informality.

Create an organization learning campaign showing how learning is different from but linked to training and education.

Publish learning dysfunctions openly.

Have an open flow of information.

Have lots of informal/face-to-face meetings.

Have a skip-level/not hierarchical structure.

Sponsor sensing meetings from below.

Encourage external benchmarking and communication.

Share information and successes.

V. **Capacity for change through work process and systems:** *To what extent does our work process and systems encourage learning?*

Table 7.2   (*continued*)

Focus

Work process: Instilling learning into management process
We often:
Commit to continuous improvement.
Reengineer all work processes.
Experiment widely.
Participate with management and employees on all business activities.
Involve customer in design and development of products.

Capacity for change: Creating catalysts for learning and improvement
We often:
Accept product challenges that we cannot yet perform—demand a stretch.
Reject business you can't learn from.
Walk away from bad clients.
Build more flexible and current information systems.
Establish a physical setting that encourages sharing.
Tie with "idea places" such as universities.
Are excellent at something functional.

VI. *Leadership:* *To what extent do leaders throughout organization demonstrate a commitment to learning?*

Leadership: Having leaders who encourage learning
We often:
Teach leaders to coach.
Have leaders who are expert.
Give leaders cross-functional experiences.
Teach leaders to facilitate.
Encourage leaders to be designers.
Have leaders who teach.
Have leaders with vision.
Walk the talk: spend time on learning.
Focus on a few key issues and actions.
Continue to learn: are open to new ideas.
Empower others and inspire commitment.
Enable others to be successful.

cise both confirms how well they're doing and informs them of what they could be doing better in the realm of organizational learning. The result is that each cell of worksheet 7.5 will contain at least two new management ideas. The worksheet becomes not only a useful blueprint but a living document on the ways to improve learning capability.

Second, we've observed that many managers feel that even the eight to 12 ideas listed on worksheet 7.5 are overwhelming and difficult to accomplish. So we ask them (or their teams) to prioritize their ideas into a learning capability plan on Worksheet 7.6. Priorities may be set in terms of timing (what should be done first, second, third, and so on), ease of implementation (which one is easiest to accomplish?), or the resources available (the level of resource availability to each idea). The bottom half of this worksheet represents the support needed to accomplish the learning improvement effort.

Our approach assumes that, in most companies, it really is hard to work on eight to 12 management initiatives simultaneously; it makes more sense to sequence or layer the actions. Making progress on change through layering has received recent attention in the strategy[10] and organization[11] literature. Various researchers believe that change is more likely to happen when success creates success, and this matches our own work.

The reason for specifying management actions in sequence, then, is that early successes (accomplishing the first layers of worksheet 7.6) may lead to ongoing success (the other layers). A company's blueprint for learning includes not only a list of new management practices but also a plan for how and when each of these practices will be implemented.

Step 4. Implement Actions for Building Learning Capability

And that brings us to the final step of the process. After management priorities have been identified, implementation can begin. For step 4, we've found that it's important to establish certain keys or processes for each priority, such as who will be responsible for the implementation, how it will become institutionalized, and how its impact will be measured. Once again, the more specific managers can be about the actions they will take, the more real-world value a learning blueprint has.

Worksheet 7.7 shows seven keys for a management priority.[12] These keys will vary depending on the breadth and complexity of an initiative. A simple action—say, "put a commitment to learning into the business strategy"—requires fewer of the keys than a more complex recommendation like "attend all training events in cross-functional teams." Worksheet 7.7 includes specific questions for assessing how these keys can be used to implement a learning capability priority. Managers can then fill in Worksheet 7.8 for that priority, numerically rate a proposed learning initiative for each of the seven keys, list ways to improve, and ultimately create a change improvement plan for all the management priorities previously identified.

To conclude, let's return to the globalization scenario described at the beginning of this chapter. By systematically going through the four-step process, this company's top management team can develop a blueprint for improving learning capability that's specifically tied to growth in emerging markets. You and other executives will openly and honestly discuss the following questions: How is learning critical to business success? How well does our company generate and generalize ideas with impact? What are our most serious learning disabilities? Your top management team will then look at the six domains of organizational learning laid out in our learning architecture—culture, competence, consequences, governance, capacity for change, and leadership—to identify specific actions you might take, and in what order.

To grow the company in the emerging markets of China and India, for example, you might consider establishing area operating councils at senior executive level to share knowledge and experiences regarding joint venture management in China and India, developing standard processes and checklists for identifying potential partners, forming centers of expertise in negotiating and structuring strategic alliances in Asia, accelerating knowledge transfer (both technical and managerial know-how) through cross-regional job assignments, and developing best-practice training courses to disseminate effective management practices. Every company's blueprint will be different, of course, but in all cases specific, and doable, management initiatives drive any successful learning effort.

CHAPTER EIGHT

Learning Matters, Warts and All

Diary of a True Learning Organization

Wouldn't it be nice to visit the inner sanctum of a true learning organization? After all, reading someone else's personal diary can be tempting, even if it brings on pangs of guilt. We want to know the "dirt"; heaven forbid if we get caught reading it, but that doesn't stop us if we have the chance. By analogy, most business leaders would like to read a diary of what worked and what didn't in other companies. It's reassuring to know that your organization is not the only one to experience difficulties in creating and retaining learning capability, to make whopping mistakes, or even to come to grips with what it means to be a learning organization.

Despite the rare success of a well-known CEO like Jack Welch, or a much ballyhooed learning giant like Motorola, few (if any) companies have "pure" learning organizations that do everything we have suggested in this book. In fact, most corporate learning diaries would show that while some activities encourage learning, others do not. That may be why corporate diaries, like personal ones, are often kept private. What company wants to reveal the warts and weaknesses behind its public persona?

Yet most of what we have done in this book amounts to opening the equivalents of such diaries, particularly those of companies we have observed in action. By flipping through the pages of company stories and case studies, we've been able to reveal some of the warts, bumps, and bruises acquired along the organizational learning way. Unlike borrowing some poor soul's personal diary to learn how to avoid mistakes in love or career, our peek into the learning sanctum is meant to be a hands-on experience for use right now. There's no time like the present to begin creating learning capability in an organization. Managers can start small or big; they can start with changes at the top or in the middle of the company—or even at the bottom, depending on what country a firm is located in.

Every company—and culture, for that matter—is different. When Motorola moved into China, for example, it entered the Chinese market at precisely the wrong time, according to P. Y. Lai, head of Motorola China.[1] It was the spring of 1989, during the infamous Tiananmen Square incident. The company had two choices, Lai notes: it could stay the course and probably suffer short-term consequences and possibly longer term problems as well; or it could flee with other U.S. multinationals and cut its losses. No one knew what the downside possibilities were in 1989, but Motorola executives made a calculated guess that this too would pass. And they were right.

More important, what they learned from that incident was indelibly etched in the firm's collective memory. After electing to remain in China, even during a terrible time of negative world opinion, the Chinese saw Motorola as a company that stuck to its guns, honored its agreements, and was willing to risk bad publicity around the globe for the principle. The net result was that Motorola is now viewed in China as the "employer of choice." P. Y. Lai says the company learned about what the Chinese valued, and the Chinese learned why Motorola has such an excellent worldwide reputation.

Does that make Motorola China a true learning organization? Does it prove Motorola China has built high learning capability? No, but this company's commitment to the Chinese market is one of many examples that collectively reinforce its reputation as a learning organization. And what does make it a learning organization is that Motorola China didn't stop with a simple decision to stay put. In this particular situation, the company took what it knew about blending different cultures and technology and assigned a cultural anthropologist to the site to try to "learn the culture." This anthropologist was on Motorola's payroll, and helped make the introduction of proposed technology a good fit with what the Chinese people needed, as well as a good business decision for Motorola. Jean Canavan, Manager of Culture and Technology, who works in the Knowledge Management Division of Motorola University, says of this learning experience:

> The adoption of a technology and how that technology is used is culture specific. Motorola learned this when they began selling pagers in China. In the U.S., pagers were designed to alert the user with a distinct tone and display a numeric call-back phone number.

That works well in an environment where telephones are in abundance and relatively inexpensive to use.

In the early 1990s in China, as you will recall, it was expensive and difficult to find a telephone. In response, Chinese salesmen developed an ingenious method to utilize their numeric pagers as message centers. They compiled a code book matching common orders with numeric codes. The numeric code could be sent by the salesman to the main office. The code, displayed on the order entry clerk's pager, was translated back into a message. This was not how the pager was originally intended to be used by the engineers who designed the technology. However, having learned that pagers were being used in this manner, the engineers worked to create a better technology to satisfy the customer's needs. Now we have pagers which are designed to specifically allow the user to send messages which are decoded automatically into text messages for the receiver.

In other words, the Chinese customers were "reinventing" paging technology to meet their needs. The evolution of paging is a good illustration of how customers of a product can drive the transformation of an industry. For Motorola, this knowledge created a shift in the traditional focus on operators and carriers as our only customers. We now understood that consumers were shaping the paging market.[2]

Motorola has learned through its various global operations that culture and technology go hand in hand; its approach to entering new national markets always combines some of the "soft stuff"—dealing with people and cultural issues—in addition to the necessary hardware. This has reinforced the company's learning capability over time. Motorola didn't start out that way, however, and true learning organizations don't evolve overnight. All of them go through stages of this process, and sometimes for the individual managers and employees involved it may feel like two steps forward, one step back. Indeed, most people in learning organizations realize that this is a process, not a static point-in-time intervention.

As we've mentioned in earlier chapters, most change initiatives in companies amount to the program du jour. This is where our concept of organizational learning capability can matter most to a firm's future success. If someone said, "You now hold in your hand the single most important thing you can do to improve not only your firm's global competitiveness but also its innovativeness and very specific performance outcomes," few managers would toss that thing away without examining it carefully. Yet as most managers also know, the concept of learning may sound nice in CEO speeches but can be very difficult to implement in the real world. Individuals resist change in all organizations, and barriers to improving a learning environment can exist in the structure of the organization itself.

An organization begins to be a learning organization when managers, especially those at the top, make a commitment to what may be a large-scale, long-term, company-wide process of organizational change. This is quite a challenge, of course, but this book has offered many practical approaches to grappling with the learning issue. In this concluding chapter, we summarize our main points and end with the diary of a hypothetical company, Zeebee Foods, a firm that has successfully achieved its learning goals.

Learning Styles Make a Difference to Business Performance

The literature documents a number of organizational learning processes that most researchers in the field accept and that have informed our own empirical work. These include discovery (people see a gap between what they want and what they have), invention (people generate ideas for how to deal with that gap), implementation (they put ideas into practice); and diffusion (the organization incorporates what has been learned and generalizes it to new situations elsewhere). The way organizations ultimately learn depends first on how they discover problems and invent solutions—what we've called idea generation. In chapter 2, we began our discussion of different organizational learning styles and then expanded on them in chapter 4.

In our empirical research, we studied more than 400 companies from 40 countries in highly diverse industries. Over 1,500 managers responded to our survey, and through statistical analyses we established that four learning styles—experimentation, competency acquisition, benchmarking, and continuous improvement—do exist.

But what academics are interested in can differ from what managers need to know. Because we thought that the whole notion of organizational learning can come perilously close to a Rorschach test that gives whatever managers want to see, we have also put some conceptual and practical meat on the bones of the idea of learning. We don't want to propagate just another fad like those that have come and gone over the years. Our intention has been to clarify what it means to be a learning organization, as well as to establish empirically the different types of learning organizations out there. While a company's learning style is only the first piece of overall learning, it appears from our survey results that all organizations rely on at least one of the styles, whether they're located in Korea, Mexico, Vietnam, or the United

States. More to the managerial point, we've demonstrated that learning styles significantly affect business performance. For that reason, executives need to identify the dominant learning style in their company and to determine whether that style is a good match for their business strategy and culture. In general, most organizations generate ideas in one preferred way, although the other learning styles may be present elsewhere in the same organization.

Experimentation isn't the most frequently used of the styles, but we believe it's perhaps the most important in enhancing a firm's competitiveness and innovation; more specifically, this style can positively affect a firm's ability to generate new product offerings. Recall that experimentation means trying out new products and processes. 3M, with its average of 600 new products a year, is the prototypical experimenter.

Competency acquisition was by far the most popular of the learning styles in our sample, and it certainly has its strengths. Skill-acquiring organizations primarily learn by encouraging individuals or teams to build new competencies. Many professional service firms like McKinsey or Anderson Consulting sell intellectual capital: acquiring new skills is the mainstay of their growth.

Another style, *benchmarking,* uses insights from other organizations as a company's primary source of information. Samsung Electronics is a premier benchmarker, having copied extensively from Japanese best practices to create its own flexible manufacturing system. However, in our survey, benchmarking was not one of the more popular or effective styles. This finding surprised us, since it seemed that benchmarking best practices had become a national pasttime in the United States. A number of busy consulting firms provide benchmarking data to just about anyone, and the sophistication of the search is high. Yet for most of the companies in our sample, benchmarking had no impact on business performance and appeared connected with the greatest number of learning disabilities. Copying from others can be cost-effective if a firm isn't focused on product innovation; but because incorporating the successful practices of others into one's own organization can be difficult, benchmarking rarely succeeds as a stand-alone learning style. We think this last point should be widely circulated to companies that insist on benchmarking everyone else ad nauseam.

Yet another style, *continuous improvement,* emphasizes improving on what has been accomplished before. Continuous improvement has been popularized recently through various reengineering efforts that focus on process improvements. Belgium's Alcatel Bell and Taiwan Semiconductor Manufacturing Company are both good examples of continuous improvers. While Alcatel Bell aims to improve its culture through the "In Charge of Change" program, Taiwan Semiconductor Manufacturing Company focuses on improving its production capability to manufacture semiconductors that are cheaper, better, and faster than those of other leading semiconductor companies.

Just knowing that organizations have different learning styles, while interesting, isn't particularly compelling. What makes this of interest to managers is that these styles significantly and differentially affect business performance all over the world. Our worldwide survey revealed that it wasn't the Americans that were best at generating new ideas. In fact, the Asian firms in our sample outperformed North American and European firms in generation of new ideas. Asian companies were also the best overall learners, which brings us to the other building blocks of organizational learning capability. Throughout this book we've pointed out that generating good ideas is necessary but not sufficient for creating long-lasting learning or a true learning organization. Companies also need to generalize those good ideas across multiple boundaries and to identify the organizational learning disabilities that may hinder either idea generation or idea generalization.

Three Building Blocks Form the Basis of Learning Capability

Becoming an idea-generating machine is the first step in a three-step process for building a learning environment. In chapter 3, we introduced a conceptual model for organizational learning capability that lays out the three building blocks—generation, generalization, and identification of learning disabilities—and indicates how these are connected with business context and performance. The second building block, generalization of ideas with impact, has to do with implementation and diffusion of ideas across many organizational boundaries. In chapter 5, we discussed how companies can successfully generalize ideas and we provided a manager's tool kit for improving generalization in an organization.

When you think of what prevents learning, you generally find that organizations have too many floors, ceilings, or walls, both internally and externally. They also have to contend with boundaries of time and geography. Sometimes, too, they must confront political boundaries or other perceived fences or hurdles that they must jump in order to generalize good ideas. A good example of this comes from Miami, Florida, where a Greater Miami Chamber of Commerce initiative called "One Community One Goal" has captured the attention of other chambers of commerce around South Florida, as well as that of other political, economic, and development groups.[3]

"One Community One Goal" was the brainchild of Jay Malina, a highly successful entrepreneur with no known political enemies who in 1995 put together a group of movers and shakers in the local Miami community with an eye toward targeted job creation in the area. Miami, of course, is a multicultural and highly politicized community, and even a good idea like targeting jobs for economic development was unlikely to be embraced by the various groups in town, much less to become a mandate for them to take action. When Malina first brought together a skeptical group of local business people, no one thought that much would happen. They looked at the guest list and decided it might be a fun afternoon and something they couldn't afford to miss in view of who else was present. But Malina in his talk not only made the idea of job creation sound possible but also convinced these other business people that it wouldn't happen without their participation and support. Through his considerable persuasive skills, he made them feel they were indispensable to creating this "One Community." He ended his afternoon presentation by showing them that Miami was losing economic ground to other cities and sent them on missions to find out why.

More to the point, Malina never gave members of this potentially fractious group too much work to do. Instead he set a very general goal: create new jobs or settle for living in a third-world city with terrible clashes. Over time, participants slowly put away their differences of opinion and began concentrating on making Miami a premier city for trade. Thus it became a question of when, not if. Over the last two years, Malina has put together task forces, all targeting specific industries and topics, and obtained the support of Miami's mayor, Alex Peneles. In a short time, all 40 of the chambers of commerce in the Miami region saw that the Greater Miami Chamber was receiving the kudos, particularly from the Mayor's Office, and they subsequently jumped on the bandwagon.

Various economic development groups insisted on participating as well. Several squabbling political groups also wanted in; much to their chagrin, they're now on the same side of an issue. The "One Community" idea was generalized to all the major players in the economic community, and in early 1998 Miami rolled out its plan of action at the mayor's Economic Summit, which featured Vice President Al Gore's endorsement of this type of community action. Initially seven key industries were targeted to address the projected shortfall of 120,000 jobs that Miami Dade County will face by the year 2005.

Those industries deemed the fastest growing which also produce high-paying jobs and the greatest opportunities for upward mobility, include biomedical, film and entertainment, financial services, information technology, international commerce, and visitors and hospitality. By 1997, three task forces were formed to investigate the biomedical, film and entertainment, and international commerce industries, and in 1998 the remaining four were initiated. Malina noted that "the work of these industry task forces is more than anything the engine that moves this initiative. They know their industries, and the obstacles they face in doing business in Miami Dade County, and they can tell us what needs to be addressed in order to increase job growth." Established in 1995 through the Annual Goals Conference of the Greater Miami Chamber of Commerce, the "One Community One Goal" is now a community-wide true learning initiative, and soon will start to give a tremendous payoff in new jobs for the local community. This example shows that generalization across numerous boundaries, including the most contentious political ones, can be accomplished, particularly if there is a champion who has power and few political axes to grind.

Beyond idea generalization, there's a final building block for creating and sustaining learning capability. Identifying an organization's learning disabilities rounds out the series, even if this is the learning step most companies are least prepared to take. Just as children and adults have learning disabilities—attention deficit disorder being one of the best known—organizations suffer from learning disabilities like diffusion deficiency, paralysis, and blindness. Unfortunately, there's no organizational equivalent of Ritalin to provide a quick fix. That's why identification is the starting place for grappling with learning disabilities. We'd like to underscore here that all organizations are prone to such barriers to learning; wherever many people work together, it's the nature of the beast to have barriers. Although the companies we surveyed reported only a moderate amount of disability, they were still often plagued by environmental blindness, diffusion deficiency, paralysis, simplemindedness, and homogeneity.

United States automobile firms in the 1970s, for example, were known to be blind to environmental threats and opportunities. In the face of increased global competition and changing customer expectations, the Big Three were not able to accurately assess the challenges posed by high-quality and efficient Japanese cars. All of them waited too long and did not react until they faced financial crisis. Blindness is a disability prevalent among companies that run into difficulties. In the 1980s, many traditionally successful companies like IBM, DEC,

Sears, Kodak, NEC, Philips, and Volkswagen also suffered blindness and other learning disabilities as they failed to swiftly respond to environmental changes.

Diffusion deficiency, another common learning disability, seems to occur all the time. This means that individual learning isn't transferred to the organization at large. Aetna is a good case in point. During an "out-of-the-box" session—Aetna's version of GE's WorkOut program—that was designed to foster large-scale culture change, it was revealed that Aetna's automotive group had generated a protocol for best practices within its unit. The HR manager for Automotive identified a series of actions they had embarked on that had produced excellent results. But the discussion among peers revealed that the rest of the organization had no idea what Automotive was talking about, even if they were impressed that there was a unit within their organization that excelled on several HR dimensions.

Our worldwide survey revealed that certain types of business strategies were better at overcoming learning disabilities than others. Companies with a product differentiation were more apt to recover from or even eliminate disabilities than were those pursuing a cost competitiveness strategy. The latter seem to suffer from almost all of the disabilities we identified. Companies with strong clan and market cultures are also more effective in reducing disabilities than companies with hierarchy and adhocracy cultures. And once again, it was the Asian firms in our sample that suffered the least from learning disabilities.

For any company, overcoming learning disabilities is not easy, but it's necessary for achieving high learning capability. That's why we can now add to our equation of $g \times g$ and write

Learning capability = *ability to* (generate ideas with impact
$\times$ generalize ideas with impact) $-$ (LD 1 + LD 2 + LD 3 . . .)

in which LD means learning disability.

Consider this an equation for thinking about how to create learning within an organizational unit. Generation of ideas is first and foremost. Then comes generalization, followed by subtracting the learning disabilities associated with any given organization. The expression $g \times g$ means that neither can exist without the other's influence. Anything times zero is always zero. If an organization's ability to generate ideas is zero, then it has no learning capability, no matter how adept it is at border crossing. Similarly, if generalization is zero, then even a torrent of good ideas won't help the learning situation. And if some measure of generation and generalization exists but a firm is still hindered by learning disabilities, its overall learning capability will be reduced by their collective weight.

In our research, the organizations that came closest to exhibiting a true learning capability were those that constantly stressed the importance of generating new ideas, as well as those that encouraged sharing ideas in all directions. Since managers must implement ideas if they are to have any lasting value, we have used our findings to help companies take a practical approach to increasing organizational learning capability. Creating a blueprint for learning, as we discussed in chapter 7, can help companies identify specific actions to take in the most effective and realistic sequence.

How to Develop Learning Capability:
One Corporate Diary

We conclude this book with a hypothetical example of a learning organization. This "diary" of Zeebee Foods indicates how a company can approach the learning issue, the specific strategies it can use, and how its HR people can help fuel the process and build commitment to learning. The Zeebee story also illustrates how long the change process can take. It's never an either/or outcome; rather, achieving learning capability occurs along a continuum, from very high (3M, GE, Motorola, HP, Samsung, Matsushita) to middling (General Motors) to low (the health care systems discussed in chapter 6). Once achieved at any level, however, it must be continuously reinforced. Nothing in the learning realm is static.

Zeebee Foods specializes in fast-food kits. Headquartered in San Antonio, Texas, it is now a multinational, with manufacturing plants in southeast Asia and the Caribbean. But Zeebee began as a childhood dream for Zelda Roning and her brother Bernard, who always wanted to run their own business. The Ronings founded the company in 1975, after completing graduate school, studying entrepreneurship, and establishing a business plan. The business started in Zelda's San Antonio kitchen and specialized in candy and desserts designed for children's lunch boxes. Bernard designed brightly colored paper to wrap the candy in; since the weather in Texas is quite warm, they also quickly learned that their products mustn't melt in anyone's hand, mouth, or lunch box. It took many trials and errors before they were successful in finding a series of desserts and candies that met the taste and melt test.

This fledgling business marketed its lunch box desserts to a local elementary school and managed to get some San Antonio shops to carry its products. To the Ronings' delight, kids loved the stuff, and the Ronings were soon asked to provide more than Zelda's small kitchen could produce. They enlarged the kitchen, hired two more cooks, and began producing candy and desserts in earnest. However, soon afterward, the Ronings grew bored with only the basic chocolate lollipop and vanilla cake Zeebee offered. Once again, they set up "taste labs" to determine what children liked and what they hated.

Going directly to the consumer source was a good idea—in theory. But by the late 1970s, razor blades and pins had started showing up in the Halloween bags of local children; few if any parents were interested in taking their kids to a "candy tasting lab." The Ronings were stumped, since children have very different tastes from adults, what adults like, children rarely do. After considerable work, Zeebee's HR group, which contained a number of psychology Ph.D.s who couldn't find academic jobs locally, discovered that lab pigeons pecked at foods most often chosen by children. (In fact, the pigeons outperformed adults two to one.) This meshed well with Zelda and Bernard's childhood experiments, when they had tried their own "taste treats" out on local children and animals. The latest round of Zeebee experiments showed that dogs didn't differentiate very much and cats couldn't be trusted; but pigeons were picky enough to match a child's taste buds.

To everyone's surprise, particularly that of the few investors involved with the company at the time, the pigeons turned out to be reliable tasters, and a whole series of candies and desserts evolved. As it turned out, San Antonio's Latin community liked products sweeter than Anglos, and so Zeebee began to differentiate product lines according to country of origin. One of the local distributors in San Antonio had contacts in Latin America, and by 1985 Zeebee had formed strategic alliances in Mexico and Barbados.

By this point, the company had made a regional name for itself. Structurally, they were very much vertically integrated, meaning that Zeebee not only carried out its own market research on what people wanted in a fast-food lunch box but also had its own kitchens for taste-testing and its own manufacturing plants for assembling the kits. Ironically, the Mexican market began to dry up about the same time that the Caribbean one took off in 1989. So Zeebee expanded its operations in the Caribbean to Grand Cayman Island and Trinidad, and one of the local Trinidadians had contacts in Singapore. Again, after considerable market research by the U.S.-based team on Singaporean tastes, the company established itself in another new market.

The Ronings' market strategy had historically been to offer good candies and desserts at a good price. To be sure, its production costs had been contained significantly by earlier decisions to use birds rather than humans as taste-testers. But a setback occurred in Singapore—the U.S. birds couldn't predict the taste preferences of Singaporean children—and thus the marketing team, now augmented by a number of ad hoc experts in animal and child behavior, as well as a virtual team of international cooks, began market research in earnest. After considerable trial and error, Zeebee researchers discovered almost serendipitously that chickens out-predicted pigeons in Singapore. Just a few months later, new taste laboratories had been created in Texas and outfitted with slightly larger areas for the chickens to perform their duties.

New problems arose. Chickens are messier than pigeons (and even children), and OSHA inspectors, along with animal rights activists, began hounding the lab. By this time, the company had received considerable attention in the media. Because an extended legal battle or PR disaster could close Zeebee down, top executives appointed an oversight group to do due-diligence, even in cases where the group wasn't sure it needed such oversight. By 1992, Zeebee had moved into different product lines with the same success, using birds to simulate children's taste preferences and making worldwide headlines. But it was the birds, not the company, that made the news, with *60 Minutes* and other TV shows eager to videotape the pigeons and chickens in action.

And here's where Bernard and the marketing team turned a potential PR problem into a gold mine. They created various "bird story" promotions as add-ons to the lunch box treats. If a parent purchased a certain amount of Zeebee food from the store, for instance, he or she could choose a videotape or a cassette that featured the birds at work. Zeebee even offered coloring books for very young children. These creative promotional projects became a huge endeavor, and Bernard gained a staff of creative writers, actors, and directors to produce the videos and cassettes.

The company has succeeded beyond the Ronings' wildest dreams. Zeebee's large R&D facility can now simulate tastes through computer modeling, eliminating the need for chickens and pigeons. The birds have been sold to animal-friendly farms and sanctuaries. This received wide recognition in the animal rights field, allowing Zeebee to bill itself as an animal-friendly company. In addition, the various lunch box treats have expanded into a whole lunch box; parents in many parts of the world can now purchase complete lunch boxes for their children that contain only natural ingredients, prepared in environmentally sound kitchens and manufacturing plants. Thus Zeebee, which began by competing on cost, ending up expanding globally through innovative products and delivery systems.

In reviewing this hypothetical success story, we'd like to capture the essence of what building and maintaining learning capability means. Zeebee Foods was the brainchild of two creative family members, who experimented, when they themselves were kids, on the products they would eventually market to the world. Did the company generate some good ideas? Here we would answer with a qualified yes. The Ronings and their researchers identified products that appealed to children, and they did so consistently in the face of many setbacks.

Did Zeebee generalize these ideas across multiple boundaries? Its move into international markets certainly indicates the company was successful at achieving this. Zeebee transferred its research into the realm of electronic communications and produced videotapes of the Zeebee "bird story" for promotional use. The company's current popularity with animal rights groups and OSHA allowed it to jump another boundary.

Finally, were Zeebee's executives able to identify and overcome its learning disabilities? Again, we would answer with a qualified yes. At a minimum, this company regrouped regularly when faced with legal and PR problems. Entrepreneurial companies can be prone, at the very least, to blindness and homogeneity, as well as diffusion deficiency, but Zelda and Bernard Roning included other managers and employees in key business decisions. While the Ronings still run the show, and the company maintains tight control of its R&D and manufacturing facilities, the organizational structure is team oriented, and experimentation is highly valued.

Zeebee Foods' corporate diary may seem a little far-fetched, but the up-and-down progress of this story does represent what learning capability looks like in action. Zeebee's strength is anticipating and reacting to issues in creative ways that are also cost conscious. At various points in its business journey, a serious lawsuit could have staggered the company, especially if researchers had erred with bird-chosen ingredients that made children sick. And in the real world of constant competitive threats and shifting market conditions, any company will face setbacks. But a learning organization like Zeebee Foods—or 3M, Hewlett-Packard, GE, or Samsung Electronics—will face such challenges and organizational disabilities head-on, reinforcing its learning capability in the process and sustaining success over the long haul.

WORKSHEETS

What Learning Means

Think of someone whom you would consider a "learner" and someone whom you would consider a "nonlearner." How would you characterize each person? For example, what are the attributes that put them in one column or the other? What do they do? What do they not do? What is the evidence that they are learners or nonlearners? What are the implications of a person's being in one column or the other?

LEARNER	NONLEARNER

A Learning Metaphor

In college, I took a class in English lierature, in which we studied Homer's *Odyssey*. As a dedicated *student*, I bought the book, read it from cover to cover, and memorized the names of the major characters in the book. I could recite the plot and even articulate the philosophical dilemmas raised. I was a good student and earned an A on the test when I recited back what I learned.

Rand was also in my class. As a *scholar*, he became enamored with the book and went beyond my student work. He read some of the book in the original Greek to become proficient in the language and the uses of language. He learned the backgrounds of the gods whom Homer worshiped to better understand the context for the journey portrayed in it. He read other works of the same period to understand the thinking of the author. He became a scholar of the *Odyssey*, not a student. He also got an A for the course.

On the surface, Rand and I were alike. We both studied hard and we both got good grades. But underneath the facade, we were quite different. As a student, I focused on the event (the exam) and did the minimum to get by; Rand focused on the learning and became enthralled with the themes and messages. Fifteen years later, I can recall that I read the book and got a good grade; Rand can still tell stories from the work as if he read it yesterday. The work affected me until it was time for the next course; it affected Rand for a lifetime—he is a professor of Latin and Greek today. Students learn words; scholars' learning is deeper (they learn more detail about the phenomenon) and broader (they learn more about the context of the phenomenon).

> ### What is the difference between Rand and me?
> ### Why would we define Rand as more of a learner than me?
> ### What are the parallels for organizations?

The Importance of Learning

What are the benefits of being learners to INDIVIDUALS?	What are the benefits of being learners to ORGANIZATIONS?

Assessment of Your Learning Culture

To what extent do the following statements characterize your organizational unit?	SCORE (1 = low; 10 = high)
1. We maintain a bias toward action.	
2. We value dialogue more than discussion.	
3. We make learning part of our cultural values.	
4. We welcome open inquiry and self-analysis.	
5. We are playful as well as serious when approaching the work endeavor (work is fun).	
6. We encourage an experimental attitude.	
7. We support failures that are the product of overreach.	
8. We perceive any change as an opportunity, not a threat.	
9. We encourage the capacity to be continually aware of internal processes and the external environment.	
10. We anticipate future demands rather than rest on past successes.	
11. We believe that knowledge is more important than job title.	
12. We encourage the norm of reciprocity.	
13. We ensure that a commitment to sharing ideas is in all formal strategic documents.	
TOTAL SCORE	

Checklist for Competence

BUY Staffing Tools to Create Competence	BUILD Training and Development Tools for Building Competence
We: ___ Hire outside experts as consultants ___ Look to acquire new competencies full time ___ Hire and promote curious chiefs ___ Seek fresh blood (from universities, oddball places) ___ Follow the whims of the stars (but insist that the stars, like all mortals, engage in sharing the norm) ___ Formally recognize learning (e.g., Director of Knowledge Management at McKinsey) ___ Hire people who are known as learners with competencies such as inquiry, reflection, system thinking, mental modeling, conflict management, disciplined postmortem process, ability to make data-based recommendations, networking ___ Outplace nonlearners and tell people about it ___ Promote learners, both in hierarchy and in public recognition events ___ Leave people in jobs long enough to demonstrate learning ___ Seek candidates for every position from many sources ___ Put people who have different backgrounds into management positions	We: ___ Attend as teams rather than as individuals and focus on learning application, not just knowledge acquisition ___ Attend in cross-functional groups ___ Invest in ongoing education throughout the organization ___ Involve customers in all aspects of training ___ Share ownership of training with line and HR ___ Guarantee that training stretches participants both intellectually and practically ___ Use training forums to challenge work assumptions and processes ___ Require systems training for all employees ___ Use postmortem format to learn from experience: What did you learn? What will you do differently as a result? ___ Sanction cross-functional moves ___ Support learning sabbaticals ___ Rotate people across jobs ___ Encourage innovative job assignments (e.g., startup, turnaround) ___ Participate in task forces ___ Practice external job sharing (share employees with customer or supplier) ___ Assign people to special projects ___ Have on-the-job apprenticeships ___ Ensure that every person has a learning plan

Learning Leader Index

To what extent do leaders in your organization possess or demonstrate the following abilities?	
ATTRIBUTE	SCORE (1 = low; 10 = high)
1. To coach others	
2. To look outside the personal domain for alternative answers (e.g., benchmark)	
3. To facilitate dialogue and exchange of ideas	
4. To teach	
5. To let go of a previous solution	
6. To experiment with new ideas	
7. To share information	
8. To learn from mistakes	
9. To set a vision	
10. To share rewards for sharing knowledge	
11. To walk the talk: to spend time on learning	
12. To enable others to be successful	
TOTAL SCORE	

Learning Matrix

In each cell, please score the extent to which a critical factor is done well in a specific business: 0 = not applicable; 1 = not good at all; 2 = sort of good; 3 = average; 4 = we think we are good; 5 = others think we are good.

QUESTION To be world class as X, we must ...								
		Critical Success Factors for X						
		a	b	c	d	e	f	g	etc.
	1								
	2								
Businesses	3								
	4								
Where	5								
	6								
Work Is	7								
Done	8								
	etc.								

Learning Criticality

ASSESSMENT QUESTIONS	RATING (1–10)	RATIONALE
1. To what extent is learning capability aligned with our business strategy?		
2. To what extent does learning capability enable us to serve customers better and faster?		
2. To what extent does learning capability enable us to serve customers better and faster?		
3. To what extent does learning capability differentiate us from competitors?		
4. To what extent is learning capability likely to have financial impact?		
TOTAL		

Auditing Idea Generation Capability

Learning Styles	Current Capability as of Today	Required Capability for Future Success	Areas for Improvement
Experimentation			
Competency acquisition			
Benchmarking			
Continuous improvement			
AVERAGE SCORE			

On a 10-point scale, please honestly assess the ability of your organization to generate new ideas through the four learning styles.

Auditing Idea Generalization Capability

On a 10-point scale, please honestly assess the ability of your organization to generalize new ideas across the following five boundaries.

Organizational Boundaries	Current Capability as of Today	Required Capability for Future Success	Areas for Improvement
Temporal boundaries			
Vertical boundaries			
Horizontal boundaries			
External boundaries			
Geographic boundaries			
AVERAGE SCORE			

Auditing Organizational Learning Disabilities

On a 10-point scale, please honestly assess the extent to which your organization suffers each of the following learning disabilities.			
Learning Disabilities	Current Level as of Today	Required Level for Future Success	Areas for Improvement
Environmental blindness			
Simplemindedness			
Homogeneity			
Tight coupling			
Paralysis			
Superstitious learning			
Diffusion deficiency			
AVERAGE SCORE			

Improving Learning Organization
Management Practices to Generate and Generalize Ideas

CULTURE How can we build a learning culture?			
COMPETENCE How can we ensure that we have individual, team, and organizational competencies for learning?	CONSEQUENCE How can we ensure that our performance management systems encourage learning for individuals, teams, and processes?	GOVERNANCE How can we ensure that our organization structure and communication processes encourage learning?	CAPACITY FOR CHANGE/WORK SYSTEMS How can we ensure that our work process and systems encourage learning?
LEADERSHIP How can we ensure that our leaders throughout the organization demonstrate a commitment to learning?			

Learning Capability Plan:
Priorities and Support

Priorities

```
**************************
*        Learning        *
*        Capability       *
*                         *
**************************
```

Time

Ongoing
Support
Activities

Keys and Processes for Making Learning Capability Happen

KEY/PROCESS FOR CHANGE	QUESTIONS TO ASSESS AND ACCOMPLISH THE KEY/PROCESS
Leading change (WHO is responsible)	Do we have a leader . . . who owns and champions the priority? who makes a public commitment to making it happen? who will garner resources to sustain it? who will put in personal time and attention to following it through?
Creating a shared need (WHY do it)	Do employees . . . see the reason for the priority? understand why the priority is important? see how it will help them and/or the business in the short and long term?
Shaping a vision (WHAT it will look like when we are done)	Do employees . . . see the outcomes of the priority in behavioral terms (what they will do differently as a result of the priority)? get excited about the results of accomplishing the priority? understand how the priority will benefit customers and other stakeholders?
Mobilizing commitment (WHO ELSE needs to be involved)	Do the sponsors of the priority . . . recognize who else needs to be committed to the priority to make it work? know how to build a coalition of support for the change? have the ability to enlist support of key individuals in the organization? have the ability to build a responsibility matrix to make the priority happen?
Using multiple levers (HOW it will be institutionalized)	Do the sponsors of the priority . . . understand how to link the priority to other HR systems, e.g., staffing, training, appraisal, rewards, structure, communication, etc.? recognize the systems implications of the priority?

continued

KEY/PROCESS FOR CHANGE	QUESTIONS TO ASSESS AND ACCOMPLISH THE KEY/PROCESS
Monitoring progress (HOW it will be measured)	Do the sponsors of the priority . . . have a means of measuring the success of the priority? plan to benchmark progress on both the results of the priority and the process of implementing the priority?
Making it last (HOW it will get started and last)	Do the sponsors of the priority . . . recognize the first steps in getting started? have a short- and long-term plan to keep attention focused on the priority? have a plan to adapt the priority over time?

These processes have been developed in work with General Electric and a design team including Steve Kerr, Dave Ulrich, Craig Schneier, Jon Biel, Ron Gager, and Mary Anne Devanna (outsiders to GE) and Jacquie Vierling, Cathy Friarson, and Amy Howard (GE employees).

Learning Capability:
Change Improvement Plan–Keys to Success

Describe the Priority for Building Learning Capability (based on layers of priority in Worksheet 7.6)		
PROCESS	RATING (how we do today) (0–100)	WAYS TO IMPROVE
Leading change		
Creating a shared need		
Shaping a vision		
Mobilizing commitment		
Using multiple levers		
Monitoring progress		
Making it last		

APPENDIX 1

Notes on
Research Methodology and
Participating Companies

The purpose of research is to answer questions systematically. This appendix lays out the methods and processes we used to answer the overall question "How can organizations build a learning capability?" There are different research methods to answer our research questions, each entailing different strengths and weaknesses. Therefore, we have followed the logic of "triangulation," which means using multiple research methods to answer research questions. To build the conceptual framework, we relied heavily on a thorough literature review. To provide in-depth knowledge of how organizations learn, we prepared several extensive case studies in which we interviewed employees and studied the internal firm processes. To understand the practice of learning capability across multiple companies and countries, we used a survey. Each of these three methods led to management implications on building learning capability.

The goal of the case study approach was to examine several companies with demonstrated excellence in learning. We used two approaches to this case study research. First, we studied in detail Alcatel Bell, Samsung Electronics, Motorola, Hewlett-Packard, and 3M. We selected these companies because they were known for their commitment to learning and because they represented multicultural insights on how organizations learn. Second, in our work within companies on other projects over the last two years, we have been aggressively looking for "best practices" in learning and a commitment to it. While this work has not been systematic and did not follow a prescribed interview format, we have gained enormous insights about learning from seminars and work with many companies, including AlliedSignal, AT&T, Boeing, Bank1, BellSouth, Canada

Life, Champion, Columbia Gas, Coca-Cola, General Electric, Hallmark, Harley-Davidson, Honeywell, Lucent, Marriott, Motorola, Praxair, Rockwell, Royal Bank, Sony, Southern Company, TRW, Union Carbide, and *USA Today*. We list these companies to acknowledge that many of our ideas on learning capability have been shaped by discussions about learning in each of these firms. We feel that through our independent and related work in firms, we could extract some of the management practices and implications for learning.

In addition to case study research, we conducted a worldwide survey of learning capability among 400 firms in 40 countries. This appendix offers detailed information on how we conducted our survey research and analyzed the data.

Survey Development and Administration Process

In our literature review we found an amazing dearth of empirical research on learning capability. Arguments against empirical work on learning capability exist. One was that learning capability occurs differently within each organization. Learning capability represents such latent and core values of the organization that it is difficult to create survey instruments that apply across organizations. The same argument has been used against cross-firm, empirical studies of corporate culture.[1] Second, learning must be seen as a flow, not a snapshot, and any one-time empirical study of learning would distort the overall and long-term process of learning capability.

Realizing the danger of not tapping into the unique and deeper insights that came from case studies and of having a snapshot picture of learning, we felt that empirical research across a large set of firms would help understand learning processes. In particular, our overall question of how organizations can build learning capability can be answered systematically through cross-firm, cross-cultural research. The steps we used were these:

1. We created a framework that led to the concepts we wanted to test, the relationships between the concepts, and the questions we wanted to answer. This framework is laid out in figure 3.1.

2. We designed an instrument to measure the concepts in the framework (see appendix 2). Our instrument was designed based on (1) previously tested constructs where possible, e.g., business strategy, business culture, organizational competitiveness, (2) literature and concepts discussed by others, but not fully tested, and (3) our best estimate of the items that would describe a factor, e.g., learning type and learning disability. We reviewed the instrument with members of our research team and with targeted experts in learning to ensure that our questions made sense.

3. We designed a data collection methodology and sample. Our goal was to collect data from a large range of companies. We realized

that many companies are inundated with surveys and that often it is difficult to get a high response rate from a blind survey received in the mail. Therefore, we wanted to focus our data collection on our contacts and enlist them to distribute surveys more broadly within their firms.

We concluded that we would send five surveys to our contact list. Our contact list was about 2,000 people and was obtained from each member of the research team, the International Consortium on Executive Development Research, and the IBEAR Program at the USC School of Business. Most of these contacts are HR professionals. We asked these contacts to fill out a survey and to give the survey to four other individuals who knew their business. We were particularly interested in collecting data from firms outside the United States.

4. We selected a unit of analysis for the results. Since we were studying the learning capability of a business, it was appropriate to use a business as the unit of analysis. We defined a business as the organizational unit in which the contact person worked, which could be a corporation, a division, a function, or a plant. The survey focused on the learning capability that occured within the organizational unit.
5. We proceeded with data collection, given the above decisions and the administrative process. Surveys were sent to participants and returned to Questar, the data processing subcontractor for this research.

Sample

In total, 1,532 surveys were received from 460 businesses in 382 companies, representing a response rate of about 38 percent from more than 40 countries. Table A.1 lists the names of participating companies.

The unit of analysis in this study was the business, the primary organizational unit within which a respondent worked. To understand the organizational learning capability of a business, data from individual respondents was averaged to form scores at the business level.[2] The number of respondents in each business ranged from one to 37, with an average of 3.28 respondents. To minimize the misrepresentation of business level data by one or two key informants, only businesses with at least three respondents were retained. As a result, 268 businesses out of 460 were retained for subsequent analysis in this book.

Tables A.2 through A.9 give characteristics of the data set. Tables A.2 through A.5 describe the characteristics of the businesses we examine in this book. Tables A.6 through A.9 describe the demographics of the individual respondents who participated in our study. Highlights of each table follow.

Table A.2. The sample is heavily weighted to North America (75 percent of total businesses). However, this means that 25 percent of the businesses in our sample are outside North America. We believe this is both the largest empirical study of learning organizations and the largest non–North American sample.

Table A.3. The range of business age is quite large. Given that the majority of businesses are smaller and younger today, our data set proportionally consists of older businesses. There are 49 businesses over 100 years old (18 percent of 268 businesses). Most of them are some of the oldest businesses in Asia and Europe.

Table A.4. The range of business size is also quite diverse, though it appears that we have a sample of mostly larger businesses. Some 37 percent of the businesses in our sample employ over 10,000 employees. The diversity of business size is useful to our study because we can examine whether learning processes of smaller businesses are different from those of larger businesses.

Table A.5. We have a large range of industries within the data set. The sample cuts across ten major industry groups, with high representation in all groups except aircraft, automobiles, and energy (petroleum, gas, and coal).

In brief, our sample is diverse in its geographical regions, age, size, and type of industry. However, compared with businesses in today's economy, the businesses in our sample appear to be larger and more mature. These business characteristics may bias the overall results toward learning processes within large and mature businesses.

Table A.6. Respondents have a normal age distribution around 45 years. They are typically middle managers who have a broad knowledge of organizational processes. As Nonaka points out, they are also the critical people who share information within the business.[3]

Table A.7. As expected with the age results, respondents have been with their businesses for some time (on the average, 16 years). These data support the use of these respondents as key informants. In general, their perceptions of organizational practices are based on long-term relationships with the businesses. They should be able to speak with some insight about the business's learning processes.

Table A.8. Respondents in the data base are generally senior managers. There are only 175 nonmanagement contributors (11 percent of the respondents), whereas 89 percent of the respondents are in management positions. Managers probably speak with more authority about organizational processes, which supports our key informants' data collection and analysis strategy.

Table A.9. Respondents represent an array of functions. We are pleased that only 34 percent of the sample comes from the Human Resource/Personnel function. Since most of our key contacts were within the HR function, we are glad that they were able to distribute surveys to individuals outside the function as we requested.

In brief, our respondents are generally managers who have been with the business for about 16 years and who are in middle or upper/middle management positions. We are happy with this sample because these people are more likely to have accurate perceptions of learning processes. In addition, we are pleased with the cross-functional distribution of the respondents.

Concepts and Measures

Consistent with our organizational learning model in chapter 3, we are interested in the relationships among three sets of variables: business context, learning capability, and business performance. The challenge, then, is to measure these concepts accurately and reliably. Table A.10 summarizes the measures used in our research. To assess the reliability of some measures, some multivariate statistics (e.g., factor analysis and reliability analysis) are reported based on the sample. Readers who are interested in how we measure each construct can further refer to tables A.11 through A.16 and figure A.1 in this appendix and other chapters in the book.

Statistical Analysis

To assess the relationships among business context, learning capability, and organizational performance, a variety of statistical techniques are used, including descriptive statistics, ANOVA, bivariate correlation, exploratory factor analysis, confirmatory factor analysis, multiple regression, and structural equation model (i.e., LISREL). The choice of statistical analysis depends on the research question to be answered.

Table A.1   Companies Participating in Our Worldwide Survey Research
($N = 382$)

ABB Power T&D Company Inc.	Allen Group PR	Anderson Consulting
Abbot Laboratories	Allied-Signal	Applied Power
Aetna Institute for Corporate Education	Allstate Insurance	ARA Holding
	Altron Inc.	Arrow-Molded Plastics
Agfa-Gevaert	Amdahl Company	Asea Brown Boveri
AGT	American Express	Asoc Venexolano-
Alcalis de Colombia	American Capital Man-	Americana de Amistad
Alcatel	agement & Research	ASTRA-CALVE
ALCO Aluminio S.A.	American President	AT&T
ALCO Health Services Corp.	Companies Ltd.	Atlas Consolidated Mining Development
	Amoco Chemical Company	Austrian Industries
ALCOA	AMP Incorporated	Avco Lycoming/Textron
Alexander Hamilton Life Insurance	Amperex Electronic Corporation	Avon Products
Algonquin Gas Transmission Company	Analog Devices	Banc Consolidado
	Analysis & Technology	Bangkok Bank

continued

Bangkok Weaving Mills
Bank of Yokohama
Bank of Boston
Bank of Thailand
Bank of Montreal
Bank of Ireland
Barclays Bank PLC
Battelle
Bausch & Lomb
Baxter Healthcare
Bell Labs
Bell South
Ben & Jerry's Home-
made
Best Western Interna-
tional
Bethlehem Steel
Beverly Enterprises
Biologic Systems
BMW
Boeing
Boise Cascade
Borden
Bose
Brecker & Merryman
Bristol Myers
Bull
Bundy
Burlington Northern
Railroad
Burroughs Wellcome
Butterworth Hospital

C. Itoh
Calgon Vestal Laborato-
ries
Camp Dresser & McKee
Canada Post
Canadian General Insur-
ance Group
Canadian Utilities
Limited
Cargill
Carnation Company
Caterpillar Inc.
Cathay Pacific Airways
Central Life Assurance
Central Hudson Gas
Electric

Centro Analisi Strate-
giche
Champion Interna-
tional
Chartered Industries
of Singapore
Chase Manhattan
China Steel
Chubb & Sons
Cigarette Manufacturers
CIGNA
Citibank
Citizens Gas and Coke
Utility
Citytrust Banking
Cobe Laboratories
Coca Cola
Colgate Palmolive
Comerica Inc.
Consumers Power
Continental AG/Werk
Limmer
Coors Brewing
Coraza Corporation
Corning
Coulter Electronics
CPC International
Cyclops
Cyprus Minerals

D.C. Health
DANA Corporation
Dayton Hudson
DDB Needham World-
wide
Deere & Company
Delta
Den Danske
Dharmala Group
Diamond Shamrock
Digital Equipment
Dow Chemical
Dragados Y Construc-
ciones
Dresser Industries
Dresser-Rand
Du Pont
Dun & Bradstreet
Duracell International

Eastman Kodak
Eisai
ELEC-TEC
Eli Lilly
Employee Assistance
Enron
Equitable Financial
Ernst & Whitney
Executive Forum
Exxon

Farm Credit Corporation
of America
Farm Credit Bank
Federal Express
Federal Reserve Bank of
Philadelphia
Federal Sign
Federal Mogul
Fiat
Fidelity Investments
Finance Corporation of
Thailand
Firestone Tire
First of America, South-
east Michigan
First Source Bank
Fleming Companies
FMC
Ford
Foremost
Frequency & Time
Systems

Gen-Probe
Gencorp Polymer Prod-
ucts
General Motors
General Electric
GENMIN
Genuine Parts
Gnaden Huetten Memo-
rial Hospital
Goodyear Tire & Rubber
GrowMark
Grupo ICI de Mexico
Grupo Cere S.A. de C.V.
Grupo Bufete Industrial
GTE

continued

178

Hallmark Cards
Hamilton Standard
Harley-Davidson
Haworth
Heineken International
Herman Miller
Hewlett Packard
Hitachi Ltd.
Hoechest Celanese Corporation
Hoechst Japan
Hoffmann-La Roche
Holiday Inn
Holiday Corporation
Honeywell
Hoteles Quinta Real
Hungarian Telecommunications
Hussey Seating Company
Hyde Group
Hyundai Business Group

ICI (Malaysia) Holding
IDS Financial Services
Imatran Volma Oy
Inchcape Pacific
Indal Limited
Industrial Bank of Japan
Ingersoll-Rand
Institute Manajemen Prasetiya Mulya
Institute for International Economics
Intermedics
Intermountain Health Care
Internal Revenue Service
International Paper
International Business Machines
International Search Associates

Japan External Trade Organization
John Deere
Johnson & Johnson

Jossey-Bass
Joyo Bank

Kaiser Aluminum & Chemical
Kansai Economic Federation
Kellogg Company
Korea Computer
Korea Stock Exchange
Kraft General Foods
Kroger

L.J. Minor Corporation
L'Oreal
Lafarge Canada
Lancaster General Hospital
Levi Strauss
Loctite Corporation
Long Island Lighting
Loral Infrared & Imaging
Lotte Group
Lufkin Industries

Mahanager Tel. Nigam
Manila Electric
Manulife Financial
Manville Institute
Marathon Oil
Marion Merrell Down
Marriott
Masco
McDonnell Douglas
MCI
Mead
Merck
Merck, Sharpe & Dohme
Metropolitan Life
Mexinox
Michcon
Milk Marketing
Mitsubishi
Mobil
Monsanto
Morgan Guaranty Trust
Motorola

NAC Reinsurance
Nacional Financlierra
NASA
National Australia Bank
National Westminster
NCR
Nebraska Public Power
NEC
Neste OY
New Jersey Bell
Newport News Shipbuilding
Nihon Keizai Shimbun
Nikko Petrochemicals
Nissan Motors
Nitto Agency
Nomura
Nordata Vestadata
Norrell
North Carolina Memorial Hospital
Northern Telecom
Northwest Natural Gas
Norton Company
Nova Corporation
Nuclear Fuel Industries
Nuclear Support Services
Nutrasweet
Nynex
NYSEG
NZR

Ocean Spray Cranberries
ODR
Oki Electric
Omron
Outboard Marine Corporation

Paccar Incorporated
Pacific Gas & Electric
Pacific Bell
Parke-Davis
Payless Shoes
PD Soedarpo
Pepsi Cola
Perini
Permodalan Naxional Berhad

continued

179

Pfizer
PhilAm Life Insurance
Philip Morris
Philippine Long Distance Telephone
Pinkerton Tobacco
Pitney Bowes
Pittsburgh National Bank
Potomac Electric Power
PPG Industries
Price Waterhouse
Prince
Promus
PT Swadhama Suta Data
PT Pembangunan Jaya
PT Hasfarm Dian Konsultan
PT Astra International
PT Humpuss
PT Muladaya Adipratama
PT Caltex Pacific Indonesia
PT Federal Motor
Public Service Company

Rhodia
Rolls Royce PLC
Royal Bank
Ryder System

Safety Harbor Spa & Fitness Center
San Miguel
Sann Aung Imaing
Saudi Arabian Oil
Security Pacific Company
Seiko Epson
Serigraph
Shell

Shimizu
Shin Caterpillar Mitsubishi
Sibson
Siemens
Signetics
Silicon Graphics
Singapore Airline
Skandia Insurance
Sony Corporation
Southam
Southern California Edison
Southern Indiana Gas & Electric
Spandoz
Sprague Semiconductor
SPX Group
Srithai Marketing
SSangyyong Group of Companies
Sterile Design
Sterling Jersey
Stolle Corporation
Stratus Computer Sumitomo
Supermarkets General
SWIFTSA
Swiss Bank
Taiwan Power
Taiwan Cement
Tandem Computers
Tenneco
Texaco
Thomaston Mills
TN Soon & Company
Tokai Lippo Bank
Tokyo Electric Power

Toppan Printing
Toronto Dominion Bank
Toyota Motor
Trak International
Travelers Express
TRW

Unibanco-Uniao De Bancos Brasileiros
Union Carbide
Unisys
United Telephone Company
United Brands Company
United Microlectronics
United Parcel Service
United States Army
UNUM Corporation
Upjohn
US Postal Service
USI/IBM Indonesia

Valmet
Volkswagen
Vulcan Material

Wang Laboratories
Wargo & Company
Warner-Lambert
Welch's
Wellcome Foundation
Westinghouse
Westpac Banking
Weyerhaeuser
Whaman
Whirlpool

Yukong
Yunbo Industrial

Table A.2 Distribution of Businesses in our Sample by Geography

Region	Frequency
North America	199
Asia	39
Western Europe	17
Australia / New Zealand	4
Africa / Latin America / Middle East	3
Eastern Europe	2
TOTAL	268

Table A.3 Distribution of Businesses by Years of Business Establishment

No. of years established	Frequency
0–10 years	18
11–20 years	20
21–20 years	26
31–40 years	21
41–50 years	21
51–60 years	22
61–70 years	21
71–80 years	12
81–90 years	24
91–100 years	26
101–150 years	42
Over 150 years	7
Not identified	8
TOTAL	268

Table A.4 Distribution of Businesses by Size

No. of employees	Frequency
1–1,000	62
1,001–2,000	22
2,001–4,000	30
4,001–6,000	23
6,001–8,000	15
8,001–10,000	9
10,001–15,000	9
15,001–25,000	23
25,001–35,000	12
35,001–50,000	19
50,001–100,000	19
Over 100,000	17
Not identified	8
TOTAL	268

Table A.5 Distribution of Sample by Industry

Industry type	Frequency
Miscellaneous manufacturing	50
Petroleum, gas, coal	7
Chemical, pharmacy	28
Electronics, computer	25
Automobiles	6
Aircraft	5
Utilities	31
Wholesaling, retailing	30
Finance	39
Services	27
Not identified	20
TOTAL	268

Table A.6 Distribution by Age of Respondent

Age	Frequency
20–30 years old	58
31–40	333
41–50	769
51–60	316
Over 60	26
Not identified	30
TOTAL	1532

Table A.7 Distribution of Tenure of Respondents

Tenure	Frequency
Less than 1 year	86
2–5 years	245
6–10 years	254
11–15 years	248
16–20 years	241
21–25 years	205
Over 25 years	253
TOTAL	1532

Table A.8 Distribution of Role of Respondents

Role	Frequency
Individual contributor	175
Manager of individual contributor	350
Director of managers	566
General manager	411
Not identified	30
TOTAL	1532

Table A.9 Distribution by Functional Specialty of Respondent

Specialty	Frequency
Finance/accounting	99
General management	294
HR/Personnel	515
Manufacturing/production	118
Marketing/sales	177
Planning	66
Research and development	75
Others	125
Not identified	63
TOTAL	1532

Table A.10 Operationalization of Concepts and Measures

Concepts	Measures	Questions of the measures
Business context		
Industry characteristics	Six factors are used to measure industry characteristics: market concentration, customer relationship, supplier relationship, technological interdependence, environmental predictability, and industry type.	See table 3.1 for the listing of questions.
Business strategy	Fifteen alternative strategies are identified based on Porter's competitive strategies. Factor analysis indicates that two dominant competitive strategies exist.	See table 3.2 for the listing of questions and table A.11 for the results of factor and reliability analyses.
Business culture	Sixteen questions are used to measure four culture types as developed by Quinn.	See table 3.3 for the listing of questions.
Learning capability		
Learning styles	Twenty-four questions were generated based on six learning dimensions.	See table A.12 for the six learning dimensions and table A.13 for the listing of questions.
	Statistical analysis confirmed the existence of four organizational learning types derived from the 24 questions.	See figure A.1 for the results of confirmatory factor analysis and table A.14 for the factor items.
Learning disabilities	Thirty-four questions were developed based on the learning disabilities suggested in existing literature.	See table A.15 for the listing of 34 questions.
	Confirmatory factor analysis identified eleven learning disabilities, seven of which have the most significant relationships with business context and performance and are reported on in this book.	See chapter 6 for the listing of questions under seven learning disabilities.

continued

Concepts	Measures	Questions of the measures
Business performance		
Competitiveness	A composite measure of 15 performance dimensions in comparison to major competitors.	For both competitiveness and innovativeness measures, see table A.16 for the list of questions and the results of factor and reliability analyses.
Innovativeness	A composite measure of four innovation indicators in comparison to major competitors.	

Table A.11 Factor and Reliability Analyses of Competitive Strategy Measures

Questionnaire items	Product differentiation	Cost competitiveness[a]
Generic question: To compete successfully, our business strategy focuses on (1 = to a very small extent; 5 = to a very large extent)		
Quality of products or services	.70	.21
Providing specialized products or services	.69	−.14
New products or service development	.68	−.16
Improving relationships with customers	.64	.27
Differentiating products or services from competitors	.62	−.07
Building employee commitment	.54	.28
Developing/refining existing products	.42	.04
Cost reduction	−.07	.80
Operating efficiency	.22	.80
Competitive pricing	−.02	.68
Developing operating technology[b]	.34	.40
Eigenvalue	3.60	2.31
Percentage of variance explained	24.00	15.40
Alpha reliability coefficient	.78	.76

a. A third factor related to marketing differentiation strategy was identified. As this strategy did not have any strong relationship with learning capability, it was dropped from further analysis in this book

  Boldface indicates which items are best explained by a given factor.

b. This item was deleted from the final scale as suggested by reliability analysis.

Table A.12   Dimensions of a Learning Organization

Question	Learning dimensions	Definition
Where learning occurs	Within boundaries	We primarily learn new ideas within the boundaries of our organization unit, e.g., team, function, division, geography.
	Across boundaries	We explicitly go outside the boundaries of our organization unit to seek new ideas and information.
Who does the learning	Individuals	We focus learning on individual learning, e.g., attend training as individuals.
	Teams (collectives)	We focus learning on teams, e.g., attend training as teams.
When learning occurs	Mastery	We work to master new ideas before trying something new.
	Ongoing	We constantly seek new ideas, even before old ones are fully implemented.
What learning focuses on	Improving existing processes	We work to upgrade the way that we do existing work until we have it right.
	Inventing new processes	We constantly seek for new ways to do work.
How we learn	Expert	We work to be analytical about how we learn; we are known as technological masters.
	Experimenter	We work to try a lot of new ideas, even at the risk of implementing them before they are fully articulated.
	Innovator	We want to be the first in the market with a new idea or concept.
	Copier	We want to learn from others and enter a market with a tested product.
Why we learn	Strategic	Learning is integrated into the strategy and overall mission of the business.
	Operational	Learning is not necessarily a central factor for the mission and vision of the organization.

Table A.13   Measures of Organizational Learning Types

To what extent do the following statements characterize your business? (on a 5-point scale)

Where learning occurs

We primarily learn new ideas within the boundaries of our team.

We primarily learn new ideas within the boundaries of our organization but outside our team.

We primarily learn new ideas outside the boundaries of our organization.

We deliberately go outside the boundaries of our organization unit to seek new ideas and information.

We primarily benchmark competition and measure progress against competitors' performance.

We primarily benchmark ourselves and measure progress against our previous performance.

Who does the learning

We encourage individuals to acquire new competencies.

We encourage teams to acquire competencies.

Our rewards primarily focus on individual performance.

Our rewards primarily focus on team performance.

We promote individuals who are strong individual contributors.

We promote individuals who are strong team players.

When learning occurs

We work to master new ideas before trying something new.

We constantly seek new ideas even before old ones are fully implemented.

What learning focuses on

We work to upgrade the way that we do existing work until we have it right.

We constantly seek new ways to do work.

How we learn

We work to be masters at what we do; we want to be known as the best technical experts in our industry.

We try a lot of new ideas; we want to be known as experimenters within our industry.

We want to be the first in the market with a new process or product.

We want to learn from others and enter a product or apply a process after it has been fully tested.

We learn by scanning broadly what other companies do.

We learn by focusing our scanning on specific activities done by other companies.

We learn by hiring people from other companies who have skills we need.

Why we learn

Learning is a critical part of our business strategy.

Table A.14 Indicators of Four Organizational Learning Types

Confirmatory factor 1: Experimentation (alpha = .78)

We constantly seek new ideas even before old ones are fully implemented (Q1).

We try a lot of new ideas; we want to be known as experimenters within our industry (Q2).

We constantly seek new ways to do work (Q3).

Confirmatory factor 2: Competency acquisition (alpha = .87)

We encourage individuals to acquire new competencies (Q4).

We encourage teams to acquire competencies (Q5).

Learning is a critical part of our business strategy (Q6).

Confirmatory factor 3: Benchmarking (alpha = .68)

We learn by scanning broadly what other companies do (Q7).

We learn by focusing our scanning on specific activities done by other companies (Q8).

Confirmatory factor 4: Continuous improvement (alpha = .60)

We work to upgrade the way that we do existing work until we have it right (Q9).

We work to be masters at what we do; we want to be known as the best technical experts in our industry (Q10).

Table A.15 Measures of Organizational Learning Disabilities

To what extent do the following statements characterize your business? (on a 5-point scale)

1. We are good at scanning the external environment for opportunities and potential problems.
2. We are active in finding/creating new markets.
3. We are good at perceiving long-term environmental threats, and opportunities.
4. We are good at scanning in the internal workings and processes of this organization for areas that can be improved upon.
5. We work to insure that all employees can recognize or discover the information that they need to perform the job.
6. In general, our work procedures have functioned well, so we see little need of pervasive change.
7. "If it ain't broke, don't fix it" would represent the general attitude here pretty well.

continued

8. We intentionally create small "false alarms," "crises," etc. in the workplace to stimulate improvements or problem solving.

9. Political considerations of important stakeholders influence the actions of our organization.

10. We try to uncover and communicate all relevant facts, not just those that are politically acceptable.

11. We work to insure that employees are directly exposed to the variation and complexity of the environment.

12. We are good at determining the causes of unexpectedly low and high levels of performance.

13. We are good at deciding on plans of action to redress performance shortfalls.

14. We try to insure that all employees have access to more information than the minimum required to perform the job.

15. We are good at generating and evaluating a wide variety of alternative solutions to performance shortfalls.

16. We encourage diversity in people and ideas within our organizations.

17. Intelligent risk taking that results in failure is not punished.

18. There is a lack of coordination between multiple, competing perspectives at this organization.

19. Groups and departments in this organization function fairly independently without much integration.

20. We tend to over-analyze problems before implementing ideas—and thus miss opportunities for improvement.

21. Employees have a significant say in how their work is done.

22. We have trouble implementing new procedures.

23. We seem to be always implementing new changes and technology without giving serious thought to the implications of each change.

24. New procedures come and go without making much of a difference in the organization.

25. We have had trouble ensuring that our actions are consistent with organizational goals.

26. In this firm once a given course of action gains momentum it is difficult to change direction.

27. We often make the same mistakes over and over.

28. Good ideas tend to disappear if they are not in regular use.

29. Our experiences are not documented or encoded in procedures here.

30. The rationale we give for our performance outcomes often has little to do with the actual causes of these outcomes.

31. The actions we take to impact performance often have little effect on the performance outcomes.

32. We work to continually decrease the time between employee actions and feedback on those actions.

33. Learning in one group or unit is not spread throughout the organization.

34. Even though individuals here learn, this learning is not transmitted up to the organizational level.

Table A.16   Factor and Reliability Analyses of Organizational
Competitiveness and Innovativeness

Questionnaire items	Organizational competitiveness	Organizational innovativeness[a]

How does your business compare to competitors for each of the following functions or activities? (1 = much worse; 5 = much better)

Human resource practices	.68	
Customer relations	.61	
Marketing and sales	.61	
Production capability	.56	
Customer buying criteria	.56	
Business financial performance in the last three years	.53	
Research and development	.52	
Financial management	.51	
Organizational structure	.50	
Computer/management information system	.48	
Government relations	.47	
Globalization	.46	
Distribution channels	.44	
Mergers/acquisitions[b]	.32	
Divestitures[b]	.25	

Compared to your major competitor, how would you rank yourself on (1 = much worse; 5 = much better)

Willingness to experiment		.86
Willingness to take risks		.83
Reputation as an innovator		.80
Cycle time for innovation		.78
Eigenvalue	3.83	2.67
Percentage of variance explained	29.40	66.70
Alpha reliability coefficient	.78	.83

a. Separate factor analyses were conducted for organizational competitiveness and innovativeness because the questions were developed to measure the two different constructs and were asked in different sections of the survey.

b. This item was deleted from the final scale because of low factor loading.

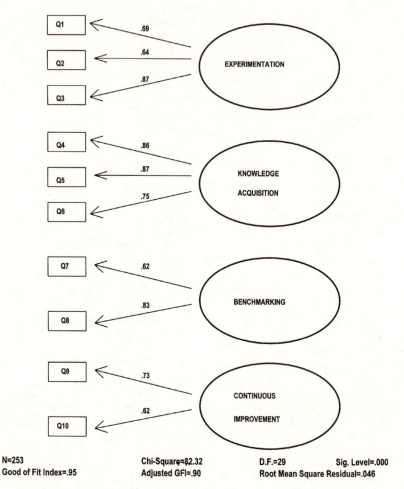

N=253   Chi-Square=82.32   D.F.=29   Sig. Level=.000
Good of Fit Index=.95   Adjusted GFI=.90   Root Mean Square Residual=.046

Figure A1.1   Confirmatory Factor Analysis of Four Learning Types

APPENDIX 2

Survey Research Instrument

ORGANIZATIONAL LEARNING AND COMPETITIVENESS:

AN INTERNATIONAL STUDY

Dear Participant:

Thank you for participating in this study entitled Organizational Learning and Competitiveness. This information will provide an international database that helps understand how organizations compete through learning, culture change, and management practices.

Please answer honestly every question. If you are unsure of an answer, please provide your best estimate. All responses will be completely confidential.

Please complete the survey and return it in the self-addressed return envelope within three weeks. If there is no return envelope, please mail the completed questionnaire to Questar Data Systems, Inc. for scanning:

> Questar Data Systems, Inc.
> 2905 West Service Road
> Eagan, Minnesota 55121-2199

If you have any questions about this survey, please contact Arthur Yeung at (415) 338-2255 (phone) or (415) 355-1723 (fax).

Sincerely,

Project Directors: Dave Ulrich, University of Michigan
Todd Jick, INSEAD
Mary Ann Von Glinow, University of Southern California
Bob Quinn, University of Michigan

Project Managers: Arthur Yeung, San Francisco State University
Steve Nason, University of Southern California
Ron Bendersky, University of Michigan

Sponsors: International Consortium for Executive Development Research
University of Michigan, School of Business

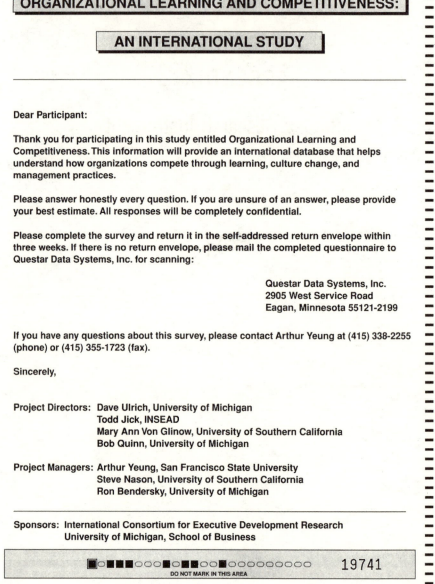

DO NOT MARK IN THIS AREA   19741

192

This survey is divided into seven sections: strategy, culture, learning organization types, learning disabilities, capacity for change, human resource practices, and business context. Many of the questions refer to your "business". "Business" refers to the *primary organizational unit* within which you work. "Business" should be an identifiable unit which is commonly understood in your corporation. Depending on your organizational level and responsibility, it may be a plant, a branch office, a regional office, a division, a subsidiary, a group, or an entire corporation. "Business" does not refer to your functional department; rather it refers to the organizational unit to which you generally apply your knowledge and skill. For example, if you work in human resources in a plant, division, group, or product line, "business" refers to the <u>organizational unit</u>, not the human resource function.

MARKING INSTRUCTIONS

- Use a No. 2 pencil.
- Fill in the oval completely.
- Erase cleanly any marks you wish to change.
- Do not make any stray marks on this form.

CORRECT MARK
○●○○
INCORRECT MARKS
⊘⊗⊙◓

BUSINESS STRATEGIES

Below are a series of questions that describe alternative strategies a business may follow to compete successfully in its market. Please indicate the extent to which each statement describes the current strategy of your business.

1. To compete successfully, our business strategy focuses on:

To Very Large Extent
To Large Extent
To Some Extent
To Little Extent
To Very Little Extent
Don't Know/Not Applicable

a. Advertising .... ⓪①②③④⑤
b. Brand identification .... ⓪①②③④⑤
c. Building employee commitment ..... ⓪①②③④⑤
d. Competitive pricing .... ⓪①②③④⑤
e. Controlling channels of distribution ... ⓪①②③④⑤
f. Cost reduction .... ⓪①②③④⑤
g. Developing operating technology .... ⓪①②③④⑤
h. Developing/refining existing products . ⓪①②③④⑤
i. Differentiating products or services
   from competitors .... ⓪①②③④⑤
j. Improving relationships with
   customers .... ⓪①②③④⑤
k. Innovation in marketing techniques
   and methods .... ⓪①②③④⑤
l. New products or service development . ⓪①②③④⑤
m. Operating efficiency .... ⓪①②③④⑤
n. Providing specialized products or
   services .... ⓪①②③④⑤
o. Quality of products or services ...... ⓪①②③④⑤

BUSINESS CULTURE

The following statements describe types of operating values which may exist in your business. Please indicate the extent to which each item is valued.

	Minimally Valued		Extensively Valued

1. Control, centralization .... ①②③④⑤⑥⑦

2. Flexibility, decentralization ..... ①②③④⑤⑥⑦

3. Empowerment of employees
   to act .... ①②③④⑤⑥⑦

4. Task focus, accomplishment,
   goal achievement .... ①②③④⑤⑥⑦

5. Efficiency, productivity,
   profitability .... ①②③④⑤⑥⑦

6. Predictable performance
   outcomes .... ①②③④⑤⑥⑦

7. Participation, open discussion .. ①②③④⑤⑥⑦

8. Outcome excellence, quality .... ①②③④⑤⑥⑦

9. Innovation and change .... ①②③④⑤⑥⑦

10. Assessing employee concerns
    and ideas..................... ①②③④⑤⑥⑦

11. Human relations, teamwork,
    cohesion .... ①②③④⑤⑥⑦

12. Stability, continuity, order ...... ①②③④⑤⑥⑦

| | Minimally
Valued | Extensively
Valued |

13. Expansion, growth and
development .... ① ② ③ ④ ⑤ ⑥ ⑦

14. Routinization, formalization,
structure .... ① ② ③ ④ ⑤ ⑥ ⑦

15. Direction, objective setting,
goal clarity .... ① ② ③ ④ ⑤ ⑥ ⑦

16. Creative problem solving
processes .... ① ② ③ ④ ⑤ ⑥ ⑦

LEARNING ORGANIZATION TYPES

To Very Large Extent
To Large Extent
To Some Extent
To Little Extent
To Very Little Extent
Don't Know/Not Applicable

To what extent do the following
statements characterize your business?

1. We primarily learn new ideas within
the boundaries of our team. .... ⓪ ① ② ③ ④ ⑤

2. We primarily learn new ideas
within the boundaries of our
organization, but outside our team. ... ⓪ ① ② ③ ④ ⑤

3. We primarily learn new ideas
outside the boundaries of our
organization. .... ⓪ ① ② ③ ④ ⑤

4. We explicitly go outside the
boundaries of our organization unit
to seek new ideas and information. ... ⓪ ① ② ③ ④ ⑤

5. We primarily benchmark competition
and measure progress against
competitor performance. .... ⓪ ① ② ③ ④ ⑤

6. We primarily benchmark ourselves
and measure progress against our
previous performance. .... ⓪ ① ② ③ ④ ⑤

7. We encourage individuals to acquire
new competencies. .... ⓪ ① ② ③ ④ ⑤

8. We encourage teams to acquire
competencies. .... ⓪ ① ② ③ ④ ⑤

9. Our rewards primarily focus on
individual performance. .... ⓪ ① ② ③ ④ ⑤

To Very Large Extent
To Large Extent
To Some Extent
To Little Extent
To Very Little Extent
Don't Know/Not Applicable

To what extent do the following
statements characterize your business?
(Continued)

10. Our rewards primarily focus on team
performance. .... ⓪ ① ② ③ ④ ⑤

11. We promote individuals who are
strong individual contributors. .... ⓪ ① ② ③ ④ ⑤

12. We promote individuals who are
strong team players. .... ⓪ ① ② ③ ④ ⑤

13. We work to master new ideas before
trying something new. .... ⓪ ① ② ③ ④ ⑤

14. We constantly seek new ideas even
before old ones are fully implemented. . ⓪ ① ② ③ ④ ⑤

15. We work to upgrade the way that we
do existing work until we have it right. . ⓪ ① ② ③ ④ ⑤

16. We constantly seek new ways to
do work. .... ⓪ ① ② ③ ④ ⑤

17. We work to be masters at what we
do; we want to be known as the best
technical experts in our industry. ...... ⓪ ① ② ③ ④ ⑤

18. We try a lot of new ideas; we want to
be known as experimenters within
our industry. .... ⓪ ① ② ③ ④ ⑤

19. We want to be the first in the market
with a new process or product. ...... ⓪ ① ② ③ ④ ⑤

20. We want to learn from others and
enter a product or apply a process
after it has been fully tested. .... ⓪ ① ② ③ ④ ⑤

21. We learn by scanning broadly what
other companies do. .... ⓪ ① ② ③ ④ ⑤

22. We learn by focusing our scanning
on specific activities done by other
companies. .... ⓪ ① ② ③ ④ ⑤

23. We learn by hiring people from other
companies who have skills we need. . ⓪ ① ② ③ ④ ⑤

24. Learning is a critical part of our
business strategy. .... ⓪ ① ② ③ ④ ⑤

- 3 -

To Very Large Extent
To Large Extent
To Some Extent
To Little Extent
To Very Little Extent
Don't Know/Not Applicable

To what extent do the following statements characterize your business?

1. We are good at scanning the external environment for opportunities and potential problems. ⓪ ① ② ③ ④ ⑤

2. We are active in finding/creating new markets. ⓪ ① ② ③ ④ ⑤

3. We are good at perceiving long term environmental threats, opportunities. ⓪ ① ② ③ ④ ⑤

4. We are good at scanning the internal workings and processes of this organization for areas which may be improved upon. ⓪ ① ② ③ ④ ⑤

5. We work to insure that all employees can recognize or discover the information that they need to perform their job. ⓪ ① ② ③ ④ ⑤

6. In general, our work procedures have functioned well so we see little need of pervasive change. ⓪ ① ② ③ ④ ⑤

7. "If it ain't broke, don't fix it" would represent the general attitude here pretty well. ⓪ ① ② ③ ④ ⑤

8. We intentionally create small "false alarms," "crises," etc. in the work place to stimulate improvements or problem solving. ⓪ ① ② ③ ④ ⑤

9. Political considerations of important stakeholders influence the actions of our organization. ⓪ ① ② ③ ④ ⑤

10. We try to uncover and communicate all relevant facts, not just those that are politically acceptable. ⓪ ① ② ③ ④ ⑤

11. We work to insure that employees are directly exposed to the variation and complexity of the environment. ⓪ ① ② ③ ④ ⑤

12. We are good at determining the causes of unexpectedly low and high levels of performance. ⓪ ① ② ③ ④ ⑤

13. We are good at deciding on plans of action to redress performance shortfalls. ⓪ ① ② ③ ④ ⑤

14. We try to insure that all employees have access to more information than the minimum required to perform their job. ⓪ ① ② ③ ④ ⑤

15. We are good at generating and evaluating a wide variety of alternative solutions to performance shortfalls. ⓪ ① ② ③ ④ ⑤

To Very Large Extent
To Large Extent
To Some Extent
To Little Extent
To Very Little Extent
Don't Know/Not Applicable

To what extent do the following statements characterize your business? (Continued)

16. We encourage diversity in people and ideas within our organization. ⓪ ① ② ③ ④ ⑤

17. Intelligent risk taking which results in failure is not punished. ⓪ ① ② ③ ④ ⑤

18. There is a lack of coordination between multiple, competing perspectives at this organization. ⓪ ① ② ③ ④ ⑤

19. Groups and Departments in this organization function fairly independently without much integration. ⓪ ① ② ③ ④ ⑤

20. We tend to over analyze problems before implementing ideas--and thus miss opportunities for improvement. ⓪ ① ② ③ ④ ⑤

21. Employees have a significant say in how their work is done. ⓪ ① ② ③ ④ ⑤

22. We have trouble implementing new procedures. ⓪ ① ② ③ ④ ⑤

23. We seem to always be implementing new changes and technology without giving serious thought to the implications of each change. ⓪ ① ② ③ ④ ⑤

24. New procedures come and go without making much of a difference in the organization. ⓪ ① ② ③ ④ ⑤

25. We have had trouble insuring that our actions are consistent with organizational goals. ⓪ ① ② ③ ④ ⑤

26. In this firm once a given course of action gains momentum it is difficult to change direction. ⓪ ① ② ③ ④ ⑤

27. We often make the same mistakes over and over. ⓪ ① ② ③ ④ ⑤

28. Good ideas tend to disappear if not in regular use. ⓪ ① ② ③ ④ ⑤

29. Our experiences are not documented or encoded in procedures here. ⓪ ① ② ③ ④ ⑤

30. The rationale we give for our performance outcomes often has little to do with the actual causes of these outcomes. ⓪ ① ② ③ ④ ⑤

31. The actions we take to impact performance often have little effect on the performance outcomes. ⓪ ① ② ③ ④ ⑤

32. We work to continually decrease the time between employee actions and feedback on those actions. ⓪ ① ② ③ ④ ⑤

To Very Large Extent
To Large Extent
To Some Extent
To Little Extent
To Very Little Extent
Don't Know/Not Applicable

To what extent do the following statements characterize your business? (Continued)

33. Learning in one group or unit is not spread throughout the organization. .⓪①②③④⑤

34. Even though individuals here learn, this learning is not transmitted up to the organizational level. ....⓪①②③④⑤

CAPACITY FOR CHANGE

1. What is the percent of sales (revenue) of your business based on products introduced in the last three years?

① Less than 5%	⑧ 35-39%	⑮ 70-74%
② 5-9%	⑨ 40-44%	⑯ 75-79%
③ 10-14%	⑩ 45-49%	⑰ 80-84%
④ 15-19%	⑪ 50-54%	⑱ 85-89%
⑤ 20-24%	⑫ 55-59%	⑲ 90-94%
⑥ 25-29%	⑬ 60-64%	⑳ 95-100%
⑦ 30-34%	⑭ 65-69%	

2. How long is your product development cycle (from concept to introduction of new product or service)?

a. Three years ago:

MONTHS
Write in number of months here. ➔ [ ][ ]
Then fill in the appropriate ovals. ➔
⓪ ⓪
① ①
② ②
③ ③
④ ④
⑤ ⑤
⑥ ⑥
⑦ ⑦
⑧ ⑧
⑨ ⑨

b. Today:

MONTHS
Write in number of months here. ➔ [ ][ ]
Then fill in the appropriate ovals. ➔
⓪ ⓪
① ①
② ②
③ ③
④ ④
⑤ ⑤
⑥ ⑥
⑦ ⑦
⑧ ⑧
⑨ ⑨

3. Compared to your major competitor, how would you rank yourself on:

Much Better
Better
Same
Worse
Much Worse

a. Response time to customers ....①②③④⑤
b. Cycle time for innovation ....①②③④⑤
c. Willingness to experiment ....①②③④⑤
d. Willingness to take risks ....①②③④⑤
e. Reputation as an innovator ....①②③④⑤

4. For each of the following items, please indicate the extent to which the behavior represents the leadership within your business:

To Very Large Extent
To Large Extent
To Some Extent
To Little Extent
To Very Little Extent
Don't Know/Not Applicable

1. Seeks and supports process innovations that improve productivity. .⓪①②③④⑤

2. Finds opportunities in change rather than excuses for avoiding change. ...⓪①②③④⑤

3. Pays attention (time, energy) to change. ....⓪①②③④⑤

4. Leads by example. ....⓪①②③④⑤

5. Clarifies role and responsibilities for accomplishing change. ....⓪①②③④⑤

6. Sets high expectations around accomplishing change. ....⓪①②③④⑤

7. Generates data that shows a need for change. ....⓪①②③④⑤

8. Sees the business from the customer's point of view. ....⓪①②③④⑤

9. Creates a bold and clear sense of purpose that energizes others. ....⓪①②③④⑤

10. Articulates a vision that others can readily embrace. ....⓪①②③④⑤

11. Creates enthusiastic support for business objectives. ....⓪①②③④⑤

12. Forms a coalition of key players who are central to change. ....⓪①②③④⑤

13. Determines the causes of resistance to change. ....⓪①②③④⑤

14. Recognizes alternative ways of dealing with conflict. ....⓪①②③④⑤

15. Engages in appropriate problem solving activity. ....⓪①②③④⑤

16. Acts in ways that demonstrates public commitment to change. ....⓪①②③④⑤

17. Transfers learning from one site to another. ....⓪①②③④⑤

18. Assigns responsibility for making change last. ....⓪①②③④⑤

19. Leverages symbols, language, and culture to support change. ....⓪①②③④⑤

20. Encourages empowered leadership throughout the organization. ....⓪①②③④⑤

21. Integrates any one change to overall business process.................⓪①②③④⑤

22. Establishes milestones toward objectives..........................⓪①②③④⑤

23. Tracks progress on business changes. ....⓪①②③④⑤

24. Shares results widely. ....⓪①②③④⑤

25. Holds people accountable for results...⓪①②③④⑤

26. Selects most talented people available. ....⓪①②③④⑤

27. Coaches others to improve..........⓪①②③④⑤

	To Very Large Extent
	To Large Extent
	To Some Extent
	To Little Extent
	To Very Little Extent
	Don't Know/Not Applicable

28. **Ensures employees have competencies to do their job.** .... ⓪ ① ② ③ ④ ⑤

29. **Establishes relevant, challenging objectives for self and unit.** .... ⓪ ① ② ③ ④ ⑤

30. **Provides specific frequent feedback that improves team performance.** .... ⓪ ① ② ③ ④ ⑤

31. **Shares credit and recognition with others.** .... ⓪ ① ② ③ ④ ⑤

32. **Shares and seeks information widely.** .... ⓪ ① ② ③ ④ ⑤

33. **Listens effectively.** .... ⓪ ① ② ③ ④ ⑤

34. **Communicates openly and candidly...** ⓪ ① ② ③ ④ ⑤

HUMAN RESOURCE PRACTICES

For each practice, please indicate the extent to which the business allocates resources (time and money) and focuses attention on the practice.

	To Very Large Extent
	To Large Extent
	To Some Extent
	To Little Extent
	To Very Little Extent
	Don't Know/Not Applicable

Staffing

a. Attract appropriate people .... ⓪ ① ② ③ ④ ⑤

b. Promote appropriate people .... ⓪ ① ② ③ ④ ⑤

c. Outplace appropriate people .... ⓪ ① ② ③ ④ ⑤

Development

a. Offer training programs .... ⓪ ① ② ③ ④ ⑤

b. Design development programs that facilitate change .... ⓪ ① ② ③ ④ ⑤

c. Prepare talent through cross functional moves or task force assignments ..... ⓪ ① ② ③ ④ ⑤

d. Offer career planning services .... ⓪ ① ② ③ ④ ⑤

Performance Appraisal

a. Facilitate establishment of clear performance standards .... ⓪ ① ② ③ ④ ⑤

b. Design feedback processes .... ⓪ ① ② ③ ④ ⑤

c. Design performance appraisal systems to differentiate performance .. ⓪ ① ② ③ ④ ⑤

d. Design performance appraisal systems for career planning .... ⓪ ① ② ③ ④ ⑤

Rewards

a. Design compensation systems .... ⓪ ① ② ③ ④ ⑤

b. Design benefits systems .... ⓪ ① ② ③ ④ ⑤

c. Design non-financial reward/ recognition systems .... ⓪ ① ② ③ ④ ⑤

	To Very Large Extent
	To Large Extent
	To Some Extent
	To Little Extent
	To Very Little Extent
	Don't Know/Not Applicable

Communication

a. Facilitate design of internal communication processes .... ⓪ ① ② ③ ④ ⑤

b. Help explain why business practices exist .... ⓪ ① ② ③ ④ ⑤

c. Work with managers to send clear and consistent messages .... ⓪ ① ② ③ ④ ⑤

Organization Design

a. Help create reporting relationships .... ⓪ ① ② ③ ④ ⑤

b. Help design self-managing/autonomous work groups .... ⓪ ① ② ③ ④ ⑤

c. Facilitate the process of restructuring the organization .... ⓪ ① ② ③ ④ ⑤

d. Facilitate the integration of different business functions .... ⓪ ① ② ③ ④ ⑤

NATIONAL CULTURE

The descriptions below apply to four different types of managers. Please read through these descriptions:

A. **Usually makes decisions promptly and communicates them to subordinates clearly and firmly. Expects them to carry out decisions loyally and without raising difficulties.**

B. **Usually makes decisions promptly, but before going ahead tries to explain them fully to subordinates, then gives them the reasons for the decisions and answers whatever questions they may have.**

C. **Usually consults with subordinates before reaching a decision. Listens to their advice, considers it and then announces the decision. Expects all to work loyally to implement it whether or not it is in accordance with the advice they gave.**

D. **Usually calls a meeting of subordinates when there is a decision to be made. Puts the problem before the group and invites discussions. Accepts the majority viewpoint as the decision.**

1. **What of the above four types would you prefer to work under?** .... Ⓐ Ⓑ Ⓒ Ⓓ

2. **Which one of the above four types of managers would you say your own superior most closely resembles?** .... Ⓐ Ⓑ Ⓒ Ⓓ

3. How frequently in your work environment are subordinates afraid to express disagreement with their superiors? (mark correct answer)

○ Very frequently
○ Frequently
○ Sometimes
○ Almost never
○ Never feel this way

Please think of an ideal job - disregarding your present job. In choosing an ideal job, how important would it be to you to:

Of Utmost Importance
Very Important
Of Moderate Importance
Of Little Importance
Very Little Importance

1. Have sufficient time left for your personal or family life? .... ① ② ③ ④ ⑤

2. Have good physical working conditions (good ventilation and lighting, adequate work space, etc.)? .... ① ② ③ ④ ⑤

3. Work with people who cooperate well with one another? .... ① ② ③ ④ ⑤

4. Live in an area desirable to you and your family? .... ① ② ③ ④ ⑤

5. Have little tension and stress on the job? . ① ② ③ ④ ⑤

6. Have security of employment? .... ① ② ③ ④ ⑤

7. Have an opportunity of high earnings? . ① ② ③ ④ ⑤

8. Have an opportunity for advancement to higher level jobs? .... ① ② ③ ④ ⑤

Using the same scale above, please indicate how important each of the following items are to you:

1. Persistence .... ① ② ③ ④ ⑤

2. Protecting your "face" (dignity, self respect, maintaining appearances and prestige) .... ① ② ③ ④ ⑤

3. Respect for tradition .... ① ② ③ ④ ⑤

4. Short term results versus a long term focus .... ① ② ③ ④ ⑤

5. How often do you feel nervous or tense at work?

○ Never
○ Seldom
○ Sometimes
○ Usually
○ Always

6. A company or organization's rule should not be broken - even when the employee thinks it is in the organization's best interest:

○ Strongly disagree
○ Disagree
○ Undecided
○ Agree
○ Strongly agree

7. How long do you think you will continue working for the organization or company you work for now?

○ Two years at the most
○ From two to five years
○ More than five years (but I will probably leave before I retire)
○ Until I retire

BUSINESS CONTEXT

This set of questions asks for information about the industry in which your business operates.

1. To the best of your knowledge, what has been the growth or decline of the industry in which your business operated in the last three years?

① Not applicable/Don't know
② Decline more than 10%
③ Decline 5-10%
④ Stable
⑤ Growth 5-10%
⑥ Growth more than 10%

2. To the best of your knowledge, what percent of the industry in which your business currently operates is accounted for by the four largest competitors? (this may or may not include your business)

① Less than 5%	⑧ 35% to 39%	⑮ 70% to 74%
② 5% to 9%	⑨ 40% to 44%	⑯ 75% to 79%
③ 10% to 14%	⑩ 45% to 49%	⑰ 80% to 84%
④ 15% to 19%	⑪ 50% to 54%	⑱ 85% to 89%
⑤ 20% to 24%	⑫ 55% to 59%	⑲ 90% to 94%
⑥ 25% to 29%	⑬ 60% to 64%	⑳ 95% to 100%
⑦ 30% to 34%	⑭ 65% to 69%	

3. To what extent are the changes predictable for the industry in which your business operates over the next three years?

① Not applicable/don't know ④ To some extent
② To very little extent ⑤ To large extent
③ To little extent ⑥ To very large extent

This set of questions asks for information about your business.

To Very Large Extent
To Large Extent
To Some Extent
To Little Extent
To Very Little Extent
Don't Know/Not Applicable

4. To what extent do the customers of your business work to maintain a long-term relationship with your business? .. ① ② ③ ④ ⑤ ⑥

5. To what extent does your business work to maintain a long-term relationship with its key suppliers? ... ① ② ③ ④ ⑤ ⑥

6. To what extent does the accomplishment of the major operational work within your business require interdependence among the employees?

① Not applicable/don't know
② To very little extent
③ To little extent
④ To some extent
⑤ To large extent
⑥ To very large extent

7. To what extent are the following functions or activities changing for your business.

	To Very Great Extent	To Great Extent	To Some Extent	To Little Extent	To Very Little Extent	Don't Know/Not Applicable
a. Computer/management information system						⓪①②③④⑤
b. Customer buying criteria						⓪①②③④⑤
c. Customer relations						⓪①②③④⑤
d. Distribution channels						⓪①②③④⑤
e. Divestitures						⓪①②③④⑤
f. Financial management						⓪①②③④⑤
g. Globalization						⓪①②③④⑤
h. Government relations						⓪①②③④⑤
i. Human resource practices						⓪①②③④⑤
j. Marketing & sales						⓪①②③④⑤
k. Mergers/acquisitions						⓪①②③④⑤
l. Organization structure						⓪①②③④⑤
m. Production capability						⓪①②③④⑤
n. Research and development						⓪①②③④⑤

8. How does your business compare to competitors for each of the following functions or activities?

	Much Better	Better	Same	Worse	Much Worse
a. Computer/management information system					①②③④⑤
b. Customer buying criteria					①②③④⑤
c. Customer relations					①②③④⑤
d. Distribution channels					①②③④⑤
e. Divestitures					①②③④⑤
f. Financial management					①②③④⑤
g. Globalization					①②③④⑤
h. Government relations					①②③④⑤
i. Human resource practices					①②③④⑤
j. Marketing & sales					①②③④⑤
k. Mergers/acquisitions					①②③④⑤
l. Organization structure					①②③④⑤
m. Production capability					①②③④⑤
n. Research and development					①②③④⑤

9. Compared to the major competitor in your business in the last three years, how has your business performed financially?

○ Much worse
○ Worse
○ Same
○ Better
○ Much better

10. Industry code of your business. (Please refer to enclosed list of SIC codes)

Write in your number → starting at the top and continuing to the bottom. Then fill in the matching ovals.

⓪①②③④⑤⑥⑦⑧⑨
⓪①②③④⑤⑥⑦⑧⑨
⓪①②③④⑤⑥⑦⑧⑨
⓪①②③④⑤⑥⑦⑧⑨

11. Approximate year your business was established.

Write in your number → starting at the top and continuing to the bottom. Then fill in the matching ovals.

⓪①②③④⑤⑥⑦⑧⑨
⓪①②③④⑤⑥⑦⑧⑨
⓪①②③④⑤⑥⑦⑧⑨
⓪①②③④⑤⑥⑦⑧⑨

12. Approximate number of employees in your business. (full-time equivalent)

Write in your number → starting at the top and continuing to the bottom. Then fill in the matching ovals.

⓪①②③④⑤⑥⑦⑧⑨
⓪①②③④⑤⑥⑦⑧⑨
⓪①②③④⑤⑥⑦⑧⑨
⓪①②③④⑤⑥⑦⑧⑨
⓪①②③④⑤⑥⑦⑧⑨

DEMOGRAPHICS

A. Age

Write in your number → starting at the top and continuing to the bottom. Then fill in the matching ovals.

⓪①②③④⑤⑥⑦⑧⑨
⓪①②③④⑤⑥⑦⑧⑨

B. Years at Present Corporation

Write in your number → starting at the top and continuing to the bottom. Then fill in the matching ovals.

⓪①②③④⑤⑥⑦⑧⑨
⓪①②③④⑤⑥⑦⑧⑨

C. Primary role:

○ Individual Contributor
○ Manager of Individual Contributors
○ Director of Managers
○ General Managers

D. Functional Speciality:

① Finance/Accounting
② General Management
③ Human Resource/Personnel
④ Manufacturing/Production
⑤ Marketing/Sales
⑥ Planning
⑦ Research & Development
⑧ Others

R6299-Questar/8210-54321

199

NOTES

CHAPTER 1

1. Presentation made by Mr. Teerlink within the company. Heard by one of the authors (D. Ulrich).

2. Some of the classic studies of organizational learning are J. G. March and H. A. Simon, 1958, *Organizations.* (New York: Wiley); R. M. Cyert and J. G. March, 1963, *A Behavioral Theory of the Firm* (Englewood Cliffs, N.J.: Prentice Hall); C. Argyris and D. A. Schon, 1978, *Organizational Learning: A Theory of Action Perspective* (Reading, Mass.: Addison-Wesley); C. M. Fiol and M. A. Lyles, 1985, "Organizational Learning," *Academy of Management Review* 10(4): 803–813.

More recent works that have focused on learning include P. M. Senge 1990, *The Fifth Discipline: The Art and Practice of the Learning Organization* (New York: Doubleday/Currency); D. Garvin, 1993, "Building a Learning Organization," *Harvard Business Review* (July–August): 78–91; C. Wick, 1993, *The Learning Edge: How Smart Managers and Smart Companies Stay Ahead* (New York: McGraw-Hill).

3. I. Nonaka, 1991, "The Knowledge Creating Company," *Harvard Business Review* (November–December): 96.

4. Statistics compiled from the Department of Education and the teaching notes of Kim Cameron, a professor at the University of Michigan.

5. R. Stata, 1989, "Organizational Learning: The Key to Management Innovation," *Sloan Management Review* (Spring): 64.

6. Personal conversation between Jack Welch and one of the authors (D. Ulrich).

7. P. Vaill, 1989, *Managing as a Performing Art: New Ideas for a World of Chaotic Change* (San Francisco: Jossey-Bass).

8. C. Wick, 1993, *The Learning Edge: How Smart Managers and Smart Companies Stay Ahead* (New York: McGraw-Hill), p. 4.

9. C. M. Fiol and M. A. Lyles, 1985, "Organizational Learning," *Academy of Management Review* 10(4): 803–813.

10. B. Hedberg, 1981. "How Organizations Learn and Unlearn," in Nystrom and Starbuck (eds.), *Handbook of Organizational Design* (Oxford: Oxford University Press), p. 6.

11. J. Slocum and C. Dilloway, 1992, "Discussion Group Report: The Learning Organization," Working paper, Southern Methodist University, School of Management, p. 45.

12. R. B. Shaw and D. Perkins, 1991, "Teaching Organizations to Learn," *Organization Development Journal* 9(4): 1.

13. C. M. Fiol and M. A. Lyles, 1985, "Organizational Learning," *Academy of Management Review* 10(4): 803.

14. P. M. Senge, 1990, *The Fifth Discipline: The Art and Practice of the Learning Organization* (New York: Doubleday/Currency), p. 14.

15. C. Wick, 1993, *The Learning Edge: How Smart Managers and Smart Companies Stay Ahead* (New York: McGraw-Hill), p. 5.

16. On the importance of culture change, see A. L. Wilkins, 1989, *Developing Corporate Character* (San Francisco: Jossey-Bass). On the logic of culture change, see E. G. Schein, 1985, *Organizational Culture and Leadership* (San Francisco: Jossey-Bass); T. E. Deal and A. A. Kennedy, 1982, *Corporate Cultures: The Rites and Rituals of Corporate Life* (Reading, Mass.: Addison-Wesley); S. Davis, 1984, *Managing Corporate Culture* (Cambridge, Mass.: Ballinger). On the financial impact of culture change, see J. Kotter and J. Heskett, 1992, *Culture and Performance* (New York: Free Press).

17. I. Nonaka and H. Takeuchi, 1995, *The Knowledge-creating Company* (New York: Oxford University Press).

CHAPTER 2

1. J. Collins and J. Porras, 1994, *Built to Last: Successful Habits of Visionary Companies* (New York: HarperCollins).

2. Ibid., p. 158.

3. F. W. Taylor, 1911, *The Principles of Scientific Management* (Norwood, Mass.: Plimpton Press).

4. J. G. March and H. A. Simon, 1958, *Organizations* (New York: Wiley).

5. W. G. Chase and H. A. Simon, 1973, "The Mind's Eye in Chess" in W. G. Chase (ed.), *Visual Information Processing* (New York: Academic Press); J. H. Larkin, J. McDermott, D. Simon, and H. A. Simon, 1980, "Expert and Novice Performance in Solving Physics Problems," *Science* 45: 208.

6. H. A. Simon, 1955, "A Behavioral Model of Rational Choice," *Quarterly Journal of Economics* 69: 99–118.

7. B. Levitt and J. G. March, 1988, "Organizational Learning," *Annual Review of Sociology* 14: 319–340.

8. C. Argyris and D. A. Schon, 1978. *Organizational Learning: A Theory*

of Action Perspective (Reading, Mass.: Addison-Wesley); G. Bateson, 1972, *Steps to an Ecology of Mind* (New York: Ballentine).

9. W. Snyder and S. Nason, 1992, "Organizational Learning Disabilities," Working paper, School of Business Administration, University of Southern California.

10. C. Argyris, 1990, *Overcoming Organizational Defenses: Facilitating Organizational Learning* (Boston: Allyn and Bacon); C. Argyris, 1982, *Reasoning, Learning, and Action* (San Francisco: Jossey-Bass); C. Argyris, 1991, "Teaching Smart People How to Learn,"*Harvard Business Review* (May-June): 99–109.

11. G. P. Huber, 1991, "Organizational Learning: The Contributing Processes and the Literatures," *Organization Science* 2(1): 88–115.

12. P. M. Senge, 1990, "The Leader's New Work: Building Learning Organizations,": *Sloan Management Review* (Fall 1990): 7–23; P. M. Senge, 1990, *The Fifth Discipline: The Art and Practice of the Learning Organization* (New York: Doubleday/Currency).

13. J. Kotter, 1996, *Leading Change* (Boston: Harvard Business School Press), p. 4.

14. J. Kotter and J. Heskett, 1992, *Culture and Performance* (New York: Free Press).

15. I. I. Mitroff and F. Betz, 1972, "Dialectical Decision Theory: A Metatheory of Decision-Making," *Management Science* 19: 11–24.

16. C. Argyris and D. A. Schon, 1978, *Organizational Learning: A Theory of Action Perspective* (Reading, Mass.: Addison-Wesley) G. P. Huber, 1991, "Organizational Learning: The Contributing Processes and the Literatures," *Organization Science* 2(1): 88–115.

17. P. M. Senge, 1990, *The Fifth Discipline: The Art and Practice of the Learning Organization* (New York: Doubleday/Currency), p. 12.

18. Ibid., p. 68, p. 73.

19. M. Hammer, 1990, "Reengineering Work," *Harvard Business Review* (July–August).

20. AT&T, 1991, *Reengineering Handbook* (Indianapolis, Ind.: AT&T Customer Information Center).

21. W. Snyder and S. Nason, 1992, "Organizational Learning Disabilities," Working paper, School of Business Administration, University of Southern California, Los Angeles.

22. C. M. Fiol and M. A. Lyles, 1985, "Organizational Learning," *Academy of Management Review* 10(4): 803–813.

23. S. B. Sitkin, 1992, "Learning Through Failure: The Strategy of Small Losses," *Research in Organizational Behavior* 14: 231–266.

24. Some authors, including Chris Argyris, claim that the learning steps occur simultaneously, not sequentially; still, for clarity's sake, they present the learning process sequentially.

25. I. Nonaka and H. Takeuchi, 1995, *The Knowledge-Creating Company* (New York: Oxford University Press); J. M. Dutton and R. D. Freedman, 1985, "External Environment and Internal Strategies: Calculating, Experimenting,

and Imitating in Organizations," in R. Lamb and P. Shrivastava (eds.), *Advances in Strategic Management*, vol. 3 (Greenwich, Conn.: JAI Press).

26. D. Ulrich and H. Greenfield, 1995, "The Transformation of Training and Development to Development and Learning," *American Journal of Management Development* 1(2): 11–22.

27. R. Duncan and A. Weiss, 1979, "Organizational Learning: Implications for Organizational Design," *Research in Organizational Behavior* 1: 75–123; P. Shrivastava, 1983, "A Typology of Organizational Learning Systems," *Journal of Management Studies* 20(1): 7–27.

28. D. Epple, L. Argote, and R. Devadas, 1991, "Organizational Learning Curves: A Method for Investigating Intra-plant Transfer of Knowledge Acquired Through Learning by Doing," *Organization Science* 2(1): 58.

29. M. Imai, 1986, *Kaizen: The Key to Japan's Competitive Success* (New York: Random House); J. P. MacDuffie and J. Krafcik, 1992, "Integrating Technology and Human Resources for High-performance Manufacturing: Evidence from the International Auto Industry," in T. Kochan and M. Useem (eds.), *Transforming Organizations* (Oxford University Press).

30. E. Abrahamson, 1991, "Managerial Fads and Fashions: The Diffusion and Rejection of Innovations," *Academy of Management Review* 16(3): 586–612; G. P. Huber, 1991, "Organizational Learning: The Contributing Processes and the Literatures," *Organizational Science* 2(1): 88–115; B. Levitt and J. G. March, 1988, "Organizational Learning," *Annual Review of Sociology* 14: 319–340.

31. P. DiMaggio and W. Powell, 1983, "The Iron Cage Revisited: Institutional Isomorphism and Collective Rationality in Organizational Fields," *American Sociological Review* 48: 147–160; J. W. Meyer and B. Rowan, 1977, "Institutionalized Organizations: Formal Structure as Myth and Ceremony," *American Journal of Sociology* 83: 440–463.

32. L. Bourgeois and K. Eisenhardt, 1988, "Strategic Decision Processes in High Velocity Environments: Four Cases in the Microcomputer Industry," *Management Science* 34(7): 816–835; J. M. Dutton and R. D. Freedman, 1985, "External Environment and Internal Strategies: Calculating, Experimenting, and Imitating in Organizations," in R. Lamb and P. Shrivastava (eds.), *Advances in Strategic Management*, vol. 3 (Greenwich, Conn.: JAI Press; P. DiMaggio and W. Powell, 1983, "The Iron Cage Revisited: Institutional Isomorphism and Collective Rationality in Organizational Fields," *American Sociological Review* 48: 147–160; E. Abrahamson, 1991, "Managerial Fads and Fashions: The Diffusion and Rejection of Innovations," *Academy of Management Review* 16(3): 586–612.

33. J. G. March, 1991, "Exploration and Exploitation in Organizational Learning," *Organizational Science* 2(1): 71.

34. M. Tushman and P. Anderson, 1986, "Technological Discontinuities and Organizational Environments," *Administrative Science Quarterly* 31: 439–465.

35. W. Powell, K. Koput, and L. Smith-Doerr, 1994, "Technological Change and the Locus of Innovation: Networks of Learning in Biotechnol-

ogy," Unpublished manuscript; M. Tushman and P. Anderson, 1986, "Technological Discontinuities and Organizational Environments," *Administrative Science Quarterly* 31: 439–465; M. E. Porter, 1980, *Competitive Strategy* (New York: Free Press); M. E. Porter, 1986, *Competitive Advantage* (New York: Free Press).

36. I. Myers, 1962, *Manual: The Myers-Briggs Type Indicator* (Palo Alto, Calif.: Consulting Psychologists Press); D. Keirsey and M. Bates, 1984, *Please Understand Me* (Gnosology Books Ltd.)

CHAPTER 3

1. From R. Kanter, J. Kao, and F. Wiersema, (eds.), 1997, *Innovation* (New York: HarperCollins), p. 151.

2. S. Covey, 1989, *The Seven Habits of Highly Effective People: Powerful Lessons in Personal Change* (New York: Simon and Schuster).

3. This quotation came from a personal conversation that one of us (Ulrich) had with Chris, but the logic can be found in his work on double-loop learning: C. Argyris, and D. A. Schon, 1978, *Organizational Learning: A Theory of Action Perspective* (Reading, Mass.: Addison-Wesley) or C. Argyris, 1982, *Reasoning, Learning and Action* (San Francisco: Jossey-Bass).

4. W. M. Snyder and T. Cummings, 1992, "Organizational Learning Disabilities: Guidelines for Organizational Development Interventions," Working paper, University of Southern California, 1–22.

5. G. P. Huber, 1991, "Organizational Learning: The Contributing Processes and the Literatures," *Organization Science* 2(1): 88–115.

6. K. E. Weick, 1979, *The Social Psychology of Organizing* (New York: Random House).

7. C. Argyris, 1990, *Overcoming Organizational Defenses: Facilitating Organizational Learning* (Boston: Allyn and Bacon); W. M. Snyder, and T. Cummings, 1992, "Organizational Learning Disabilities: Guidelines for Organizational Development Interventions," Working paper, University of Southern California, 1–22.

8. H. Hornstein, 1986, *Managerial Courage* (New York: Wiley).

9. S. B. Sitkin, 1992, "Learning Through Failure: The Strategy of Small Losses," *Research in Organizational Behavior* 14: 231–266.

10. M. E. Porter, 1980, *Competitive Strategy* (New York: Free Press); G. G. Dess and P. Davis, 1984, "Porter's Generic Strategies as Determinants of Strategic Group Membership and Organizational Performance," *Academy of Management Journal* 27: 467–488.

11. R. E. Quinn, and J. Rohrbaugh, 1983, "A Spatial Model of Effectiveness Criteria: Toward a Competing Values Approach to Organizational Analysis," *Management Science* 29(3): 363–377; R. E. Quinn, and K. S. Cameron, 1988, *Paradox and Transformation: Toward a Framework of Change in Organization and Management* (Cambridge, Mass.: Ballinger); R. E. Quinn, 1988, *Beyond Rational Management* (San Francisco: Jossey-Bass).

CHAPTER 4

1. These quotes are from J. Kao, 1996, *Jamming* (New York: Harper-Business), pp. xv–xvi.

2. J. Collins, and J. Porras, 1994, *Built to Last: Successful Habits of Visionary Companies* (New York: HarperCollins).

3. "Masters of Innovation," 1989, *Business Week* (10 April): 62.

4. V. Huck, 1995, *Brand of the Tartan—The 3M Story* (New York: Appleton-Century-Crofts), pp. 189–190.

5. 3M Company, 1977, *Our Story So Far* (St. Paul, Minn.: 3M Company).

6. Collins and Porras, ibid., p. 140.

7. See R. Pascale, and E. T. Christiansen, 1983, "Honda (B)," Harvard Business School Case #9–384–050.

8. 3M Company, ibid., p. 70.

9. From *In Motion*, HP's corporate publication (September 1994): 62.

10. Some of the background for this case is drawn from J. F. Miraglia, 1994, "An Evolutionary Approach to Revolutionary Change and the Implications for Human Resources Practice," in C. Schneier, (ed.), *Managing Strategic Change* Human Resource Planning Society).

11. Mentioned in a presentation by Dan Halloran, regional HR director of Motorola's Paging Business in the Asia-Pacific region, March, 1997.

12. H. M. Petrakis, 1965, *The Founder's Touch* (New York: McGraw-Hill), p. xi.

13. R. Galvin, 1991, *The Idea of Ideas* (Schaumburg, Ill.: Motorola University Press), p. 45.

14. W. Wiggenhorn, 1990, "Motorola U: When Training Becomes an Education," *Harvard Business Review* (July–August).

15. Based on a presentation by William Wiggenhorn, President of Motorola University, at China-Europe International Business School, Shanghai, on October 23, 1997.

16. Based on a personal interview with Ken Hansen, Director of Strategic Education at Motorola University, September 9, 1994.

17. Based on a phone interview with Ramli Abbas, Vice President and Country Manager of Motorola Malaysia, conducted by Arthur Yeung on June 16, 1997.

18. P. Woolcock, A. Yeung, and J. Gee 1994, "Motorola University: Education as a Source of Competitive Advantage," Research Report, California Strategic Human Resource Partnership.

19. From an interview Patty Woolcock conducted with Ken Hansen at Motorola University in 1994.

20. From T. Jick, 1993, "Alcatel Bell." This case was written as part of the ICEDR-funded project on organizational learning.

21. T. Jick, op. cit., p. 1.

22. P. Block, 1988, *The Empowered Manager: Positive Political Skills at Work* (San Francisco: Jossey-Bass).

23. T. Jick, op. cit., p. 9.

24. T. Jick, op. cit., p. 9.

25. These quotes are extracted from T. Jick, op. cit., pp. 14–16.

CHAPTER 5

1. Information on boundaryless organizations can be found in R. Ashkenas, D. Ulrich, T. Jick, and S. Kerr, 1995, *Creating the Boundaryless Organization* (San Francisco: Jossey-Bass).

2. G. Hofstede, G. 1980, *Culture's Consequences: International Differences in Work Related Values* (Beverly Hills: Sage); Geert H. Hofstede, 1997, *Cultures and Organizations: Software of the Mind* (New York: McGraw-Hill); J. Milliman, S. Nason, M. A. Von Glinow, P. Huo, K. Lowe, and N. Kim, 1995, "Best Strategic Pay Practices: An Exploratory Study of Japan, Korea, Taiwan, and the U.S.," *Advances in International Comparative Management,* Vol. 10 (JAI Press).

3. K. Carrig, 1997, "Reshaping Human Resources for the Next Century: Lessons from a High-flying Airline," *Human Resource Management Journal* 36(2): 277–289.

4. We have compiled the worksheet items for a generalization culture from the following sources: R. Aubrey and P. Cohen, 1995, *Working Wisdom: Timeless Skills and Vanguard Strategies for Learning Organizations* (San Francisco: Jossey Bass); C. Argyris, 1991, "Teaching Smart People How to Learn," *Harvard Business Review* (May–June): 99–109; C. Argyris, 1982, *Reasoning, Learning, and Action* (San Francisco: Jossey-Bass); Delta Consulting Group, 1990, "Organizational Learning Case Studies," unpublished study; C. M. Fiol and M. A. Lyles, 1985, "Organizational Learning," *Academy of Management Review* 10(4): 803–813; G. P. Huber, 1991, "Organizational Learning: The Contributing Processes and the Literatures," *Organization Science* 2(1): 88–115; C. Wick, 1993, *The Learning Edge: How Smart Managers and Smart Companies Stay Ahead* (New York: McGraw-Hill).

5. "Career Architect" was originally developed by Eichinger and Lombardo. Lominger combined individual competencies developed in "Career Architect" with his "Organization Architect." In "Organizational Architect," one of the sixteen organizational capabilities deals with the ability to share information (cluster 7). Lominger identifies a set of eight individual competencies most likely to make this organizational capability happen.

6. These concepts on measures and rewards are drawn from E. E. Lawler, 1990, *Strategic Pay* (San Francisco, Calif.: Jossey-Bass); S. Kerr, 1989, "Some Characteristics and Consequences of Organizational Rewards," in B. Schoorman, and B. Schneider (eds.), *Facilitating Work Effectiveness*, chapter 3 (New York: Lexington).

7. Many good books have been written on teams, including S. Mohrman, S. Cohen, and A. Mohrman, Jr., 1995, *Designing Team-Based Organizations: New York Forms of Knowledge Work* (San Francisco: Jossey-Bass); C. Larson and F. LaFasto, 1989, *Teamwork* (Newbury, Calif.: Sage Publications); R. Guzzo, E. Salas and Associates, 1995, *Team Effectiveness and Decision Mak-*

ing in Organizations (San Francisco: Jossey Bass); J. R. Katzenbach and D. Smith, 1993, *The Wisdom of Teams: Creating the High-performance Organization* (Boston, Mass.: Harvard Business School Press).

8. Current thinking on change in organizations is discussed in P. F. Drucker, 1997, "Toward the New Organization," *Leader to Leader,* Number 3, Winter (San Francisco: Jossey-Bass), pp. 6–8; CSC Index, 1996, "The 21st Century CEO: Organizational Agility," monograph prepared for CSC Index, Cambridge, Mass.; P. F. Drucker, 1995, *Managing in a Time of Change* (New York: Penguin Books); R. Kanter, B. A. Stein, and T. D. Jick, 1992, *The Challenge of Organizational Change* (New York: Free Press).

9. The learning matrix described here is based on a personal conversation between Steve Kerr and one of the authors (Ulrich).

CHAPTER 6

1. C. Argyris, 1991, "Teaching Smart People How to Learn," *Harvard Business Review* (May–June): 99–109; P. M. Senge, 1990, *The Fifty Discipline: The Art and Practice of the Learning Organization* (New York: Doubleday/Currency).

2. J. Kotter and J. Heskett, 1992, *Culture and Performance* (New York: Free Press).

3. For example, see G. P. Huber, 1991, "Organizational Learning: The Contributing Processes and the Literatures," *Organization Science* 2(1): 88–115; P. M. Senge, 1990, *The Fifth Discipline: The Art and Practice of the Learning Organization* (New York: Doubleday/Currency).

4. S. B. Sitkin, 1992, "Learning Through Failure: The Strategy of Small Losses," *Research in Organizational Behavior* 14: 231–266.

5. I. Nonaka, 1988, "Creating Organizational Order Out of Chaos: Self-Renewal in Japanese Firms," *California Management Review* (Spring): 57–73; I. Nonaka, 1990, "Redundant, Overlapping Organization: A Japanese Approach to Managing the Innovation Process," *California Management Review* (Spring): 27–38; I. Nonaka, 1991, "The Knowledge-Creating Company" *Harvard Business Review* (November–December): 96–104.

CHAPTER 7

1. From a speech Jack Welch gave at GE's Annual Meeting, April 23, 1997.

2. The learning architecture we present here is taken from D. Ulrich, 1997, *Human Resource Champion* (Boston: Harvard Business School Press).

3. J. R. Phillips, and A. A. Kennedy, 1980, "Shaping and Managing Shared Values," McKinsey staff paper, internal document; D. Nadler and M. Tushman, 1980, "A Model for Diagnosing Organizational Behavior," *Organizational Dynamics* 9(2): 35–51; J. R. Galbraith, 1977, *Organization Design* (Reading, Mass.: Addison-Wesley).

4. See T. E. Deal, and A. A. Kennedy, 1982, *Corporate Cultures: The Rites and Rituals of Corporate Life* (Reading, Mass.: Addison-Wesley); A. L. Wilkins, 1984, "The Creation of Company Culture: The Role of Stories and Human

Resource Systems," *Human Resource Management* 23(1): 41–60; A. L. Wilkins, 1989, *Developing Corporate Character* (San Francisco: Jossey-Bass); E. G. Schein, 1985, *Organizational Culture and Leadership* (San Francisco: Jossey-Bass).

5. Competence has come to refer to both individual knowledge and skills and organizational capabilities that are bundles or collections of individual knowledge and skills. See C. K. Prahalad, and G. Hamel, 1990, "The Core Competence of the Corporation," *Harvard Business Review* (May–June): 79–91; J. B. Quinn, 1992, *Intelligent Enterprise* (New York: Free Press). We focus here on individual-level competencies for learning capability.

6. W. Davidow, and M. Malone, 1992, *The Virtual Organization: Lessons from the World's Most Advanced Companies* (New York: Harper Business).

7. D. Meiland, B. Wieczerek, and D. O'Brien, 1997, "Face to face: Jack Welch," *Focus*, p. 12.

8. From Jack Welch's speech at GE's Annual Meeting, April 23, 1997.

9. P. M. Senge, 1990, "The Leader's New Work: Building Learning Organizations," *Sloan Management Review* (Fall): 7–23. P. M. Senge, 1990, *The Fifth Discipline: The Art and Practice of the Learning Organization* (New York: Doubleday/Currency); R. Stata, 1989, "Organizational Learning: The Key to Management Innovation," *Sloan Management Review* (Spring): 63–74; C. Wick, 1993, *The Learning Edge: How Smart Managers and Smart Companies Stay Ahead* (New York: McGraw-Hill).

10. C. K. Prahalad, and G. Hamel, 1990, "The Core Competence of the Corporation," *Harvard Business Review* (May–June): 79–91; G. Hamel, and C. K. Prahalad, 1991, "Corporate Imagination and Expeditionary Marketing," *Harvard Business Review* (July–August): 81–92; G. Hamel, and C. K. Prahalad, 1994, *Competing For the Future* (Boston, Mass.: Harvard Business Press).

11. D., Nadler, M. Gerstein, R. Shaw, and Associates, 1992, *Organizational Architecture: Designs for Changing Organizations* (San Francisco, Jossey-Bass).

12. This frame comes from GE's "Change Acceleration Process," developed by a design team lead by Steve Kerr and David Ulrich.

CHAPTER 8

1. From a personal conversation between Mary Ann Von Glinow and P. Y. Lai in Beijing in 1995 at Motorola China.

2. From a personal conversation between Mary Ann Von Glinow and Jean Canavan in 1996 in Hong Kong.

3. Information about "One Community One Goal" comes from Mary Ann Von Glinow, who serves on the OCOG Board of Advisors (1995–present) and from various press releases in the *Miami Today*.

APPENDIX 1

1. A. Wilkins, 1989, *Developing Corporate Character* (San Francisco: Jossey-Bass).

2. Before aggregating individual data to business data, one-way ANOVAs were conducted to ensure that the within-group variance of respondents was significantly smaller than the between-group variance in all variables.

3. I. Nonaka, 1991, "The Knowledge-Creating Company," *Harvard Business Review* (Nov.–Dec.): 96–10.

INDEX